A History of
HANDGUNS

A History of

HANDGUNS

Frederick Wilkinson

The Crowood Press

First published in 2010 by
The Crowood Press Ltd
Ramsbury, Marlborough
Wiltshire SN8 2HR

www.crowood.com

British Library Cataloguing-in-Publication Data
A catalogue record for this book is available from the British Library.

ISBN 978 1 84797 225 5

FRONTISPIECE: The Webley self-loading .32 pistol, which was for
many years the official firearm available to many police forces until
replaced by various revolvers that in turn have been withdrawn.
Many forces now use the latest Austrian Glock 9mm self-loader.

Typeset by Bookcraft Ltd, Stroud, Gloucestershire
Printed and bound in India by Replika Press

Contents

Acknowledgements

Over many years I have had the privilege and pleasure of knowing and working with some of the outstanding experts in the fields of modern and antique firearms. The late, great H.L. Blackmore, Claude Blair and Herb Woodend were especially helpful for many, many years. David Penn, George Geear, David Winks, the staff at the Royal Armouries and the Imperial War Museum, as well as collectors, members of various specialist societies, academics, auctioneers, shooters and police officers have continued their good work. The author owes them a debt of gratitude for their encouragement, help and teaching. They have shared their time, their knowledge and their enthusiasm for the study of a fascinating subject and it gives me great pleasure and satisfaction to dedicate this book to them as a token of my gratitude.

However, my biggest thanks must go to my late wife, Teresa, who sacrificed her time and effort, generously encouraged and cheerfully supported me in all my ventures and never complained. It is stating the obvious to say that without her love, tolerance and support very little would have been achieved.

Copyright

Every effort has been made to acknowledge the use of illustrations but since many are from my own collection, built up over many years, some details may have been missed or overlooked. In any such case, I offer my sincere apologies and will make efforts to correct the details.

Permission to include the illustrations of the various locks was generously given by the late Claude Blair. They were first published in his book *European and American Arms* (London 1962).

Introduction

Handguns have been around for hundreds of years and during that time have brought pleasure and, sadly, pain and death to thousands of people. They have been given as prizes or rewards and marks of respect to the famous. They have been embellished and turned into works of art and triumphs of craftsmanship, but they have also been produced as crude, basic, 'throw-away' weapons. They have made the fortune of inventors whose names are now familiar all over the world.

As a weapon, the pistol has gained a reputation with the public which, in some respects, is very over-inflated. Handguns have featured in so many films, television shows, illustrations and stories that most people are probably more casually familiar with this type of weapon than with any other. They are often seen in the hands of notorious villains and fabulous heroes, many of whom demonstrate great skill in their use, and this has created an exaggerated image of a pistol's capabilities. As a consequence they are, possibly, one of the most widely misunderstood of all the weapons in the armoury.

In Western films heroes and villains draw a revolver, usually a Colt, from a belt holster and, without taking aim, shoot a hat from the head, a buckle from a belt, a cigarette from the mouth or a gun from an enemy's hand. Show people have performed similar feats, sometimes with a little technical help, unbeknown to the audience. In real life such shooting is not totally impossible, but it is the province of just a few, a very few, talented shooters, such as the exceptional and gifted Annie Oakley and Ed McGivern. Annie (1880–1928), a performer with Buffalo Bill's Wild West Circus, is credited with some incredible target shooting, while, more recently, McGivern was the author of the *Book of Fast and Fancy Revolver Shooting* (Chicago 1987) and *Triggernometry*.

Such feats of marksmanship are beyond the ability of any normally competent shooter. Even in a quiet, custom-built shooting range with a fixed target, good lighting and plenty of time to take careful aim, only the most proficient marksman would shoot a perfect score. New aiming techniques, such as 'sense of direction' or instinctive shooting that involve gripping the butt of the handgun with both hands, have led to an increased proficiency in some styles of shooting, but results still vary.

Another technique featured in many Western films is high-speed firing with a revolver using a technique known as 'fanning'. Instead of the trigger being squeezed for each shot, it is held back and the hammer, which fires the shot, is struck many times in rapid succession with the flat of the other hand. Every shot generates recoil, which makes the weapon move in the hand and this, coupled with the impact of the striking hand, is extremely likely to move the pistol and so throw the shot off target. To maintain a steady accurate aim it is vital to have a very firm grip on the gun, and this is always a difficult task with one hand. Any gain in speed generated by fanning would almost certainly be counterbalanced by a diminishing of accuracy.

In the hands of an average shooter the handgun is not a particularly accurate weapon. To achieve consistently good results, frequent practice and training are vital but, despite all the training, mechanical aids and sighting devices, accuracy cannot be guaranteed. Stress can undo all the training and skill of a good marksman. This has happened when skilled shooters, dealing with an emergency, have opened fire and missed their target. In tense incidents, even specially highly trained armed police officers may fire several rounds yet fail to score any significant hits.

Characters on television and in films are also remarkably good at hitting a moving target at long range using a conventional handgun. The relatively short barrel of this weapon rather limits its power and, consequently, its range. Most are essentially close-range, almost hand-to-hand combat or defensive weapons, with an effective range that is seldom more than 25 to 50 metres. Beyond that distance, an aimed shot is quite likely to land off target.

The necessity to reload a handgun is so often ignored in films. The maximum number of rounds that most revolvers can normally hold is six, but, in the hands of the film actor, they seem to be able to fire almost continuously without being reloaded. The ability to increase the number of rounds held by a handgun was one of the goals of many inventions and devices but few were really successful, prior to the appearance of the semi-automatic pistol. Despite some experimental models, six shots was the maximum practical capacity of the vast majority of revolvers. Even the modern self-loading pistol can carry only a maximum of about fifteen or twenty rounds, unless it is fitted with one of a number of specially extended magazines.

Handguns are not always the most reliable of weapons and many a life has been spared because of a malfunctioning pistol or revolver. Revolvers may misfire and self-loading pistols can jam and fail to fire a shot. This is far less likely with a modern handgun than with a flint or percussion model, but it can and still does happen.

As far as historical accuracy is concerned, many film-makers and directors have had a cavalier attitude where handguns are concerned. In films featuring the Wild West it was common practice for nearly every shooter to be armed with the Colt Single Action Army revolver, which was adopted in 1873, despite the fact that the film or drama may have been set in a period prior to this date. One result of this 'fixation' has been to give the impression that the Colt was the only revolver that saw action in the West. Research has shown this was certainly not the case and that, in fact, many makes of handgun were eagerly bought, sold and used by the pioneers. Similar anachronistic errors in the fictional use of handguns may well be spotted by the eagle-eyed student. One or two film directors of Western films did make an effort and, to their credit, armed their characters with examples of other contemporary handguns, including those made by Smith & Wesson, Remington, Tranter, Webley, and others.

The handgun features so often in crime, both in fact and fiction, that, unfortunately, it has been somewhat demonized by association. Supporters of the anti-gun lobby link it almost wholly to violence and condemn it by saying that it has only one function – to kill or wound. A moment's thought must surely lead to the realization that a gun can have no purpose of its own. Its function is determined by the human being in whose hands it rests; indeed, this is true of every object, be it a baseball bat, a knife or a pistol. If a handgun has any function, it is simply to discharge a missile; the target of that missile is determined by the user.

Despite all the misconceptions and errors associated with the handgun, it has a fascinating history and for hundreds of years people have sought to improve its accuracy, its firepower and its reliability. As a weapon it has always had a rather special personal significance and in some circumstances it does offer advantages (such as portability) over all others. However, if it is to prove really effective, it demands skill, training, dedication and plenty of sustained practice.

The gun-making industry has been (and, in some cases, still is) an important sector in the economy of several nations. That industry over the years has proposed some brilliant innovations, while other modifications have bordered on the ridiculous. Successful inventors associated with guns include Colt, Luger, Browning, Webley, Mauser and Winchester, all world-renowned names.

During its history the handgun has sometimes been seen as an object deserving special

BARNEY fighting a DUEL.

Engraving by the famous cartoonist George Cruikshank (1792–1878), rather mocking the duel, which was increasingly being condemned by the public.

care and top-quality decoration, so that at times it became a status symbol. The manufacture of such a handgun would involve not only the mechanics and metal-workers, but also a number of other craftsmen, including jewellers, engravers, wood-workers, goldsmiths and leather-workers. Decorated and embellished, it would be considered a suitable presentation piece for the rich and famous. Many were engraved with appropriate patterns and sentiments and fitted into elaborate cases, together with all manner of accessories such as cleaning items or tools for making cartridges. Until the mid-nineteenth century and the introduction of mechanization, each pistol was unique. It was largely hand-made and, although apparently identical, close inspection may reveal even a matched pair of pistols to differ slightly in decoration and styling.

In the eighteenth century the handgun gradually replaced the sword on the field of honour and most men with any pretensions to gentility would own a cased set of duelling pistols. There were those who argued that duelling with pistols was fairer than with swords since there was little to be learned about their use, whereas sword play demanded intricate and extensive training. By the early nineteenth century, the concept of the duel had largely been rejected by British society and duelling pistols were replaced by target pistols. By the late nineteenth and early twentieth centuries, pistol shooting had become an established sport and was included in the new Olympic Games, inaugurated in 1896.

During the later part of the nineteenth century there were great developments in self-loading pistol design. A wide variety of such pistols became available on the market, in a wide range of calibres. In order to improve the pistol's scoring potential, some gunmakers devoted much time and effort to producing special barrels, contoured grips, intricate sights and, later, various electronic aiming and firing devices that were intended to offer reliable and consistent accuracy. Some pistols became little more than electronic aiming items rather than effective, practical handguns. As a self-defence item the handgun was sometimes disguised as an item of cutlery, a belt buckle or a walking stick, or was concealed in a purse. It was also combined with one or more other weapons in an effort to expand its usefulness.

Unfortunately, the misuse of handguns over the years by a minority of thoughtless or criminal individuals created fear among the public and civic authorities, which led to demands to increase restrictions on their private ownership. The attempts to control private possession were sometimes overhasty and ill thought-out and, consequently, achieved little, beyond restricting their perfectly legitimate use by ordinary citizens. In Britain today, largely as the result of several terrible and tragic events, the private ownership of a handgun is virtually forbidden and native pistol shooting has ended[1].

This book seeks to put the handgun into some perspective by tracing its broad history and detailing some highlights as well as the tragedies and the ingenuity of its story. It does not attempt to record in detail the innumerable types, patterns, mechanisms, styles and names of the various models – the bibliography lists several excellent reference books that have done that job. Instead, it hopes to explain some of the aspects of its use that are often neglected by technical histories. It will introduce some villains and some heroes and hopefully shed light on the ways in which society has tried to reconcile the difficult problems of public safety and private ownership of firearms.

CHAPTER I

The Beginning

The Longbow and the Crossbow

In any combat situation there is an obvious advantage for the side that can get the first blows in as early as possible and, preferably, when the enemy is still some distance away. Missiles are the obvious means of achieving this and primitive men no doubt hurled rocks and cudgels at their foes, later graduating to longer-range weapons such as spears, javelins, slings, catapults and, eventually, the bow. For centuries, whether the long European version or the short, recurved, composite style of Asia, the bow was the supreme missile weapon. The shower of English, bodkin-pointed arrows played a decisive part in many battles and the skirmishing, mounted archers of Asia were a constant threat to the Crusading armies. Apart from its lethal capability, the bow obviously had a greater range than hand-thrown missiles and the enemy were therefore under attack for a longer period before they were able to respond. Range continued to be an important consideration in later combat. It was one feature that was well understood by gunmakers and designers and, consequently, affected the development of handgun ammunition.

There is one serious limitation to the use of the bow – proficiency in its use can be achieved only by experience and constant practice. During the Middle Ages it was never easy to persuade the potential archer, invariably men of the peasantry and other labourers, to spend time at the butts learning how to shoot well. Monarchs such as Henry VIII, anxious to maintain bodies of archers available for service in their armies, had to coax or bully men into giving up their leisure time to practise their skills. Laws prohibited the playing of games at times when the men should have been practising their archery and local officials were charged with implementing these rules. Penalties were imposed upon those who failed to attend for practice. Restrictions on the time spent at the inn were also proclaimed and at this period there was a legal obligation on the men of the house to supply the young boys of the family with a bow and encourage them to practise.

The other missile weapon of this period was the crossbow, which was more powerful than the longbow and mechanically much more complex. Less skill was required to

The longbow was a deadly weapon in the hands of a skilled archer. This representation of fifteenth-century bowmen shows them wearing little armour and loosing bodkin-pointed arrows. (Hewitt)

Although spanning the crossbow was difficult and time-consuming, the weapon did offer another great advantage in that aiming it was much simpler than aiming the longbow. The spanned crossbow, with a bolt in place ready to be loosed, could be held in the aiming position whilst a target was selected and the lever or trigger was pressed to release the bolt. The archer drawing a very powerful longbow could only hold that aiming position for a short time. A war bow required a pull of something in excess of one hundred pounds to draw back the string to a position ready for loosing the arrow.

Gunpowder

Missile technology stayed as it was until early in the fourteenth century when a new and revolutionary weapon, the firearm, first made its presence known in Europe. The driving force for the weapon was a mixture of three chemicals, of which the prime ingredient was saltpetre, nitre or potassium nitrate. This chemical occurred naturally, often as a salt deposit on damp walls, but it could be extracted from organic materials such as compost and urine. Large quantities of scrapings from walls and elsewhere were needed to produce just a few ounces of the chemical. The acquisition of saltpetre was a constant problem for the powder-makers and regulations were periodically enacted in an attempt to ensure regular supplies. For centuries saltpetre and barrels of gunpowder were stored in the basement of the White Tower in London so that there was one enormous, potential explosion at the very centre of the capital. Fortunately it never happened, although the chemical effects of saltpetre caused serious, long-lasting damage to the basement walls.

use it well, which was a great advantage, but there was a significant disadvantage in the time it took to bend, or span, the bow when preparing to discharge a bolt. The bow was so strong that the cord could not easily be pulled back by hand alone. The earliest types of crossbow could be spanned with the aid of a hook attached to a waist belt and by using the legs to give extra power. As the bows became even more powerful, especially when steel bows replaced wooden ones, it took more and more effort and, consequently, more time to span. Indeed, armourers soon had to develop mechanical aids such as the capstan and goat's-foot lever, to help with spanning. A skilled archer with his longbow could loose several arrows whilst the crossbow man struggled to loose just one bolt.

As firearms came to play a more important part in war so the demand for saltpetre increased. There were frequent official proc-lamations concerned with the production and supply of gunpowder and the collection of the chemical. In 1626, the Gunpowder Men of Southwark, London, were given the legal right to visit the site of any demolished house within a three-mile radius and take away any earth from which they could extract the saltpetre[2]. In 1636 the import of saltpetre was forbidden and in the following year controls were put on the sale of gunpowder[3]. In 1666 Commissioners for Saltpetre were appointed by Parliament and given powers to comman-deer carts to transport their materials. They were allowed to enter private premises to dig up the floors of latrines in order to extract the chemical from the earth and later regu-lations stipulated that urine was to be stored for their collection[4]. In later centuries bulk saltpetre was exported to Britain by the East India Company from naturally occurring supplies in Bengal but, since it was rather impure, it had to be refined before it could be used.

When saltpetre burns it does so very quickly and generates large amounts of gas. In China, possibly whilst searching for various magical substances, alchemists became aware of this and began to experiment with the chemical. At some point they mixed it with sulphur, a yellow, crystalline substance commonly associated with volcanoes (in later centuries the best quality sulphur was imported from Sicily). The two substances were subsequently mixed with a third – charcoal, created from heating and charring wood, preferably from alder or willow trees. In later centuries the charcoal was ground into a fine powder by great rollers and mixed with the sulphur and then the saltpetre was added. The end product was gunpowder, also known as 'black powder' or 'the devil's powder'. The combination remained in use until the nineteenth century.

At different periods other components were tried in the mixture and the proportions of the three main materials were also varied over the centuries, but the most commonly used basic formula was 75 per cent saltpetre, 15 per cent charcoal and 10 per cent sulphur. When ignited the interaction between the materials produces a high temperature, a rapid flaring flame and a burst of gas and smoke. This spectacular reaction obviously impressed the Chinese for at an early date they adapted it in various ways and its first use appears to have been in the manufacture of incendiary devices, fireworks and rockets.

It was obvious that, if the powder was packed into a tube that had one end blocked off and was then ignited, the generated gas would blast out of the open end and propel the tube along like a rocket. If however the tube was firmly secured then the gas would project a jet from the open end. If any type of projectile – a stone or an arrow, for example – were placed on top of the charge of powder inside the tube, it would be expelled at speed. As the gas would also exert outward pressure on the container, especially in that section holding the powder, this part would have to be strengthened to withstand that pressure. It has been suggested that hollow bamboo stems with some binding at the breech-end could well have served as the first gun barrels. When this vital step was first taken is unclear but there is no doubt that the Chinese were using rockets by the early tenth century. By the thirteenth century, they had developed crude guns and there is at least one example that is reputedly dated 1288.

One problem affecting the use of gun-powder soon emerged – the separation of the constituents. It became apparent that, if the three chemicals were simply mixed together, there was a tendency over time for the components to separate, especially if the mixture was subjected to movement. This separation changed the consistency of the mixture in a random manner so that similarly sized scoops of powder from the same source could vary slightly in composition. This could lead to variations in the rate of burning and hence the amounts of gas generated. This would alter the power generated, which, in turn, would affect the range, speed and impact of the missile.

By the early fifteenth century the powder men had developed an improved method of preparing and stabilizing the consistency of gunpowder. Instead of simply dry-mixing the chemicals to produce what was known as 'mealed powder', the components were now mixed with a liquid base such as vinegar or, occasionally, other, stranger liquids. The resulting sludge or paste was spread out in sheets and left to dry. These were then broken up and crushed back into a powder, using specialized rollers and mills that were designed to produce a constant quality. The resultant grains, known as 'corned powder', were found to be more stable and remained more consistent in quality. This process remained as the basic system of production for the rest of the gunpowder era, although some fine-grained, rather slow-burning mealed powder, known as 'serpentine powder', was still produced and continued in use for priming.

When and how the knowledge of gunpowder first reached Europe is still open to debate. The general opinion is that it travelled across Asia from China via the Mongols and through trading links between China and India. Its secret had also probably been acquired by the Moors, who conquered much of Spain in the eighth century, and had been passed on to Europe, again through trade and cultural contacts, presumably by the eleventh or twelfth centuries.

Although the exact date of its first arrival may be uncertain, there can be little doubt that some in the West knew about the existence of gunpowder by the thirteenth century. The writings of Franciscan monk and Oxford academic Roger Bacon (1214?–1294?) refer to explosions, loud noise and flashes of light, indicating that at the very least he knew of its power. Indeed, there are claims, although these are not accepted by all scholars, that among his written works Bacon includes, in an anagram form, a formula for the composition of gunpowder. Even if the anagram is genuine, unfortunately, much of the evidence for its dating is literary based. Such evidence is always difficult to date precisely, and some academics believe that the text may well have been added to Bacon's work at a later date.

Another character associated with the early history of gunpowder is a monk known as Black Berthold, who is believed to have lived in Germany. The story goes that, whilst conducting an experiment, Berthold combined the three 'magic' components in a mortar. During the mixing of the powders, friction ignited the gunpowder and so a small explosion was generated, blowing the pestle out of his hand. The accident is said to be the origin of the concept of a gun. It is a feasible story and Berthold's discovery is commemorated in the town of Freiburg by a statue, as well as a Schwarz Berthold Institut. Unfortunately, his very existence is questioned by most scholars[5] and little or no firm credible evidence of his life has yet been found.

Early Guns

Proof of the early use of guns in Europe is based on much firmer evidence. Surviving records kept by the Council of the Italian city of Florence clearly show that, in 1326, men were being paid to maintain cannon and ammunition, held for the defence of the state. Further confirmation of the presence of guns

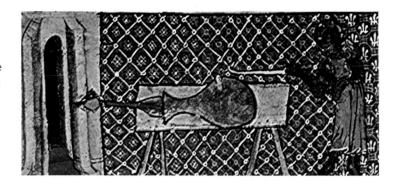

The cannon illustrated in the Milemete manuscript of 1346. The knight uses a rod, perhaps heated or holding a glowing match, to ignite the priming powder. The illustration is vague on details – there is no indication of how the cannon was held in place on the platform. (Christ College, Oxford)

around this date comes from a British source, a manuscript written in the same year, 1346[6], by a monk named Walter de Milemete, as a guide for King Edward III (1327–1377). Although there are no references to them in the text, the manuscript does include two detailed illustrations of what must surely be cannon.

The better-known illustration shows a vase-shaped container lying on a table, with the point of an arrow projecting from its open end. At the rear of the table and to one side stands a mail-clad knight. In one hand the knight holds out a rod of some sort, the end of which is presumably hot, or perhaps holding a glowing ember or a length of smouldering cord. He has directed the tip of the rod towards a small hole at the neck of the gun from which a puff of smoke is emerging. If, as it surely must, this drawing depicts a cannon, this hole would have passed through the wall of the vase down to the main charge or powder, which would have been housed in the breech of the gun. A pinch of powder placed at the mouth of this aperture could be ignited by the heat source and, as it flared up, the flame would go through the wall to ignite the main internal charge. The resulting blast of gas would fire the shot and expel the arrow at speed. The effectiveness of such a system has been demonstrated by experiments using modern reconstructions.

Whilst there are some anomalies and questions relating to the details of this illustration, there is sufficient supporting evidence to suggest that it is, in fact, a fair depiction of an early cannon. Seventeenth-century records in the Tower of London mention the discharge of arrows from cannon and the vase shape is basically the same as a short, bronze cannon barrel found in Loshult, Sweden, and dated to the early fourteenth century. The vase shape accords with the idea of the breech end of a cannon being thicker than the rest of the barrel, in order to withstand the pressure of the burning gunpowder. Looking at this evidence, it is reasonable to say that, by

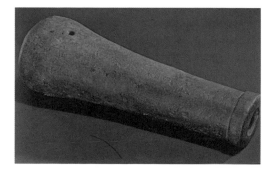

A bronze barrel found at Loshult in Sweden and dated to the early fourteenth century. The shape resembles that of the cannon from the Milemete manuscript, with a thickened section at the breech end. The touch hole is clearly visible.

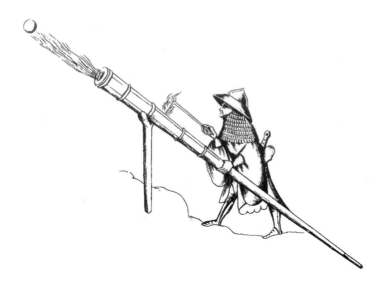

Depiction of a fifteenth-century gunner with staff-mounted hand gun. (Hewitt)

the early fourteenth century or possibly the late thirteenth century, firearms were known and probably in use in Europe.

Much of the very early history of firearms is primarily concerned with the use of gunpowder and the development of artillery when besieging castles; the massive cannonballs soon proved their ability to demolish the strongest fortifications. Although the English longbow was still the ultimate missile weapon, there are references relating to some simple cannon being used at the battle of Crécy in 1346. Those early gunners were the forerunners of the artilleryman of contemporary armies[7].

At some point, probably during the early fourteenth century, the concept of a small 'personal' cannon was developed. The term *hand gonne* is first recorded in 1339, presumably referring to a short Loshult-type barrel secured to the end of a wooden pole to produce a simple gun. (Interestingly, this was a development that apparently was not adopted by the Chinese until the fifteenth century[8].) When firing the weapon, the handler could tuck the wooden stock under the arm, rest it on the shoulder or perhaps support it on a wall. Another version of the hand gun was an all-metal construction with the barrel and stock cast as one, with a short arm projecting from beneath the barrel. This could be hooked over a wall or fence to give the gunner a firm firing base. Such weapons must have been very inaccurate and were basically incapable of aimed fire; nevertheless, if deployed in numbers, they would be a powerful deterrent to an enemy.

The short barrel of the earliest hand gun was charged with a set measure of powder poured in at the muzzle, and a wad of hemp, hay, grass or similar material rammed down on top to hold the powder in place. On top of that was placed the projectile, which might be made of stone, lead or other material. It was important for the gunner to ensure that wad and bullet were firmly seated on top of the charge of powder and sometimes a second wad was pressed home to ensure that the missile stayed in the barrel. The fit of the bullet in the barrel was later found to be very important – a tight fit meant that, when the powder was ignited, the gas was confined, allowing pressure to build up in the chamber

Three-barrelled hand cannon of iron, probably eighteenth century and Chinese, but virtually identical to the earlier medieval type. Mounted on a pole, it was turned to bring a barrel to the top position and, since there is no pan cover, it was then primed and fired. (Thomas Del Mar Ltd)

until it was sufficient to blast out both wad and bullet at speed. A poor fit allowed gas to escape around the sides of the loose-fitting missile, reducing pressure and lowering the bullet speed, range and impact.

A wooden rod, the ramrod or scouring stick, was used to press down the ball, charge and wads firmly into the breech. This was a separate item. On later guns it was firmly housed in a slot cut into the stock below the barrel and was commonly made of wood, often with a horn tip. In contemporary handbooks and manuals detailing the drill of handling a gun there were set sequences for drawing, using and replacing the ramrod.

One great advantage offered by the hand gun was the fact that minimal skill was required to carry out the firing technique. Even the simplest peasant could be trained in its use in a very short time, and anyone in possession of such a weapon had the potential to injure or kill. Despite his expensive armour and extensive martial training, the noblest knight was now vulnerable, and at risk of possible injury or death at the hands of the clumsiest, most ignorant peasant.

Armour

The advent of gunpowder and introduction of firearms were to affect not only the way that battles were fought but also the way in which the soldier was equipped. The bullet was sometimes better able to cause injury than the arrow and was easier to produce and discharge in quantity. Apart from the ability of armour to stop a projectile it could also deflect it but this advantage was somewhat diminished as the larger-diameter bullet created an area of impact that was much bigger than the point of an arrow. This meant that it would transfer more of its potential energy to the target. Even if the bullet failed to penetrate the armour, it could still deliver a heavy blow to the wearer, which might often be sufficient to incapacitate him.

It was fairly easy to prevent a bullet penetrating the armour by making the plates thicker, sometimes by using two layers, but inevitably thicker meant heavier. The soldier was now faced with a choice: insufficient protection or the inconvenience of a heavier personal load to carry and, above all, to fight in. The manufacture of armour was obviously also affected. Most soldiers chose to reduce the overall weight of their armour by discarding those pieces that would save them only from wounds that were less likely to be life-threatening. Leg defences were the first to be discarded, with the lower sections of the armour being supplanted by long leather boots, and arm defences were the next to go.

By the time of the English Civil Wars (1642–49), most horse soldiers were wearing armour that consisted simply of a thick breast- and thinner back-plate, a helmet, and perhaps a bridle gauntlet covering his left arm, which held the reins of the horse. Most cavalrymen placed their trust in a thick leather coat, the buff coat, which was capable of offering some protection against sword cuts. The infantryman serving as a pikeman retained rather more extensive personal armour; he was obliged to stand firm in formation in the face of the enemy, and consequently was more exposed to enemy fire. In addition to his helmet, breast- and back-plate, he was also fitted with a pair of skirt-like tassets to guard the lower part of his body. Some cavalry units, such as the heavy cuirassiers, continued to wear full armours but they were the exception. They were referred to as 'lobsters'.

A practice that became more common in the seventeenth century was the proving of armour. This involved taking a finished breast-plate, standing it against a post or wall, and firing a musket at it. The dent made by the ball showed convincingly that it had failed to pierce the armour, thus proving that the plate was bullet-proof. Helmets were proved in the same way, using a pistol. Although the dent might look impressive it could be rather misleading for the proof test does not appear to have been standardized. The size and depth of the dent would be affected by the range at which the shot was fired, and the size of the powder charge used in the testing. It seems that there were no set conditions established as to the size of the proving charge, which might well be below that likely to be encountered in battle. So far, no recorded set of regulations for proof procedure appears to have survived, even if such a protocol existed. Thus, a proof dent was no real guarantee that the armour would in fact stop a bullet.

Ignition

Firing a hand gun was simple but awkward. A heat source to ignite the priming was hand-held; in the early days it was possibly a piece of rod with the tip heated, or perhaps holding a glowing ember. The gunner simply touched the tip of the rod into the priming and, as the match was touched into the priming powder, it started the firing sequence and discharged the shot. Aiming was largely a matter of luck, but if the barrel was pointed in the direction of the opposing troops the projectile was likely to hit something that might well be an enemy soldier.

The necessity of having to hold the ignition device in readiness at all times was tedious, awkward and inconvenient for the musketeer. Clearly, a mechanical system of ignition needed to be developed, to simplify the firing sequence of the gun; this was to remain in use until the eighteenth century. It comprised a length of cord, known as the 'match', which had been soaked in a strong solution of saltpetre and then allowed to dry. If the match was ignited it smouldered, burning slowly with a glowing tip, and this end was applied to the priming at the touch hole, which was now countersunk to form a shallow saucer. The first recorded example dates back to 1411. Fitted on the side of the wooden stock of the gun, adjacent to the touch hole, was a metal arm called the 'serpentine', shaped rather like the letter 'Z' reversed and pivoted at the centre. In the upper arm of the serpentine, held in place by two adjustable jaws, was the smouldering end of a length of match. Upward pressure on the lower part of the arm caused the upper section to swing forwards and downwards, to press the burning tip of the match into the priming pan.

The adoption of the serpentine led to a change in the general design of the gun. The

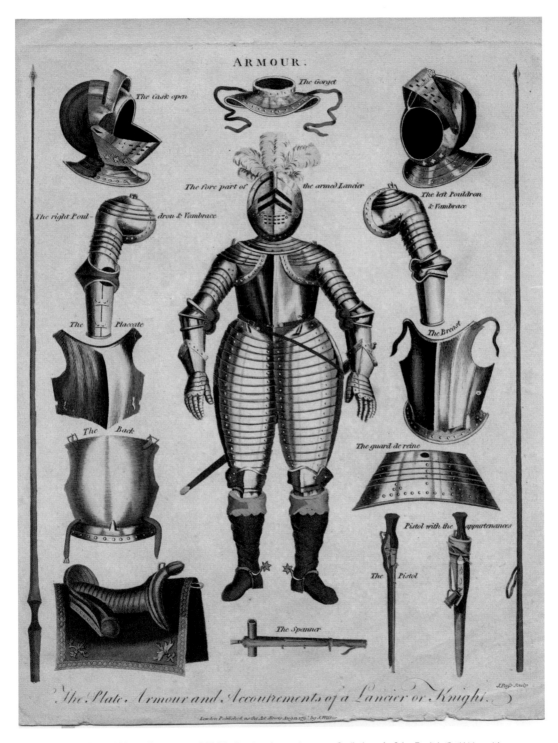

Engraving from Grose Military Antiquities of 1801, showing the equipment of a 'Lobster' of the English Civil Wars. He was armed with two wheel-lock pistols, lance and sword and was unusual in that he still wore full armour.

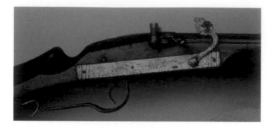

The matchlock mechanism of an early seventeenth-century musket. The serpentine holding the match is at rest and swings forward when the trigger is pressed. The pan cover, closed to protect the priming powder, had to be pushed open before the shot could be fired.

A musketeer of the early seventeenth century, as depicted by Dutch artist Jacob de Gheyn. Note the loop on the rest and the double-ended burning match in the left hand. The musketeer wears a bandoleer from which hangs a small flask of priming powder and some spare match.

touch hole, which had been mounted on top of the breech on the earliest guns, was now moved to the side, and a small, shelf-like projection was set just below it. The priming powder was placed in this side-mounted pan and was protected from wind and rain by a pivoting cover, which obviously had to be moved prior to firing a shot. About the same time, illustrations show that the stock was beginning to acquire a butt shape, allowing the gun to fit to the shoulder so that it was more easily aimed. The matchlock musket or 'arquebus' had been created. Despite the fact that most contemporary illustrations appear to show the musket being held to the shoulder, it is of interest to note that, in a manual of 1680, *English Military Discipline*, the aiming position is defined as follows: 'the butt of the musket must be on the breast, half a foot below the chin.' Indeed, this was the position adopted for use with a form of musket known as a 'petronel'.

The military authorities soon evolved set sequences of drill movements to be followed when loading and firing the musket. In *Mars his Triumph*, an account of an exercise performed in October 1638 at the Merchant Taylors Hall in London and described by K. Bariffe, there are twenty-four separate commands listed. It was very important to follow the drill sequence, as failure to do so could result in a misfire or a situation that might prove serious in battle. Without the glowing tip or other heat source the musket could not be fired so, as a precaution, the length of match was lit at both ends. One end was held in the serpentine and the other was held between the fingers of the left hand of the musketeer, ensuring a reserve ignition source should one be extinguished. Drill discipline was important. In the heat of battle, it was not unknown for a soldier to forget to withdraw the scouring stick from the barrel after ramming home the charge. As he

Sequence of some of the prescribed moves for firing a musket. The arquebusier was drilled to follow the set routine and each movement was prescribed, since any mistake could render the musket useless.

pressed the trigger and the charge was fired, the ramrod was sent whistling through the air; it might serve as an arrow, but it now left the shooter unable to reload properly.

Despite the obvious advantages of this new weapon, the arquebus was not without its problems. The presence of numerous sparks and glowing embers from the pan or muzzle being generated amongst quantities of gunpowder was not a very safe situation. A sudden gust of wind could send a shower of sparks in all directions, perhaps with dire results. A sudden shower of rain could extinguish the glowing match, effectively disarming the shooters. Without any means of ignition, or after it had been discharged, the musket was useful only as a cudgel, although the subsequent development of the bayonet extended its lethal capability.

Although the serpentine was sometimes slightly modified, it was to remain as the basic firing system in Europe until the late seventeenth and into the early eighteenth century, and even longer in Asia and Africa. In areas where materials might be scarce and technical facilities limited, the matchlock had much to offer. Damage and repairs were generally fairly basic and easily dealt with and, in the event of a complete breakdown of the mechanism, the match could still be applied manually. For these and other reasons, the matchlock remains in use in some areas of the world even now.

Although the matchlock system remained basically constant, some differences in design did evolve across the world. One of the most obvious was the movement of the arm of the serpentine and the development of two main types of mechanism to control this. One type was the snap-lock, in which the arm holding the match was held at rest by a spring in the down position, pressing into the pan. To prepare for action, the arm was lifted clear of the pan and locked in place by a small spring-operated sear or arm, which engaged with the arm of the serpentine. Pressure on a stud released the arm, which allowed the serpentine to swing forwards to ignite the priming. The snap-lock was simple and worked well but it was risky. An accidental nudge of the stud or button would cause the serpentine to move forwards to ignite the priming.

A second, safer system involved the serpentine pushing the match into the pan while moving backwards, in the direction of the butt end of the stock. Apart from a few very early examples and some target arquebuses, the vast majority of European matchlocks had this system, in which the normal position of the arm holding the match was well back from the pan. It was held thus by the tension of a small spring and a simple mechanism, which, operated by pressure on a long lever set below the stock, pushed the arm back towards the butt and then down to fire the

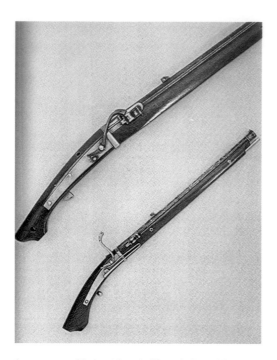

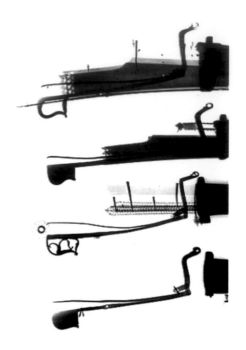

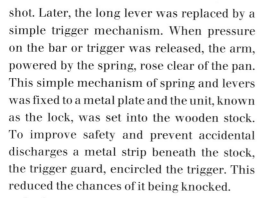

Japanese matchlocks with typical brass locks and forward-swinging serpentines. The barrels are octagonal, unlike the usual European ones, which are tubular. Triggers are of the button form and the lack of a trigger guard is a feature of many Japanese weapons. (Private collection)

X-ray of an Indian matchlock mechanism, showing the simple arrangement of levers used to activate the serpentine that still occupied a limited space. Note that on these locks the serpentine swings in a forward direction, unlike the European style.

shot. Later, the long lever was replaced by a simple trigger mechanism. When pressure on the bar or trigger was released, the arm, powered by the spring, rose clear of the pan. This simple mechanism of spring and levers was fixed to a metal plate and the unit, known as the lock, was set into the wooden stock. To improve safety and prevent accidental discharges a metal strip beneath the stock, the trigger guard, encircled the trigger. This reduced the chances of it being knocked.

In the vast majority of matchlocks developed in Asia and the Far East, a similar lever system is used but in this case the serpentine arm swings in the opposite direction to European examples, that is, towards the muzzle. Part of the reason for this difference

lies in the size and shape of the wooden stock of the gun. Some early fifteenth-century European matchlocks have rather narrow stocks and use this same type of movement, but the stock was later widened. By the early seventeenth century the musket has assumed a conventional, more modern-shaped stock with a wider rear section – the butt – designed to fit against the shoulder when aiming.

The European stock is broad and is capable of accommodating the lock plate with its spring and lever assembly. Most Asiatic matchlock stocks are generally much slimmer and lack the space needed to fit the European lock. A simpler, narrow spring and lever mechanism was evolved to fit the limited space of the Asiatic stock. As a result

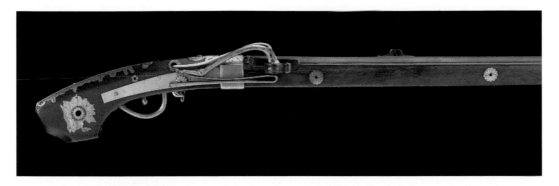

Japanese matchlock musket with octagonal barrel and brass snap-lock mechanism. The cherry wood stock has applied brass plaques. The short butt is typical of Japanese muskets of the Edo period, which lasted from the 17th to the 19th century.

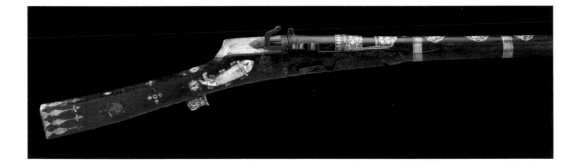

An eighteenth-century Indian matchlock with typical, slim, angular butt. The barrel is covered with decorative gold plaques and the stock is fitted with similar panels including a silver fish. The trigger is of the common flat-plate style. (Thomas Del Mar Ltd)

of the adaptation and simplification, the serpentine moves in the reverse direction to that of the European model, that is, forwards towards the muzzle. Some muskets of typical Indian form with a narrow stock were fitted with a typical European-style flintlock but they appear to overcome the lack of space by using a lock of a smaller size.

Many of the Japanese matchlocks differ in another respect: the arm holding the match is usually made of brass, as are the springs. Despite the superb Japanese mastery of metal-working, they seem to have had something of a problem with spring-making,

although their brass springs do operate quite well. Most Japanese guns use the snap-lock system, operated by a button trigger with the match-holding section normally in the down position.

To operate a matchlock musket a number of accessories are required. When action was imminent the match had to be kept burning continuously, ready for instant use. As it burned, its length gradually diminished so that it had to be adjusted in the serpentine until eventually, after some time, it was so burnt out that it had to be replaced by a new length of match. Spare lengths of match were always carried by musketeers – some hung them in loops from their belt while others coiled them round the brim of the hat. The match was obviously vitally important and on campaigns it was essential to ensure that the troops had an adequate reserve supply of match at all times.

Loading and Reloading

When loading the musket the ball had to be pushed down the barrel to sit firmly on top of the powder in the breech. This was done using the scouring stick or ramrod, which was normally housed in a slot cut in the stock beneath the barrel. A handy supply of powder was obviously a necessity and musketeers usually carried their own stock in a flattened, triangular-shaped wooden box. At the narrow end was a metal spout with a spring-operated cut-off at the base; the nozzle held just the right amount of powder for one shot. If the end was closed off by a finger and the flask upended and the cut-off opened, the spout was filled with powder ready to be poured down the muzzle.

When speed in reloading was more important, the musketeer used a bandoleer. Edward Davies, writing in 1619, recommends having '16 or 18 charges or mates at the least hanged thereunto'[9]. Worn across the chest, the bandoleer was a belt from which were suspended small, wooden, corked containers. Davies' number seems high – later only twelve containers were generally carried, known, with typical soldier's irony, as the 'twelve apostles'. Each of these capped containers was filled with one charge of powder and it was a matter of seconds to take a container, remove the stopper and empty some of the powder into the pan, and pour the rest down the barrel. A second, smaller flask was sometimes carried at the belt and this held a supply of priming powder.

Musketeer's powder flask of the early seventeenth century. The wooden body is covered in vellum and bound in iron. (Thomas Del Mar Ltd)

Developments

The musket or arquebus was a popular success with the troops. Paul Ive in his book *Instructions for the Warres* (1589) declared that the *harquebus hath been invented these feive years and is very good*, but his dating is perhaps a little out. He also claimed that everybody wanted to be an arquebusier, musing, somewhat cynically, whether this was because their wages were better, because they fought the enemy from afar, or because they were less laden with equipment than the pikemen.

In December 1642, a foot soldier with his musket was paid six shillings a week by the King. In comparison, a trooper with a horse, saddle and bridle with pistol or carbine

Hofoever will ferve the KING as a foot Souldier, and bring his Muf-ket, fhall have pay 6ſ. per weeke.
Whofoever will ferve upon any Nagge or Mare of 3ˡ. price or up-ward as a Dragoon, and will bring a Musket: fhall have pay 12ſ.10d. per weeke.
If he bring a Gun of any other kind that is foure foot long hee fhall have 11ſ. 8d. per weeke.
Without a Gun 10ſ. 6d. per weeke.
Whofoever will bring a ferviceable Horfe, faddled and bridled, with Piftoll or Carabin fhall have 3ˡ. towards his Horfe, and his Horfe his owne at the end of the fer-vice, and 17ſ. 6d. per weeke.

Let them repaire to Sir IOHN BYRON Colonell of a Regiment of Horfe for His Majeftie, and all this fhall be performed.
God fave the KING.

Recruiting proclamation of Charles I setting out the rates of pay for the differing types of service. Dragoons were troops who rode into battle but fought on foot.

RIGHT: Metal shoe from a musket rest of the early seventeenth century. With its 48-inch barrel, the musket was too heavy to hold in an aiming position without some support. To reduce the chances of loss, the rest was often fitted with a safety loop to go over the wrist.

received 17s 6d a week[10]. Ive praised the bow and crossbow for being very good against armoured men especially in wet weather when the arquebus was no good. He also pointed out that both weapons were able to discharge missiles at a quicker rate than the arquebus.

The musket fired a lead ball of approximately three quarters of an inch (19mm) in diameter; if it was not a good tight fit, which was often the case, it rather bounced along the barrel and this did not make for accurate shooting. The barrel was around forty-eight inches (122cm) long and fairly heavy, so much so that the musketeer had to support it on a wooden rest when aiming.

Smaller versions of the musket, known as 'calivers', were available and these did not require the use of a rest. The wooden stocks of the musket and caliver were usually made of walnut and were quite plain. However, those issued to bodyguards or units financed by some particular groups were often embellished with inlay or carving.

The basic shape was established early in the seventeenth century, with the butt cut to give a narrow wrist, allowing the hand to get a good grip when aiming. Accuracy was not especially good and there were those who argued that if you were the intended target of a musketeer there was no need to worry – you were unlikely to be hit. This was not so important in a military situation, in which individual, aimed firing was uncommon. Most battles were fought with volley fire, with lines of musketeers firing in unison. Under this system, the balls were more likely to find a target among the close-packed ranks of opposing troops. Once the shot had been fired, and where there was no time to reload, the musket became a club and hand-to-hand combat became the order of the day.

There was another way to use an empty musket and that was to convert it into a short pike. Early in the seventeenth century, a short, broad-bladed knife with a tapering, tubular wooden hilt was developed. It became known as a bayonet, the name usually attributed to a connection with the French town of Bayonne, which was noted for its production of cutlery. Other derivations have been offered. It seems to have first appeared late in the sixteenth century and by the second quarter of the seventeenth century seems to have been generally carried by the infantry. The hilt of the bayonet could be pushed into the muzzle of the empty musket, converting it into a stabbing, thrusting weapon. Obviously with the bayonet in place the musket could not be loaded or fired. This was resolved later by the development of a special cylindrical hilt to the bayonet, which fitted round the outside of the barrel. This firearm–bayonet combination was to be used on many later patterns of long arms and even on pistols right up to the Second World War (1939–1945), although bayonet fighting was rare. The Russian Special Forces, the Spetnaz, have taken the concept a step further and developed a ballistic dagger. It looks like a conventional knife with tubular hilt but is, in effect, a small rocket projector. When activated, it propels the blade through the air rather like a spear.

The fact that ignition of the matchlock required an active source of heat meant that a length of glowing match or something similar had to be constantly to hand. This made it extremely difficult to design a pistol that was essentially a portable, concealable weapon. Using the matchlock mechanism made it almost impossible to enclose and isolate the glowing tip of the match. This meant that the handgun could not be accommodated in a pocket or purse, so removing a prime benefit of a handgun – portability. Some soldiers, such as some of Henry VIII's bodyguard, were issued with metal shields which were fitted at the centre with a matchlock pistol, but these were specialist and exceptional items. It was obviously easy to produce small versions of the musket or caliver but such weapons offered little benefit apart from size. As a consequence, matchlock handguns were rarely made but a few survive and the Royal Armouries have Indian and Japanese examples in their collection.

CHAPTER 2

Locks and Keys

~ ~

The matchlock musket was simple, sturdy and comparatively easy to manufacture, and as a result it long remained a standard issue to the military and continued to be much favoured by hunters of moderate means. Its basic design changed little during the seventeenth and early eighteenth centuries. However, apart from hunting and target shooting, there was little civilian use for it. The necessity of having the match constantly alight restricted any possible use of the matchlock as a personal self-defence weapon since it obviously could not be carried in a pocket or container. What was needed for this purpose was a firearm that could be safely carried about the person and yet still be ready for use at all times and without further preparation. What the gunmakers sought was a replacement firing system in which ignition would be generated only when it was required.

The Wheel-Lock Mechanism

The solution that came about was, in fact, an adaptation of the age-old fire-making system that used flint and steel. From the earliest time man had generated fire by striking flint against a hard surface, to generate glowing sparks that were then used to initiate combustion. Was it possible to reproduce the system mechanically? It seems highly likely that the Renaissance genius Leonardo da Vinci (1452–1519) was one of the first to point the way ahead for firearms. He was a man of immense vision and imagination, with a mind that could take a basic concept and develop it. In his notebooks he sketched and noted ideas to be explored and one of his manuscripts, *Codex Atlanticus*, generally believed to date from around 1500, contains illustrations of two spark-making mechanisms[11].

The larger drawing shows a rotating steel disc or wheel with a roughened edge, powered by means of a helical spring. Two arms are spaced around the edge of the wheel and each holds a piece of mineral, which is pressed against the rim of the disc. The idea was that, as the disc rotated, friction between steel and mineral would generate a shower of sparks. If those sparks could be directed into the priming powder of a firearm, here was a practical firing system. The design, using a coiled spring and twin arms, was certainly capable of generating sparks but it was hardly suitable for attachment to a gun.

On the same page of the manuscript da Vinci showed a sectional view of a different, smaller and much simpler version of a mechanism that would create sparks. The large wheel is replaced by a much smaller one and the helical spring by a V-shaped one, and the whole mechanism is of such a size and shape that it could be fitted into a narrow space. The original design is rather rudimentary but, with a few adaptions and modifications, the gunmaker now had a practical mechanism that could be manufactured in any size. For the first time it would be possible to construct a firearm small enough to be carried comfortably about the person or by a horseman. Here was the beginning of the first really practical, personal gun – a handgun or pistol. This connection with da Vinci would seem to indicate that the wheel-lock mechanism was an Italian invention but there is some evidence to suggest that the wheel lock may have been invented in Germany slightly earlier than 1510. Most early wheel-lock firearms use a piece of the mineral pyrites.

There is some doubt as to the origin of the name 'pistol', but it is generally thought to be derived from *pistolese*, the term for the small daggers that were made and exported in quantity from the north Italian town of Pistoia. Perhaps a connection was made because of the similarity in size between the dagger and the new handgun. In England during most of the sixteenth century these small handguns were referred to as 'dags', a word which seems to have had vague associations with points and sharp implements and so might have a loose connection with the small daggers or pistolets. Some called them 'tucks' – it has been suggested by arms historian Blair that this may have arisen from contemporary mishearing of the English word 'dag' by foreign workers.

The basic concept of the wheel lock was not solely da Vinci's, and there are illustrations and sundry literary references dating from the early sixteenth century to mechanisms that made use of friction between mineral and steel. This must surely have involved some form of sparking or wheel-lock device, probably a tinder lighter. One device associated by tradition with the ghostly Black Berthold was called the 'Monk's Gun', on which sparks were generated by pulling a roughened metal bar past a fixed piece of mineral. There may well be records of one or two other sparking devices but it was the da Vinci-style lock that set the main pattern and was the one used for the pistol.

Ironically, one of the first recorded customers for the new weapon was a man of peace, a churchman – an Italian cardinal is known to have ordered one from Germany in 1507.

The next early reference to a wheel-lock pistol concerns an unfortunate accident in January 1515, in the German town of Constance. Laux Pfister, from Augsburg, was apparently entertaining a lady of the town 'in a small room' and, perhaps to impress her with his possessions or his toughness, he appears to have shown her a firearm. Sadly, he forgot one of the basic rules when handling any firearm: check that the weapon is unloaded or at least safe. Unfortunately, this one was loaded; somehow a shot was fired and the bullet hit the lady, passing through her chin and out of her neck.

A doctor was summoned and the expense of his services and other items amounted to a total of 77 florins – clearly, it turned into an expensive event for the young man. The unfortunate lady was awarded 40 florins in compensation and a lifelong annual pension of 20 florins, which suggests that, not surprisingly, she must have suffered some permanent disability. The records state that the weapon 'ignited itself'; this is a phrase unlikely to refer to a matchlock and it is also

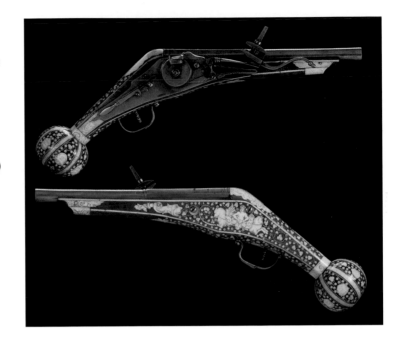

A pair of German wheel-lock pistols, known as 'puffers', dated 1586. The fruitwood angled stocks are decorated with inlaid horn flowers and monsters. The butts terminate in large, decorated ball pommels, the bases of which have inset circular plaques depicting cavalrymen. (Thomas Del Mar Ltd)

unlikely that Pfister would have had a musket in a 'small room'. The evidence points to the fact that a pistol was involved and at that date it surely cannot have been anything other than a wheel-lock.

The oldest known surviving examples of wheel-lock pistols appear to date from 1510–1520 and are held in the Palazzo Ducale in Venice. They are, in fact, support weapons, secured to the wooden tiller of a crossbow. They are of Italian manufacture and their purpose is uncertain. The crossbow was essentially a long-range weapon and it may be that the designer had visualized a scene in which the enemy had closed in and there was no time to span the bow, but the pistol was ready for use. A cover protecting the touch hole is manually operated and the entire system is a little primitive but still serviceable.

With the development of the wheel-lock system, the pistol could now be made properly portable, small enough to be carried concealed about the person and ready for immediate action. The risk of assassination and murder was significantly increased – it was now possible for an apparently unarmed individual to approach a victim, draw and fire the pistol when still a short distance away, and when least expected. The risks were further enhanced with developments in men's fashion, when male clothing went from the older robe-style of dress to breeches, which had inset pockets that were large enough to hold a pistol. The potential victims of pistol attacks soon became aware of the increased risk and quickly took steps to reduce the threat. In 1517, the Emperor Maximilian (1493–1519) issued a clear order stating that no handgun *which ignites itself* was to be carried anywhere in the Habsburg territory. This wording must surely apply to a wheel-lock weapon. Needless to say, the announcement of any new law achieves little unless it is backed by appropriate action, and a year later Maximilian forbade the manufacture of wheel locks within the Empire. Correspondence of the period does speak of the weapon being concealed under clothing, however. Other rulers took similar action and in the northern Italian town of Ferrara the Duke forbade the carrying of weapons in the streets, mentioning 'stone guns', surely a reference to the pyrites of the wheel lock.

Maximilian was not the only ruler to place restrictions on the possession and carrying of firearms. The introduction of the pistol was not welcomed by Henry VIII (1509–1547) either, who saw it as distracting the attention of men away from archery. In 1526, a proclamation was issued stressing that this must not happen. Henry banned the possession of crossbows and handguns for anyone with an income of less than 300 marks per annum; presumably this figure was set sufficiently high in order to exclude all but the wealthier yeomen and aristocracy from owning the weapons. Local officials were ordered to implement the ban or suffer penalties if they failed to do so, while in London all merchants and foreigners were required to report to the authorities anybody seen in possession of a handgun or a crossbow. In 1533 Henry relaxed the prohibition, reducing the qualifying figure to property worth more than £100; it was still quite a large sum, however, effectively limiting handgun ownership to the propertied class.

There are indications that the new pistols were popular and that people enjoyed shooting them. In 1540 Henry instructed owners to control their enthusiasm for shooting – they were apparently firing their pistols anywhere that suited them – and henceforth restricted their use to approved shooting areas. In 1541 he bemoaned the use of handguns in crime, and defined the size of the permitted weapon as a minimum of *one yarde*[12]. This stipulation would exclude all usual handguns and perhaps suggests that the main priority was to ban smaller weapons that were easy to conceal.

In 1548 Henry's son Edward VI (1547–1553) also set down rules defining the areas where shooting was permitted. In 1559 Elizabeth I (1558–1603) issued a proclamation reminding her citizens that restrictions on the ownership of handguns, proclaimed by her father, were still in force. Her concern was that the rules were being ignored:

> Many men do dayly use to ryde with handgonnes & dagges under the length of three quarters of a yarde, whereupon have folowed occasions for sundrye lewde and evyll persons, with such unlawfull gonnes and dagges now in time of peace to execute greate and notable robberies and horrible murders.

The significance of the use of both terms for pistol, 'handgonnes' and 'dagges', is unclear; perhaps there was a legal difference between the two, or maybe both names were used simply for emphasis. In 1561 Elizabeth threatened prison and fines for anyone who drew or fired a gun in a church or church-

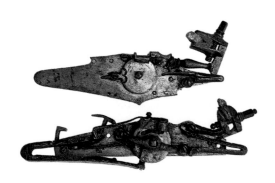

Locks from two wheel-lock pistols. Top: This one has an external wheel and a sliding pan cover with an internally mounted main spring. Bottom: This has an external wheel and mainspring and probably came from a light hunting gun called a 'Tschinke'. Both date from the mid-seventeenth century. (Thomas Del Mar Ltd)

Wheel-lock mechanism with two dog heads designed to provide back-up should the first attempt to fire a shot fail to generate sparks. Mid-seventeenth century. (Thomas Del Mar Ltd)

yard. By 1575 there was a total prohibition on carrying handguns, dags or pistols, but it seems to have had little effect. Just a few years later, in 1579, she was complaining again that too many people were carrying handguns. According to the proclamation, the high crime rate was encouraging ordinary citizens to carry handguns for self-defence. The statement suggests that pistols were now more easily available and the price of wheel-locks must surely have dropped, since the implication is that ordinary citizens could now afford them.

One group of people was given specific permission to carry pistols, defined as gentlemen *which be without spot or doubt of evil behaviour*. These honourable men were permitted to carry a dag when travelling but it had to be openly displayed in a holster carried at the front of the saddle.

These orders and proclamations were the first in a very long line of bans and restrictions on the ownership, use and manufacture of firearms. Then, as now, no matter how many proclamations are made or laws enacted, there is always the chance that someone will find a way to evade them. In 1563 Francis, Duke of Guise, was killed by an assassin using a pistol and in 1584 an even

more illustrious victim, Prince William the Silent of the Netherlands (1533–1584), suffered the same fate. Both were shot with a wheel-lock pistol that had been loaded with three bullets, with the obvious intention of increasing the chance of a hit. According to contemporary accounts, the pistol that killed Prince William was a small dag that had been sold to the killer by a servant in the palace.

By the early sixteenth century the basic wheel-lock pistol was available but its sale must surely have been somewhat limited. The mechanism was complex and demanded a high degree of time, effort and skill from the craftsmen, increasing costs and making it an expensive item. The price of these pistols was such that in the sixteenth century they were seldom issued to the military and were generally restricted to bodyguards and some select cavalry units.

Since the cost of a pistol was high, possession of a wheel-lock indicated to the world that its owner was wealthy and important. Many owners sought to emphasize this impression by increasing the amount and quality of decoration on the stock of their pistol. Wood, ivory, bone and mother-of-pearl inlay were all used on many pistols, and lock plates and barrels were chiselled and engraved. This made the pistol something of a fashion item or status symbol and, for those who could afford it, higher-quality decoration became an important feature of the early pistols. As a general rule, the later into the sixteenth century the more elaborate the pistols.

As manufacturing techniques improved and gunsmiths became more skilled, production increased, with the result that prices fell and more people were able to afford to own a pistol. This led to a reduction in the amount of decoration and by the late sixteenth century, a simpler, more functional type of pistol became available.

Military wheel-lock pistol of Dutch manufacture, circa 1650, with the conventional fish-tail butt and plain walnut stock. The mechanism is of basic form with an external wheel. The Netherlands was one of the main suppliers of such pistols. (Thomas Del Mar Ltd)

By the seventeenth century, the designs and problems of manufacture had been simplified even further, so that costs had fallen sufficiently to enable much of the cavalry to be equipped with a pair of pistols.

The majority of early wheel-lock pistols were of German origin. Many of the sixteenth-century German wheel-locks had an angled butt with a large, ball-shaped pommel, which was not only decorative but also practical. This type of pistol has long been referred to as a 'puffer'. The pommel was certainly never intended for use as a cudgel – the pistol was too valuable and the fitting too fragile for that – but it did provide an easy and convenient grip when drawing the weapon from the saddle holster. At the same period many German pistols had a stock on which the butt was straight and almost in line with the barrel. Another feature that appeared on the late wheel-lock pistols is a curved almost hook-like arm on the cock, intended to provide an easy purchase when pulling it back.

The old matchlock musket did not easily lend itself to use on horseback, and the wheel-lock pistol therefore introduced a new tactic into war. Its portability meant that a cavalry-man could now carry a pair of pistols, charge the enemy, fire the pistols, then turn and ride away. Of course, he needed some convenient way to carry the pistols and by the later part of the sixteenth century holsters were in common use. As with the pistols themselves, the wealthy owner would have his holsters beautifully decorated, while those used by the common soldier tended to be plain and simple.

Parts and Accessories

Although there were variations on the main theme, the basic wheel-lock pistol consisted of a number of standard parts. First, it required a specially made barrel, since the pan, now fitted at the side, needed an aperture at its base that would be filled by the edge of the ridged wheel. The pan had a sliding cover, which was designed to open automatically as the pistol was fired, although some less complex models required it to be pushed clear manually.

The wheel, with its roughened, grooved edge, was mounted on the lock plate and linked internally by a short chain to the end of a powerful V spring. To prepare the pistol for firing, the breech was loaded with powder and ball, and the wheel was prepared or spanned by fitting the open end of a key, the 'spanner', over the axle of the wheel and

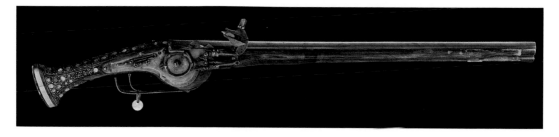

Wheel-lock pistol dating from around 1630 and slightly unusual in having an octagonal barrel. It has an external wheel and a characteristic, swelling, angled butt. The stock is decorated with inset brass scrolling and mother-of-pearl plaques. (Thomas Del Mar Ltd)

turning it. Just less than one full turn placed the spring under tension and at this point a small, spring-operated arm, or 'sear', clicked into place on the side of the wheel and locked it in position. Priming was now placed in the pan and the cover pushed forward to keep it safe from wind and weather.

A long angled arm, known as the 'cock' or 'dog head', terminated in a pair of adjustable jaws, which held the piece of pyrites (a naturally occurring iron-based mineral also known as 'fool's gold', because of its similarity to the precious metal). In order to fire a shot this arm was moved forward until the tip of the pyrites rested on the top of the pan cover. Pressure on a trigger operated internal levers, which pushed the cover clear of the pan, allowing the pyrites to drop slightly so that it was then in contact with the priming and the roughened edge of the wheel. The levers also retracted the retaining sear that was locking the wheel, so allowing the spring to turn the wheel. Friction between pyrites and wheel generated sparks directly into the priming and so fired the shot.

This was the basic wheel-lock system but there were variations in pattern and most early pistols were fitted with various safety catches. These were gradually discarded as the makers and design became more reliable. For total safety, the cock could be pulled back

so that there was no contact between pyrites and pan cover, making it impossible to generate sparks. As a very rough guide to dating wheel-lock pistols, the greater the number of buttons or studs on the lock plate, the earlier it is likely to be.

This new system made possible something that had been virtually impossible, or at least very difficult, with the matchlock. The wheel-lock pistol could be spanned, and the dog head lowered to the pan cover, and the pistol was then ready for instant action. There was no need for a glowing match, no need to check that it was alight, no need to adjust it. The loaded wheel-lock pistol was ready but quite safe and could be picked up and fired simply by a press on the trigger.

During the sixteenth century, as the knowledge of the new weapon spread across Europe, some national styles developed. On some early wheel-locks, the mainspring was fixed on the outside of the lock mechanism, but for the majority of pistols the entire lock mechanism was housed within the wooden stock. One problem encountered by early makers was that the size of the lock meant that a considerable amount of the wooden stock had to be removed to accommodate it. This obviously weakened the pistol and many early pistols have all-metal bodies. The French developed one rather unusual

A pair of mid-seventeenth-century wheel-lock pistols with typical curved stock and fish-tail butt, of Northern European origin. The wheel is, as usual, mounted externally. The spanner has been made as a turnscrew. (Thomas Del Mar Ltd)

system, whereby the mainspring was set in the stock and not attached to the plate. In another variation, the doghead was linked to the wheel and the action of pulling it back and returning it to the original position wound the wheel, so dispensing with the spanner.

The stock usually had a slightly angled butt section, often with an ovoid or multi-faceted pommel. Later in the century, the angle of the butt became sharper but the general appearance was neater and plainer. The military pistol that became common in the seventeenth century was usually straight, with only a slight down-turned curve to the butt, which terminated in a fish-tail pommel. Although the innovations generated by the introduction of the wheel-lock were probably of greater importance in the development of the handgun, the mechanism was also fitted to hunting firearms. The greater surface area offered by the larger weapon allowed even more elaborate decoration to be applied, and the hunting wheel-lock was often as much a work of art as a weapon.

With its newly acquired social status, the wheel-lock pistol's accessories were upgraded in quality to match the hand gun. The key or spanner used for rotating the wheel was chiselled, pierced and engraved to become a small masterpiece. Sometimes it was fitted with a turnscrew, while others were combined with simple powder measures. The old musketeer's wooden powder flask was supplanted by a variety of flasks, embellished with decoration such as inlay, carving, moulding and engraving.

Disadvantages

Despite its many advantages, the wheel-lock pistol was a complex piece of equipment and as such it was subject to breakdowns. The loss of the spanner meant that the gun could not be used; a break in the small chain or a broken spring could also render the weapon useless. The repair of such faults was beyond anyone but a competent gunsmith, and in this the wheel-lock was less practical than the trusty matchlock, which had been so simple to maintain. Loading could be a problem too – it was likely to take a little longer than for a matchlock and was a little more involved.

A pistol normally offered only one chance to score a hit and, once it had been fired, it became no more than an expensive bludgeon. The wheel-lock was often combined with another weapon – it may have been that the other weapon was fitted to the wheel-lock as a back-up weapon! The earliest surviving wheel-lock pistols were fitted to crossbows and there were also combination weapons, with a wheel-lock pistol fitted to a dagger, an axe or a mace. The effectiveness of such combination weapons is open to question; indeed, later experience suggests that such weapons often exhibit the worst features of each component.

If there was any chance of prolonged danger after the shot had been fired, it was as well to carry a reserve weapon. One solution to this problem was to carry two pistols, and numerous pairs of wheel-locks were produced. Interestingly, since each item was an individual production, matching pairs will sometimes be found to have minor differences of detail. Another solution was to make pistols that could fire two shots and this was achieved in various ways. One obvious method was to fit two barrels and two locks to a single stock and provide twin triggers. Such weapons were produced, but they tended to be rather cumbersome. A simpler system had twin barrels and a single lock operating both mechanisms.

Developments

Over the centuries the wheel-lock mechanism was gradually modified and simplified, and became increasingly easy to manufacture. By the early seventeenth century, the style of pistol also changed, with the butt becoming more angular and often terminating in a faceted ball shape. The stock became much slimmer, with a central extended section to accommodate the mechanism. The stock was almost straight and frequently terminated in a faceted pommel. Many were well decorated but a simpler form was beginning to make its appearance. The slim stock, usually of walnut, was plain, with the usual central section to accommodate the mechanism, and the butt was now of a gently down-curving shape with a slightly flared end, often encircled by a narrow metal band. The simplified form was adopted by the cavalry, commonly supplied in a pair, and saw service during the English Civil Wars of the 1640s. It was the adoption of the wheel-lock pistol that hastened the abandoning of armour by the majority of the cavalry.

The wheel-lock was gradually replaced by later systems and production ceased, although in the Brescia area of Northern Italy they were still being made in the early eighteenth century, when most of Europe had converted to the newer snaphaunce and flintlock mechanism. The early flint pistols tended to retain the basic shape of the wheel-lock stock, although the butt pommel was of a more rounded form, often with a decorative metal cap with small arms that extended up the sides of the butt.

Although it is likely that the wheel-lock was an Italian innovation, the majority of surviving examples are of German manufacture, with Nuremberg and Augsburg being the main centres. There are few examples that can definitely be ascribed to Italian manufacturers, while very early English-made wheel-locks are almost unknown and extremely rare.

CHAPTER 3

Flint and Steel

⌒ ⌒

Once a mechanical system of spark genera-tion was seen to be practical, similar lines of development were explored. The wheel-lock was a brilliant innovation but it was perhaps just a little too complex and a little too difficult and expensive to manufacture in quantity for it ever to become the universal handgun. Nevertheless, it had indicated the way ahead. If sparks could be generated mechanically, perhaps there was a simpler method to be discovered? The solution was an adaptation of the old, well-established system of spark production using flint and steel.

Flint, a hard, dark quartz rock, is relatively easy to work and shape, and was utilized by the earliest humans for tools, weapons and fire-making. It is found over wide areas of the world and England is fortunate in having some extensive flint deposits. There was an ancient, well-established trade in the mate-rial, and Brandon, a small town in Suffolk, had been a centre of flint-knapping – the shaping of the rock – for centuries. There is even some evidence that flint was begin-ning to replace pyrites on wheel-locks by the late sixteenth century[13]. Flint is far more common than pyrites and a flat piece of steel was much simpler to produce than a spring-operated wheel. Instead of manually striking flint and steel, was there a way to achieve the same result mechanically? Wedge-shaped flakes of flint were comparatively easy to produce in quantity and in any size, ranging from diminutive, for tiny pocket pistols, up to massive, for cannon locks.

The basic principle of the new mecha-nism was not too different from the wheel lock, and a method of using flint and steel seems to have first appeared somewhere in northern Europe, the Baltic, Scandinavia or North Germany. It is still not too clear as to precisely where it originated, but it was in that area, early in the sixteenth century, that the snaphaunce lock made its appearance. There is some controversy over the origin of this name but it is generally taken to refer to the movement of an arm, the cock, which swings forward in a movement thought to resemble the action of a hen pecking at food on the ground.

There is some academic division over the correct nomenclature of the style of locks that were developed around the mid-six-teenth century. This style of lock remained in general use in Northern Europe until well into the seventeenth century and is usually defined as the 'Baltic lock'. As commonly defined by collectors, the basic snaphaunce lock mechanism comprised a flat lock plate to which was attached a pivoted arm, at the end of which was a simple, two-jawed clamp holding a wedge-shaped piece of flint. The arm was linked to a strong spring attached to the inside of the lock plate. A second, short, pivoted arm, terminating in a small, vertical steel plate was also fitted on the outside of the lock plate. This plate was positioned to sit just above the pan and touch hole of the pistol.

To prepare the pistol for firing, a pinch of priming powder was put into the pan and retained in place by a sliding cover. The arm with the flat plate was moved forward until the plate sat vertically above the pan cover. Before the priming could be ignited, the pan cover obviously had to be pushed clear and on some early examples this was done by hand. By the second half of the sixteenth century a simple internal lever system ensured that, as the cock swung forward, the cover was automatically pushed clear.

The cock holding the flint was pulled back and this activated a small internal arm, the sear, the end of which projected through a slot in the lock plate. This sear engaged with the tail of the cock to hold it in this rear position. Pressure on the trigger withdrew the sear, allowing the spring to impel the arm forward in its pecking action. The flint scraped down the steel plate, pushing it clear of the pan and at the same time producing a shower of sparks, which fell into the priming. On the lock plate just ahead of the arm of the cock was fitted a metal block, the buffer, designed to halt the cock at the end of its swing.

The records show that by the 1580s the snaphaunce pistol was in use in England and the few recorded examples are quite highly decorated. The stock on many closely resembles that of the wheel-lock pistol, with a large, bulbous pommel.

This simple snaphaunce lock system had a comparatively short life, soon being ousted by the more sophisticated flintlock. It lingered longest with the Northern Italian gunmakers, who continued making such pistols well into the eighteenth century. Some Italian locks are recognizable by the coffin-like shape of the lock plate, which is very similar to those found on wheel-locks.

There were several variant forms of the snaphaunce lock and it was not long before the next step was taken – combining steel and pan cover into one piece. This L-shaped piece, usually known as the 'frizzen', was pivoted at the tip of the short arm which, when at rest, covered the pan. A small V-shaped spring held it in the closed position. The scraping action of the flint down the face of the frizzen tilted it forward, so lifting the section covering the pan, allowing the sparks to drop into the priming powder. This mechanism is described by most collectors as the 'flintlock', although there are those who maintain that this terminology is confusing. Whatever the quibble on definition, most collectors use the term 'flintlock' to describe actions which incorporate a combined pan cover and steel as a frizzen.

In some areas, including North Africa and parts of Asia, the snaphaunce lingered on until much later. Locks on many North African muskets are almost exactly the same in appearance as a seventeenth-century example, although they were probably made in Belgium at the Liège factories in the nineteenth century.

This fundamental development appears to have been introduced by Marin le Bourgeoys, a member of a French gunmaking family from Normandy, some time in the 1620s. It was simple, effective and from the mid-seventeenth century was gradually adopted throughout the world. As the principal lock mechanism it was to remain in common use until well into the nineteenth century. It was versatile and, although it underwent refinements and developments and was adapted for a variety of purposes, the basic system was retained. It could be adapted to any size and was used to operate devices other than firearms, such as alarm or time guns and warning guns.

The Flintlock

Whilst this new system offered undoubted advantages it removed one safety feature from the pistol. On a snaphaunce pistol, if the plate was raised clear of the pan the gun could not be fired even if the trigger were pressed, for there could be no contact between steel and flint. On the new flintlock system the frizzen had to be closed in order to retain the priming powder in the pan, which meant that the steel was in position above the pan. If the action was cocked, an accidental firing was possible. Because of this, the flintlock pistols were usually fitted with various safety catches.

THOMAS MONCK,
GUNSMITH, STAMFORD;

TAKES the liberty to acquaint his FRIENDS, and the PUBLIC in General, that he has engaged his Brother, EDMUND MONCK, Clock and Watch-maker, late Journeyman to *James Wilson*; and that he intends carrying on the Clock and Watch-making business.

Those who please to favour him with their Commands, may depend on their Orders being well executed, in the best Manner, on the lowest Terms, and the Favours gratefully acknowledged, by their most obedient Servant,

THOMAS MONCK.

STAMFORD: Printed by T. HOWGRAVE.

Eighteenth-century promotional leaflet by a Stamford (Lincs) gunmaker. It is likely that he sold pistols made in London and Birmingham rather than running a full-time gunmaking business, but at this period most towns of any size would have had one or more gunmakers.

The introduction of the flintlock was a major event and this ignition system was to remain, more or less, in universal use until the 1830s, by which time a newer system was gradually replacing it. During its long history it underwent changes in fashion, style and mechanical operation. It was incorporated into a range of combination weapons and the

A very rare pair of Dutch flintlock pistols of around 1760. The special, two-stage turn-off brass barrels are extremely heavy and it is thought that such pistols were intended to fire not only ball, but also grape and buck shot, and possibly even incendiary loads. (Thomas Del Mar Ltd)

workmanship ranged from superb quality to some rather crude, cheap, almost mass-produced pieces. The greater simplicity of the flintlock mechanism meant that it was cheaper and easier to make than the wheel lock and consequently its production costs fell and more people were able to afford to purchase a pistol. Most men of quality would probably have owned at least one pistol or gun, although their competence to use them may have been in doubt.

In January 1661 there was a minor armed uprising in London. On hearing uproar in the street, the famous diarist Samuel Pepys (1633–1703) went to investigate. He found his neighbours had armed themselves so he went back home and collected his pistol and sword, *though with no great courage at all, but that I might not seem to be afeared.* In fact he would have been fairly useless if there had been any need for action, for he then found that he could not load the pistol – *I had no powder to charge it.*

Pepys appears to have had a bit of an interest in handguns. In 1667 he purchased a repeating pistol that he described as 'very pretty', claiming that it would fire shot after shot without danger. However he later had it checked by William Trulock, a well-known London gunmaker of the period and gunmaker to Charles II, who was kind enough to take the time to strip down Pepys' pistol and explain the working to him. He praised the design and action but then, presumably, rather depressed Pepys by warning him that it was not safe to fire! Trulock made a significant contribution to gunmaking in his time, making some rather unusual flintlock pistols, experimenting with a different kind of breech mechanism, as well as producing at least one pair of long-barrelled rifled pistols.

Whilst the striking of flint on steel was basic to all forms of the flintlock, there were a number of ways of achieving the action, and these means were all subject to change. Since there is much overlap and interaction between the various styles of flintlock, it is probably simpler to detail the main patterns individually. There are, however, some expressions that are common to all the styles of lock: 'half cock' describes the mechanism when the cock holding the flint is usually upright and is locked in that position. Pressure on the trigger will have no effect, meaning that the pistol is safe. If the cock is then pulled further back it brings the

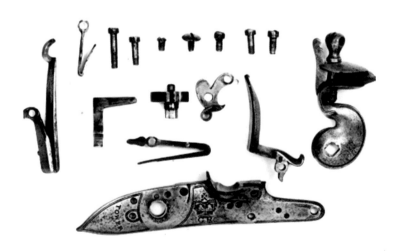

The component parts of a conventional flintlock from a Sea Service pistol of the early eighteenth century. The majority of the pieces would be either completely hand-made or at least hand-finished.

action to 'full cock'; at this point, any pressure on the trigger will allow the mechanism to operate, swing forward, strike sparks and fire a shot. If the lock is in reasonable condition there is usually an audible click from inside when each of these positions is set. When handling a flintlock pistol the trigger should never be pressed unless the frizzen is in the closed position. Failure to observe this safety measure will most likely result in the cock being damaged.

Although the basic mechanical action may have remained more or less standard, the decoration and method of construction of flintlock pistols did vary. A number of 'national' styles evolved and there were chronological differences. The different features did not start and stop on a set date but were most often in operation at the same time. When dating the various actions it must be remembered that there was never an official 'cut-off' date. Not only were differing styles of mechanism being used at the same time, but changes also occurred at different dates in different areas. The date of adoption of a new style varied from country to country and, indeed, from urban to rural areas within each country, with some provincial makers often being slow to adopt changes. There was also a certain conservatism among shooters and gunmakers, who continued to supply customers with pistols that were, by some standards, old-fashioned and dated. Fortunately, there has been a great deal of research over the past few years and there are now several reliable[14], standard reference books that give details of makers, their marks, dates and other information that is invaluable when dating a piece.

There are a few pointers that may help to suggest possible dates of manufacture of a flintlock pistol, but it must be stressed that these are very imprecise criteria, and exceptions are common. Whilst very much a 'rule of thumb', a pistol with a long barrel (say, around twelve inches or longer) is more likely to be earlier than one with a barrel of nine inches. This reduction in barrel length was partly due to an improvement in the quality of gunpowder, which later burned more quickly. The higher burning rate meant that the pressure in the barrel built up

A Police Office pistol of good quality, marked T.K. Hutchinson No 232 Borough, in reference to a street in London. The barrel is also engraved 'Union Street', the location of the Police Office. (Thomas Del Mar Ltd)

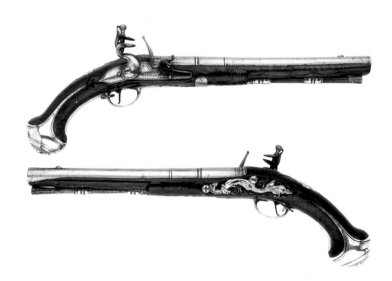

Fine pair of English flintlock pistols made about 1700 by Lewis Barbar, a French gunsmith who had settled in London. The stocks are of walnut with silver decoration. At one time their owner must have lived in Ireland for they bear the stamping required under an Act of 1841. (Thomas Del Mar Ltd)

much more rapidly, which meant that less barrel length was needed in order to achieve the same result. Military weapons tended to retain the longer barrel and they may well bear some special markings, too.

The greater the amount of decoration on a pistol, the earlier the weapon is likely to be, but this guideline is very general and other factors must be considered. A flintlock pistol of 1820 will almost certainly have a plainer stock and less decoration on the furniture than an early eighteenth-century example. There were also cycles of fashion and some decoration themes such as pineapple finials were common for a period, and then gradually disappeared from the pistol.

A lock that incorporates modifications to improve its performance will suggest later rather than earlier. On many early flintlock pistols the frizzen is usually secured to the lock plate by a single screw passing through its base. Later in the eighteenth century the fitting was made more secure and the base of the frizzen was supported between twin arms. A butt with a bulbous base and with arms extending up from the butt cap is usually an indication of an earlier date. Triggers with rear curling tips were a common feature on seventeenth-century pistols.

The English Lock

Common during the first part of the seventeenth century and used extensively on military pistols, the so-called 'English lock' was, in a way, a linking development between the original snaphaunce mechanism and the later flintlock. The main purpose was to ensure greater safety – once the pan was primed, the frizzen had to be closed or the priming would be lost. If the frizzen were closed it was possible that the cock could accidentally strike sparks and so fire a shot. What was wanted was a method to lock the cock in a safe position. (There is some academic controversy over the absolute definition of the flintlock mechanism and this volume relies on the idea that an ignition system utilizing a frizzen that combines steel and pan cover is by definition a flintlock.)

One feature that is taken by some to distinguish between most snaphaunce and flintlock mechanisms is an internal, irregularly shaped block known as the 'tumbler'.

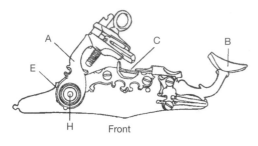

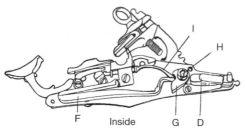

Snaphaunce. In order to prepare the lock for discharge the pan (C) is primed and the sliding cover closed. The cock (A) with a piece of flint in its jaws is then pulled back until held by the sear (D). This last projects through the lock-plate and engages in a recess cut in the inner face of the cock. The steel is then lowered onto the pan-cover, being held in that position by a spring in the same manner as the cock of a wheel-lock. Pressure on the trigger causes the sear to move laterally, so releasing the cock, which falls sharply forward under the action of the mainspring through a tumbler (G) attached to the cock spindle. As the tumbler turns it comes into contact with an arm (I) linked to the pan-cover, forcing the latter open at the same time as the flint knocks back the steel and strikes a shower of sparks from it into the pan.

This has two notches cut into the edge and these engage in turn with the tip of the main-spring, which presses down on the edge of the tumbler. The lock normally comprises a metal plate with a circular hole through which the arm of the tumbler projects; to this is attached the cock, usually by a single screw. The tumbler is held in position on the inside of the plate by a shaped fitting, the 'bridle'. The mainspring under pressure is secured

by a screw and has the tip pressing against the front edge of the tumbler. There is an L-shaped sear that is connected to the trigger and, powered by a small V-shaped spring, presses down against the edge of the tumbler. As the cock is pulled back, the tip of the sear engages, in turn, with two notches cut into the face of the tumbler.

In this first position (half cock), pressure on the trigger cannot disengage the sear because of the angle of engagement, and the action is locked. Pull the cock further back (full cock), so that, as the tumbler turns, the tip of the sear is lifted clear from the first notch and then clicks into the second notch. Pressure on the trigger can now lift the sear clear of the notch and allow the mainspring to make the cock swing forward. A small V spring holds the trigger in the forward position. Another small spring on the outside of the lock plate holds the frizzen in the closed position until it is pushed clear by the cock.

A second safety feature of many pistols with an English lock was a pivoted, hooked arm situated behind the cock. In the half-cock position it could be moved forward so that the hook engaged with a notch cut in the rear, lower section of the cock, again secur-ing it in a safe position. Pulling the cock back to the full-cock position automatically dis-engaged the hook. This feature is commonly referred to as a 'dog lock'.

The Miquelet Lock

Whilst most of Europe and America adopted the flintlock as described above, Spain and its domains were an exception. The vast major-ity of Spanish pistols have a special type of lock known as the Miquelet lock. There were two forms and, just as the dog fitting easily identifies the English lock, so the Spanish lock or patilla has a number of equally identi-fiable features. The flint is held between two

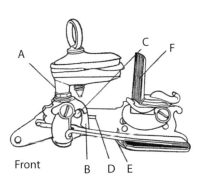

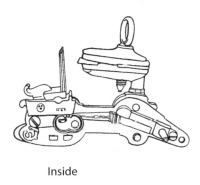

Front B D E   Inside

The Spanish Miquelet lock. The two arms of the sear project through the lock plate in front of the cock (A), the toe of which has a blade-like extension (B). The half-cock arm ends in a stud (C) which engages under the angle of the extension. The full-cock arm ends in a flat lug which engages under the blade when the cock is pulled back fully. Both arms are withdrawn laterally when the trigger is pressed. The mainspring (E) presses up on the heel of the cock.

large, square jaws through which passes a ring-neck, securing screw. The rectangular frizzen, which is deeply grooved, often has a detachable face, which, when it has been worn down by use, can be replaced by a fresh one.

The operating system of this lock is rather complex, differing considerably from the ordinary flintlock mechanism. First and most obvious is the fact that the mainspring is mounted on the outside of the lock plate. The second feature is that the mainspring pushes upwards against the toe of the cock in contrast to the flintlock, in which the spring presses down on the tumbler. The half-cock position is achieved by means of a small stud, mounted on the internal sear arm, which projects through the plate, engaging with the cock and rendering the pistol safe. Pulling back the cock to the full-cock position moves the sear bar and so withdraws the locking stud. By the same movement a flattened, thin, blade-like projection at the base of the cock engages with a second lug that also projects through the plate. Pressure on the trigger withdraws both arms on the sear, allowing the cock to swing forward and strike sparks.

This rather complicated system seems to offer little benefit, if any, over more usual systems. The cock is more complex in shape and the two locking features of bar and stud are without any great obvious advantage. The Spanish Miquelet lock is found on most pistols from Spain from the seventeenth

A pair of Continental small pocket or muff pistols of the late 18th century. They have turn-off barrels and top sliding safety catches. (Thomas del Mar Ltd)

century until the new percussion system was adopted.

Another lock that is somewhat similar to the patilla is the so-called Italian Miquelet, which was common in the south of Italy. One obvious difference is the cock, which is far more like the shape used by most European gunmakers, although the jaws still have a squarish rather than oval shape. Similarly, the frizzen is also rather squarish .The mechanism operates in a similar manner to the patilla with two studs projecting through the lock plate to engage the cock in both positions.

Madrid was the main centre of Spanish firearms production from the mid-sixteenth century, but later another centre developed at Ripoli in Catalonia, in the north-east corner of the Spanish peninsula. Many Ripoli pistols are rather short with a ball butt and are fitted with a belt hook. Another feature is that the stock is often covered with applied, pierced sheet-brass decoration.

Spanish gunmakers were greatly admired for the quality of their barrels and it was not uncommon for many English sporting guns to be fitted with Spanish barrels. This was also true of some English flintlock pistols. The Spanish gunmaker often identified his work by the addition of a small, inlaid gold poinçon, normally near the barrel breech.

Pistols of the Period

Until the mid-nineteenth century every handgun was unique – it was, to a greater or lesser degree, hand-made. Certain parts such as the brass fittings might well be cast and mass-produced, but the making of the lock and barrel, the shaping of the stock and the final assembly were all carried out by hand. The earliest gunmakers were metal-workers such as blacksmiths, armourers and lock-makers, but as the weapon technology developed other craftsmen – engravers, carpenters, gold- and silversmiths – became involved. The craftsmen eventually formed trade associations or guilds, each with its own air of mystery and set of rules, mainly designed to protect their members from competition. Not unnaturally, the guilds developed in the areas where the craftsmen were based and towns with a previous armour or edged weapons association became the earliest centres of firearm production. Nuremberg, Paris, Amsterdam, Vienna and Milan were soon as well known for their firearms trade as they had been for armour production. Guilds were set up and products were stamped with a mark identifying their place of manufacture.

In Britain, where there had never been a particularly strong armour trade, gunmakers guilds do not develop until later, beginning in the reign of Henry VIII. It took the English Civil Wars (1642–49) for the London gunmakers to establish their own Gunmakers Company, which soon included the Blacksmiths. In 1631 they, together with the Armourers, Pike and Bandolier Makers, had been granted permission to inspect and repair common weapons. The arrangement rather lapsed but in 1637 the group received a City Charter, granting it the right to establish the Gunmakers Company, which gave the guild control of the trade. It elected officials and formulated conditions and rules that members were bound to follow, and established a court to enforce the rules.

One right that the gunmakers cherished was that of testing or proving barrels. This involved taking the barrel, not yet in a finished condition, visually checking it and then loading it with a larger than normal charge of powder. It was then fired and examined for any cracks, fractures or bulges. If none was found then the barrel had passed the test, was granted proof and stamped with an

An Act for amending an Act of His present Majesty, to insure the proper and careful Manufacturing of Fire Arms in *England*, and for making Provision for proving the Barrels of such Fire Arms.

[12th *May* 1815.]

WHEREAS an Act was passed in the Fifty-third Year of the Reign of His present Majesty, intituled *An Act to insure the proper and careful Manufacturing of Fire Arms in* England, *and for making Provision for proving the Barrels of such Fire Arms* : And whereas the Powers and Provisions of the said Act have been found in some Respects defective and insufficient for the Purposes thereby intended, and the same cannot be effectually carried into Execution unless the Powers and Provisions thereof are amended : May it therefore please Your Majesty that it may be enacted ; and be it enacted by the King's most Excellent Majesty, by and with the Advice and Consent of the Lords Spiritual and Temporal, and Commons, in this present Parliament assembled, and by the Authority of the same, That from and after the passing of this Act, every Person who shall use or begin to use, or cause or procure to be used, or to be begun to be used, either by ribbing, break-off fitting, rough-stocking, or other Process, in any progressive State of Manufacture in the making, manufacturing, or finishing of any

53G.3.c.115.

Penalty for using in any of the progressive Stages of Manufacture of Fire Arms, Barrels not duly proved.

6 F

Extract from Proof Act, setting out conditions for sale and proof, and making it illegal to sell any unproved barrel.

official mark, usually near the breech. At first this mark was a crowned 'A', to represent the fact that the Armourers were officially in charge. Later, the Gunmakers took control and from 1657 barrels were stamped with the Company's marks, a 'V' to indicate that it had been viewed or examined, and a crowned 'GP' to indicate that it had passed the firing test.

Proving military weapons was not the responsibility of the gunmakers; instead, they were checked by the Government Board of Ordnance, which was responsible for all military stores. The Ordnance proof mark was first either an Irish Harp or a St George Cross, but following the Civil Wars it was changed to a royal cipher with a rose and crown. During the reign of William III (1689–1702), the rose and crown cipher was replaced by the crossed sceptres.

In the early days the English gun trade was concentrated in London, much of it in the vicinity of the Tower of London, where the offices of the Board of Ordnance were established. However, while it may have been the main centre of arms production, it was not the only one. The Midlands city of Birmingham was expanding and increasing its production of arms and the competition between the two towns became quite intense. In 1813 Birmingham finally acquired the right to set up and manage its own proof house, despite valiant efforts by the London Gunmakers to retain their monopoly. An Act of Parliament set out conditions and tables for the amount of powder to be used in the tests, stipulating also that the powder was to be of official Board of Ordnance quality. Birmingham adopted as its proof mark two sets of the crossed sceptres that were used by London, with the addition of the letters 'V' and 'BCP'. In 1815 an amending Act was passed setting out in detail the various charges to be made for proving barrels and the penalties for non-observance of the law. In 1855 the Gun Proof Act made it obligatory for every gun sold in England to be tested at one or other of the proof houses.

There were similar developments on the Continent, with each country setting up a professional body using its own marks. In Belgium the town of Liège blossomed into one of Europe's main arms produc-tion centres and the Liège mark – the letters 'ELG' in a crowned oval – is to be seen on many handguns, ranging from top-quality pieces to cheaper nineteenth-century per-cussion pistols. In North America, soon to become one of the largest producers of hand-guns, there was no development of official proof houses, although several manufactur-ers carried out their own proofing. A number of production centres and arsenals, such as Springfield, Harpers Ferry and Hartford, developed, especially during the nineteenth century.

The barrel of the weapon was obviously of prime importance and its manufacture involved much manual labour. They were made in several ways, all of which were time-consuming. Some were formed by winding a hot metal ribbon around a former and then hammer-welding it into a tube. If alternate ribbons of iron and steel were used, then the barrel acquired a pattern that could be enhanced by polishing and mildly corroding the surface. These 'Damascus' or 'stub-twist' barrels were highly prized, especially on sporting guns. Another method, apparently favoured in Spain, was to construct a number of short tubes, which were put end to end round a former and, by various methods, hammer-welded together into one full-length

barrel. It was believed that old horseshoes provided the best metal for this job as their continuous pounding on the roads resulted in a material of fine quality.

When the rough tubular barrel was com-plete it was then a matter of laboriously filing and smoothing the inside and outside sur-faces. For centuries this entire process was done by hand, using drills with special bits and files, and mounted on long benches. It was a long, tedious process until, at a later date, special mechanical drilling machines were developed. The barrels of smaller pistols were sometimes made in two pieces that screwed together. One section was the breech, which incorporated the touch hole; it was thicker and often slightly hollowed at the mouth, to allow a ball to be placed directly into it on top of the powder. The front section of the barrel was then screwed in place; this section often has a small, projecting base lug that engages with a circular key, which was slipped down over the barrel. This meant that more pressure could be applied, to ensure a tight fit between the two sections. This type is known as a 'turn-off' barrel and, as many were moulded in a similar style to that used on artillery guns, it is also known as a 'cannon' barrel.

As the century progressed, fashions changed, with the amount of moulding being reduced, so that by the turn of the eighteenth century most barrels were of plain tubular form. Towards the end of the century many pistols were fitted with octagonal barrels. A small number of pistols were made with a blunderbuss-style barrel, with a flaring muzzle, based on the rather misguided belief that this shape made for a greater spread if the pistol were loaded with shot rather than a ball.

When the barrel was nearly finished it had to be breeched and one end of the tube sealed off. On most ordinary barrels the breech

Two French powder flasks fashioned from coconut shells decorated overall with low-relief carving of costumed figures and cavalry and with white metal nozzles. Early 19th century. (Thomas del Mar Ltd)

plug usually has a rear, flat narrow extension, which is let into the body of the pistol, known as the stock, and screwed in place to secure the barrel. To hold the rest of the barrel in place, one or more small rectangular lugs, each drilled with a hole, were fitted beneath the barrel. These engaged with slots cut into the stock and small metal pins were passed through the stock and the lugs, securing the barrel. Later, on pistols of better quality, the breech plug was often fitted with a rear-projecting, stubby hook and at the back of the recess in the stock there was a metal plate into which the hook fitted. This made for a stronger union and, coupled with one cross-fitting bar and lug, rather than several pins, allowed quick and easy removal of the barrel.

On the Continent the barrel and stock were more commonly united by encircling metal barrel-bands, while the British favoured the lug and pin method for pistols. Sights were fitted on some pistol barrels – these were normally either a front bead or blade with a V-shaped back sight set above the breech, but design did vary. When smaller pistols are fitted with sights it is likely that they are cosmetic rather than practical. Until the advent of rifling, accuracy, except at close range, was not one of the main features of the early pistols.

Some pistols, especially the more expensive models, had barrels that were browned, a colour achieved by polishing and controlling the rusting process. It was not only decorative but also served to prevent further rusting. The browning was particularly attractive when applied to twist barrels as the colouring emphasized the pattern rather effectively. When pepperboxes and revolvers became fashionable, the metal parts were more often blued rather than browned. The blue colour was achieved by carefully controlled heating processes.

The accuracy of a pistol depends on many features, not least on the fit of the ball in the barrel. As the charge of powder burns, the gas pressure builds up and pushes the ball along the barrel. If the fit is loose, there is a tendency for the ball to wobble on its journey along the bore to the muzzle, and for gas to escape around the ball. At the moment when it leaves the muzzle any one part of the ball may be in contact with any area of the internal surface of the barrel. This contact can generate a slight drag at that point, giving the projectile a very slight bias in one direction or another. When that tiny deflection is extended over, perhaps, twenty yards, it results in a substantial deviation in the path of the bullet.

One of a pair of steel box-lock flintlock pocket pistols with turn-off barrels, signed 'Segallas London', but almost certainly made in Liège in Belgium. The barrels have the small lug at their base, to engage with a turning key. These pistols were produced in quantity in the early nineteenth century. (Thomas Del Mar Ltd)

One way to reduce inaccuracy was to ensure a firm fit between ball and barrel. This was sometimes done by wrapping a patch of paper, cloth or thin leather around the ball prior to loading it into the barrel, but, while this method improved the pistol's accuracy, it also slowed the rate of fire. The very tight fit of the ball made it more difficult to ram it home – the shooter often had to use a small hammer to force the ramrod down the barrel.

Although, at first, the details of the mathematics and science may not have been fully understood, it was known that, if the bullet could be made to spin as it left the muzzle, this would improve accuracy. The gyroscopic effect would help keep it on a much straighter course. The problem of how to spin the ball was eventually overcome by 'rifling' the barrel, that is to say, cutting a series of shallow, spiral grooves on the inside surface of the barrel. As long as there was a good fit, the grooves would grip the lead bullet, forcing it to follow them so that, as it emerged from the muzzle, it would be rotating about its axis and consequently more stable. It is unclear exactly when rifled barrels were first made, but there is evidence to suggest that some crude experiments were carried out as early as the fifteenth century.

With the mechanical facilities available at the time it was no easy matter to cut shallow grooves of a consistent depth on the inside surface of the barrel – it was achieved only by a process involving special drill bits and slow manual control. It was not until the seventeenth century that rifling became more generally available, and not until the nineteenth century that special machinery designed to do the job came into general use. A rifled handgun was far more accurate than the usual smooth-bore pistol and one anecdote has Prince Rupert (1618–1682), nephew of Charles I and a talented cavalry commander during the English Civil Wars, hitting the weathercock of a church in Stafford from a range of 60 paces. He was teased by friends, who claimed that his success was due more to luck than to accuracy, but the story goes on to assert that he then drew the second of his pistols and repeated the shot.

It was common practice for a gunmaker to engrave his name and address along the top of the barrel. The lock plate often carries the name of the maker and sometimes the date of manufacture. However, the presence of a name on the barrel or lock does not

Cased pair of flintlock holster pistols by John Probin, a Birmingham gunmaker circa 1780, although these are London proved. They are fairly typical with sliding bolt safety catches and slab-sided butts. (Thomas Del Mar Ltd)

necessarily mean that the pistol was made by that gunmaker. It was not uncommon for small gunmakers, especially those in the provinces, to purchase ready-made weapons or parts from London and Birmingham, and then engrave them with their own name.

The lock was obviously the most complex part of the pistol and its production called upon the skills of filers and above all spring-makers. The elasticity of a spring depended on its tempering, which was achieved by heating it to a certain temperature. The production of a good-quality spring was largely determined by an instinctive appreciation of the colour of the metal during this heating process. The colour of the hot spring was the indication of the correct working temperature and the craftsmen judged this by eye.

The shape of the spring was also vital for the correct functioning of the lock and most collectors will confirm that the number of broken springs found on antique pistols is impressively small, indicating the highly professional skills of the craftsmen. Early lock plates to which the mechanism was attached were frequently decorated with quality engraving and chiselling. With the exception of those on high-quality, expensive pistols from the eighteenth century, most lock plates are fairly plain, with decoration limited perhaps to some restrained, incised line engraving. The vast majority of flintlock pistols have the lock set on the right-hand side of the stock but occasionally a pair of pistols will be found in which one pistol has the lock fitted on the left-hand side.

Walnut was the preferred wood for pistol stocks although other, more elaborately grained woods were used on occasions. There are several types of walnut, each of which has its own characteristic colouring and graining. Black American walnut was commonly used by the American colonists for their gunstocks and was favoured for its colours, which vary from near-black or brown to almost yellow. English or Circassian walnut came from the Asia Minor area and had originally been introduced into England by the Romans. Its virtues in gunmaking were soon appreciated – once seasoned, it is remarkably stable, never shrinking or cracking even under the repeated shock of recoils[15].

At first, most pistols were full-stocked, with the wooden body extending the full length of the barrel. By the turn of the eighteenth century, there was a change and more pistols were half-stocked, with the wooden body ending half-way along the barrel. The

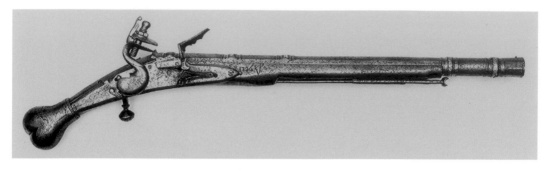

Scottish pistol of the seventeenth century with typical metal stock, pillar and ball trigger and heart-shaped butt. The thin ramrod housed beneath the stock is typical of this style of pistol.

tip of the stock was often capped with a horn end.

Whilst most early wheel-lock pistols were made with metal stocks, the majority of later pistols were fitted with wooden stocks. Scottish and Balkan pistols were commonly fitted with metal stocks and in the later part of the eighteenth century many small pocket pistols were similarly produced. A few pistols were fitted with ivory stocks and the Netherlands gunmakers of the early seventeenth century were particularly noted for their skill in this field. Some of their pistols were fitted with stocks on which the butt terminated with a pommel in the shape of a carved head.

Presentation pistols commonly had a stock embellished with carving and inlay of precious metal, but many of the smaller eighteenth-century pocket pistols had a stock decorated with inlaid silver wire. The stock was carved with narrow, slightly undercut, channels into which the silver wire was laid and then firmly pressed home to expand and sit snugly in place. Shaping the stock and seating the various parts of the pistol was a highly skilled job and on top-class pistols the fit is so good that it is difficult to feel the junction of wood and metal. Some wood-working machines were later developed but these were largely used in manufacturing long arms, on which the shape to the stock lent itself better to machine cutting.

The shape of the butt was important – in the best pistols it was set in such a way that, when the pistol was taken up in the hand for aiming, it immediately felt comfortable and secure and sat in a comfortable aiming position. The majority of flintlock pistols are fitted with a slightly angled or curved butt but other shapes were tried. It was common practice to chequer or cross-hatch the butt with a diamond pattern, to provide a slightly firmer grip.

The stock was often embellished with carving around the various pieces of metal furniture, such as the trigger guard, ramrod pipes and butt cap, but on the whole, unlike sporting guns, the decoration was restrained. Most of the pistol furniture, including trigger guards was of brass, iron, silver or, very rarely, gold. The detail of the fittings varied over the centuries and these can be a useful indication of date, with the comparatively plain style indicating a later item.

In the late seventeenth and early eighteenth centuries, pistol butts commonly terminated with a globose, bulbous shape but this feature gradually disappeared in the eighteenth century, when the butt was given a smoother, simpler shape. The butt pommel on early pistols was often covered with a metal cap of brass, silver or steel, with long side arms extending up the butt, but these were gradually shortened and the fashion

Barrel of a very rare box-lock flintlock pistol engraved with 'High Street Public Office Marylebone'. This was carried by an officer of a small group of constables based in London in the early nineteenth century.

faded away in the eighteenth century. Many of the pocket pistols of the early part of the eighteenth century were fitted with silver butt masks, usually in the form of a grotesque face. Sometimes these masks carry hallmarks and this can help date the pistol; unfortunately, not all are marked in this way.

Another feature common in the period was a small, sometimes elaborate, shield or cartouche, often of silver, set in the butt on which the owner could have his initials or crest engraved. Vanity could be an owner's

downfall. In the notorious attack on the Duke of Ormonde in December 1676, one of the clues left behind was a pistol bearing the initials 'TH'. Thus, the perpetrator was deemed to be Thomas Hunt, a known villain. (Incidentally, in contemporary accounts the pistol is described as a silver-mounted, 'screwed' pocket version, the term 'screwed' implying that the barrel may have been rifled, which was unusual for a pistol of that period.) Despite the identification, the whole mysterious affair was never really sorted satisfactorily[16].

In most gunsmiths' workshops, each worker was normally responsible for one aspect of the manufacture – some working on the stocks, some on springs, and some on the barrels – and when all the parts were finished it was the job of one or two men to put the whole thing together and finish off the job. When a pistol is stripped it is quite possible to find certain marks – a couple of parallel lines, a cross or something similar – scratched on some hidden part of the weapon. These marks would have been made by the workman to identity the various parts for a particular pistol that he was assembling.

The typical box-lock mechanism designed to fit centrally above the breech of a pistol with the trigger hanging below. It has a top sliding safety catch and the mainspring is fitted behind the action, so saving space.

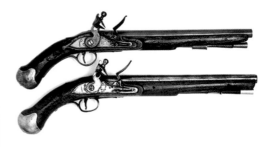

Top: A good example of the early eighteenth-century long-barrelled Sea Service flintlock pistol. Bottom: A modern replica that is just not quite right. The butt is slightly out in the angle and a close comparison of the two will reveal other minor differences. If this was capable of being fired it would be illegal in the UK.

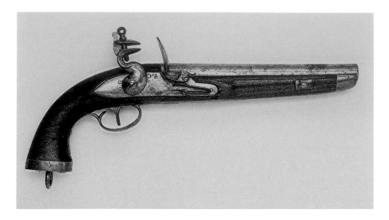

The Belgian town of Liège continued manufacturing percussion pistols long after they were considered old-fashioned and out of date. The pistols were exported to Asia and Africa but were also supplied to some armed forces. The design was simple but practical. This example dates from the later part of the nineteenth century. (Thomas Del Mar Ltd)

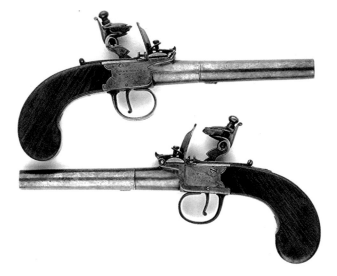

A pair of long-barrelled box-lock flintlock pistols as carried by officers of a Public or Police Office located at Worship Street, London, circa 1810. (Thomas Del Mar Ltd)

Loading the pistol required the use of a ramrod to press down the powder and ball into the breech. The majority of ramrods were of wood with a slightly flared horn tip at one end. On some of the more expensive pistols the rods were fitted, at the opposite end, with a corkscrew-like fitting, the 'worm', or a short, metal, angular section, or 'jag'. On some good-quality pistols, this worm was housed in a detachable brass cover. In the event of a problem, perhaps a misfire, the pistol needed to be unloaded. For this purpose the ramrod was pushed down the barrel and the worm screwed into the lead ball and, once firmly engaged, the rod was withdrawn complete with lead ball. The jag was used, with a piece of material wrapped around it, for cleaning the barrel.

The ramrod was housed in a slot cut into the stock beneath the barrel. It was held in place by one or two tubes, the ramrod pipes. Metal ramrods were sometimes used and on some pistols of the late eighteenth and early nineteenth centuries a special pivoted link, fitted below the muzzle, secured the ramrod to the barrel, to reduce the chances of losing it.

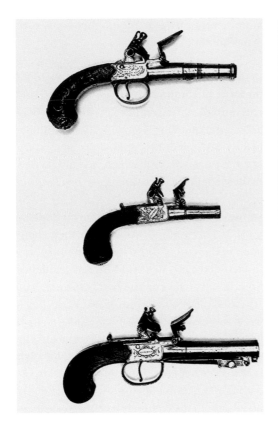

Examples of popular box-lock pocket pistols. Top: Early eighteenth-century model with silver-wire inlay decoration and turn-off barrel. Middle: Later version with top sliding safety catch and drop-down trigger. Bottom: Similar example with spring bayonet locked back by the trigger guard.

No matter how well made the flintlock pistol was, its various projections, such as the cock and the frizzen, made it difficult to carry comfortably in a pocket. One form of lock, which was very popular during the eighteenth century, had the cock set centrally above the breech rather than at the side, as on most pistols. A simple mechanism with a lever and spring was set beneath the cock and housed in the frame and stock. The frizzen and touch hole were centrally situated on top of the breech, while the trigger hung below. Known as the 'box lock', it offered certain advantages – the result was a pistol with a more confined shape. This meant that it would sit more comfortably in a pocket or pouch and was also less likely to snag on clothing when being drawn.

Since there was always a slight danger of an accidental discharge, many box-lock pistols were equipped with a sliding safety catch. Set on top of the breech, the catch fitted around the cock and, when pushed forward, engaged it in the half-cock position. On many of the pistols a small projecting rod on the front of the catch engaged with a small hole in the frizzen and locked that shut. Another safety feature often found on these pistols is a folding trigger, which folds up into the frame of the pistol; only when the weapon is cocked does the trigger drop down into position. Another safety system used a sliding trigger guard that could be pushed forward to lock the mechanism. Some larger versions of the box-lock, with turn-off, cannon barrels, are known as 'Queen Anne pistols', although they were in use long after the good queen had died, in 1714. The same style of Queen Anne pistol, often with inlaid silver wire decoration, may also be found with a less conventional side-mounted lock.

On conventional, larger flintlock pistols there is often a sliding safety catch fitted on the lock plate. It comprises a short flat bar that can be pushed forward to engage with a slot cut into the rear of the cock when it is set to the half-cock position. Prior to firing a shot, this safety catch had to be manually pulled back.

Efforts to improve the effectiveness of the conventional lock were introduced on the more expensive pistols and from around the 1770s a small roller-bearing was fitted to the toe of the frizzen. This reduced friction between frizzen and spring, speeding the action slightly and perhaps making it a little more positive. Mostly fitted to long arm locks was the detent, a small weighted lever set inside the lock. When the weapon was held with the muzzle vertical, the detent dropped into a position that prevented the lock working; when the gun was held normally it moved clear. Unfortunately, it did have a slight tendency to jam, which could be inconvenient, to say the least.

When powder burns it causes some corrosion and over a period this can build up and damage the surface of the metal. On better-quality pistols, to reduce or delay the corrosion, the surface of the pan was given a thin layer of gold, a metal which is unaffected by corrosion. The same protection was given to the touch hole, which was fitted with a lining of gold or, from early in the nineteenth century, platinum.

It was important to ensure that the priming powder was kept dry for, if it failed to burn, there was no shot. Closing the frizzen gave some protection, but rain and damp could be a problem. So-called 'waterproof' pans were produced but they were no more than the usual pan with a slightly raised rim running round the edge, which helped to reduce to a minimum any gap between frizzen and pan.

One virtue of the flintlock mechanism was that it could be made in any size, ranging from locks big enough to be mounted on cannon down to tiny locks mounted in the handle of a knife. To a lesser degree the wheel-lock pistol had the same flexibility, but most were made large rather than small. With the advent of the seventeenth century the majority were less bulky, however the same century saw a change in male fashion, with the earlier 'cloak or robe' being replaced by coats and breeches. The older, belt-attached purse was discarded. Instead, slit, inset pockets or pouches were fitted in clothes and the gun trade, no doubt, soon realized that there was

a market for pistols to fit into these new personal holders.

The seventeenth century saw a big increase in the production of pocket pistols, in a trend that was to continue into the eighteenth and early nineteenth centuries. Although there are no set standards or definitions, antique pistols are generally graded in size, starting with the smallest which are only a few inches in length. These are described as 'muff pistols', since they were allegedly carried by young ladies or gentlemen concealed inside a muff. The muff, as a hand warmer, dates back to the end of the sixteenth century but, in fact, there is a dearth of literary evidence linking the pistol and the hand warmer. The seventeenth-century muff pistol often has a neat, rather bulbous wooden stock, a short barrel and often lacks a trigger guard. The next definable size is the pocket pistol, which is around six or more inches long. The largest pistols are variously described as holster pistols, or, in the eighteenth century, as horse pistols; these are around ten, twelve or more inches long. There is an intermediate size falling between pocket and holster, and these are grouped as overcoat pistols. There are no set criteria for these names; they are simply a convenient phrasing used by collectors and those involved with the antique firearms trade.

Duelling Pistols

Honour is a vaguely defined quality, but it was to many people an incredibly valuable one. Over the centuries hundreds of men have died defending their honour against some trifling insult. To the gentleman who had become increasingly paranoid about alleged slurs upon his character, there was only one way to deal with the slight – to 'call out' the offender and challenge him to a duel. Elaborate rules gradually developed around

A flintlock Irish duelling pistol made about 1810 by Dublin gunmaker T. Pattison and later converted to percussion by the drum and nipple method. It is half-stocked and has a saw-handle butt. As it is Irish, it bears the 1841 registration mark. (Thomas Del Mar Ltd)

the rituals for the moment when matters came to the point of no return and had to be settled, either by an apology with ignominy, or by combat.

Trial by combat to settle a question of guilt had been common during the Middle Ages, based on the concept that God would protect the innocent. By the sixteenth century private duels to settle an argument were commonplace and the practice was to continue until the nineteenth century. The French and Irish seem to have been especially conscious of an insult and hundreds of them died as a result of this sensitivity.

Until the later part of the eighteenth century the duel was normally settled with the sword, although various bizarre variations did take place. From about the 1770s there was a gradual conversion from blade to bullet and the pistol became the weapon of choice. The reason for the change is not immediately obvious but no doubt it was affected by the fact that the everyday carrying of a sword by civilians had begun to go out of fashion. It was also less fashionable for a young man to learn the art of fencing, although it was often still part of his edu-

cation – more as a social grace rather than a matter of self-defence. At the same time, pistols were becoming everyday objects. It may also have been seen by some that the chances of surviving a pistol duel were slightly better than the chance of surviving a sword fight. Combatants using pistols were in mortal danger for only a very short time whereas a sword fight might continue for a long time. Whatever the reasons, the pistol took over the field of honour.

Books began to be written on the correct etiquette of arranging and fighting a duel[17]. Published in the mid-nineteenth century, *The*

Blunderbuss pistol by Galton, the lock dated 1780. The effect of the Belling barrel would only be noticeable if the pistol were loaded with shot.

Officer's percussion pistol by W. Ketland of Birmingham, circa 1830. It is half-stocked and fitted with a spur trigger guard. The octagonal barrel is fitted with sights and has gold line decoration at the breech. (Thomas Del Mar Ltd)

Code of Honour declared that the pistols should be smooth-bore and not exceed nine inches in length, but fails to clarify whether this refers to just the barrel length or the whole pistol. It also specifies that flint and steel weapons should be used, but allows percussion pistols if that option is agreed by all involved. The method of handing the loaded pistol to the duellist is clearly defined: 'in presenting the pistol … never put it in his pistol hand, but place it in the other, which is grasped midway [along] the barrel'. The ready-to-shoot stance is defined as muzzle down and barrel away, and insists that the barrel up position is not acceptable. There was however no single universal ritual for the duel and different distances at which the shots should be fired, as well as the command or signal to fire, could be decided at the time by the parties involved.

It was obvious to gunmakers and duellists alike that, if lives were at risk, then the pistol had to be totally reliable; consequently, the flintlock weapon probably reached its peak of perfection as the duelling pistol. Since the chances of each combatant had to be equal, it was important that the pistols were, as far as

Officer's pistol by William Parker, circa 1815. The lock incorporates all the finest points: sliding safety catch, roller bearings on the frizzen and platinum plug touch hole and damp-proof pan. The barrel is fitted with sights and a swivel ramrod, which suggests it was not intended as a dueller.

possible, exactly alike. Duelling pistols were normally supplied in pairs and it was customary for any gentleman of quality to purchase a cased pair of duelling pistols. Inside the case, in addition to the pistols, would be a number of accessories, including items such as a powder flask, bullet mould and turnscrew.

Part of the ritual surrounding the duel was the choice of weapons and it was normally the right of the challenged to have the first option. The friends supporting the duellists, the seconds, were supposed to supervise the loading of the weapons to ensure that there was no sharp practice. However, it is known that there were one or two little scams, such as reducing the powder charge of one pistol. Some cased pistols were supplied with a small tubular fitting which screwed on to the end of the ramrod. This was filled with the powder charge and, with the pistol held vertically, muzzle down, was pushed up the barrel until it reached the breech. Pistol and rod were then upended, depositing the charge directly into the breech. This was to overcome the chances of some powder adhering to the inside of the barrel, slightly reducing the total charge of powder.

At first, the standard officer's pistol would have been used for the duel and these were generally full-stocked. By the turn of the century most pistols specially made for the duel were half-stocked and the round

barrel had been replaced by one of octagonal section. This made the pistol a little heavier, which was thought to benefit the shooter as it made it less likely to shake. The use of rifling on a dueller was considered to be unsporting, although there are cases where the apparently smooth-bore barrel was, in fact, rifled from an inch or so down from the muzzle. How much difference this made to the aim is unknown. Most duelling pistols had sights, usually of blade and V shape, but barrels and, indeed, most fittings were blued or browned. The purists feared that silver or bright items might flash in the sunlight of early dawn and distract the shooter.

Moves to provide a firmer grip were made early in the nineteenth century and from about 1805 the base of the trigger guard was often fitted with a down-curving extension. This was positioned in such a way that, when aiming, the middle finger fitted naturally into it , which improved the grip and steadied the aim. This feature was later adopted by Smith & Wesson on their Russian Model revolver produced in the 1870s. A little later in the eighteenth century the pistol butt was modified and many pistols were then fitted with a saw-handle grip, which had a top extension that extended backwards over the web of the thumb, again to steady the grip.

Another refinement fitted to some duelling pistols and sporting guns was a hair, or

Royal Mail coach guard's flintlock pistol by H.W. Mortimer, circa 1800 and numbered 221. This would have been one of a pair of brass-barrelled pistols carried by the guard together with a blunderbuss.

In 1784 the Royal Mail started their mail coaches system. Each coach carried a guard armed with two flintlock pistols and a blunderbuss. For years these weapons were supplied by the gunmaker H. W. Mortimer.

set, trigger. This simple mechanism made the trigger very sensitive, so that only the slightest touch was sufficient to activate the lock mechanism. The set trigger had to be adjusted by means of a small lever or screw positioned near the trigger or by moving the trigger itself.

By this means, the pressure required to activate the lock could be reduced to an absolute minimum. This ensured a slightly steadier aim, since there was less time for the shooter to impart any possible bias to one side or the other as he pressed the trigger.

A good-quality pair of officers' pistols by William Parker of Holborn, London, circa 1820. The locks have sliding safety catches, and roller bearings on the frizzens ensure a smooth action. The barrels are fitted with swivel ramrods to prevent any chance of loss.

A good cased set of duelling pistols was expensive but they were considered part of a gentleman's fixtures. They were supplied by many of the finest gunmakers in London, including Egg, Manton, Mortimer, Nock, Harding and Parker. One maker, Wogdon, achieved a somewhat exalted reputation as one of the best makers for duelling pistols and was hailed as Wogdon, 'patron of the leaden death'.

Public support for the practice of duelling waned from early in the nineteenth century, especially as there were one or two unpleasant incidents. If one contestant was killed in the duel, technically the winner was likely to be charged with murder, but many fled the country immediately after the event. In the 1840s the British Army and Navy forbade officers from taking or making challenges to duels and the whole system began to fade away. On the Continent duelling lingered on, although in Germany the sword retained pride of place. In France pistols were often favoured and French makers supplied cased pairs of duelling or target pistols. These are usually far more elaborate than the English versions, with more decoration and extra tools in the case. One big difference was that most French pistols were rifled and the tight fit of the bullet necessitated the inclusion of a small hammer to drive home the load.

Scottish Pistols

Scotland's early history was violent, and continued to be so until the nineteenth century, so it is not surprising that a small but strong weapons industry developed. The basket-hilted sword and the dirk are probably the weapons most associated with the country, but Scottish firearms form a very distinctive group. Although literary evidence clearly shows that wheel-lock pistols were in use in Scotland at an early date, unfortunately none is known to have survived.

Early proclamations sought to forbid the carrying and use of firearms. In November 1567 a proclamation from the Regent and Secret Council forbade carrying of any *daggis, pistolettes and uthe sic ingynis*. It apparently had little effect, for in July 1568 another proclamation spoke of brawling and

Scottish flintlock pistol of the third quarter of the eighteenth century. The steel stock and barrel both have engraved decoration. There is a slender belt hook and the butt is of ram's-horn style with a central ball pricker. (Thomas Del Mar Ltd)

An early eighteenth-century Scottish flintlock pistol. The original barrel has been replaced by one of Continental manufacture. The brass stock is fitted with a long belt hook. The butt is of the typical ram's-horn style and at the centre of the scrolls is the ball-mounted pricker for clearing the touch hole. (Thomas Del Mar Ltd)

carrying of arms during the coronation of James VI. In 1580, 1593 and 1595, there were further proclamations banning the carrying of *dags*. In 1597/98, the sternest proclamations threatened death for those making and mending *pistolets*[18].

These proclamations were almost certainly referring to wheel-lock pistols but the earliest surviving Scottish pistols are fitted with snaphaunce locks. Examples date from the early seventeenth century and most have similar features: they have no half-cock position and the pan cover is connected to the lock, ensuring that it is automatically pushed clear when the trigger is pressed. The pistols also have a circular cover, or 'fence', at the end of the pan that is often engraved with a date of manufacture. However, as this can be easily replaced, such dates must be considered speculative. The early versions of the lock had a sear, which engaged with the rear of the cock, but from the late 1640s there was a change, with the sear now engaging with a tumbler rather than directly with the cock. Scottish gunmaking seems to have been

a local skill, with one craftsman working on the whole pistol. This differs from the English trade, in which specialist craftsmen each worked on one particular part of the pistol (although later there was apparently a change to the English system). In Scotland, Dundee, Doune and Edinburgh were centres of production.

Another common feature appears about the same period: stocks of the pistol that had been of wood and metal were now all metal, and the flat-sided butt terminated in a metal butt cap of a style known as 'fish-tail'. One unusual feature found on these Scottish pistols is that some pairs were made with one right- and one left-hand lock. Most pistols are also fitted with belt hooks and this arrangement of the locks may possibly have been designed so that the two pistols could sit comfortably one on each side of the waist belt or sash. Yet another particular feature is that these early pistols are seldom fitted with trigger guards and, instead of being narrow and flat, the triggers are moulded rather like small columns.

Around the middle of the century the butt's shape underwent a change and the 'ram's-horn' style came into fashion. Around the same date, many Scottish pistols, possibly through English influence, now had a lock with the combined L-shaped frizzen. At the base of the butt and situated between the incurving horns was a small ball that unscrewed to reveal a fitted pin used to clean out the touch hole. This style was to persist and formed the basic style of Scottish pistols for the rest of their working lives, including the dress pistol that was favoured during the nineteenth century.

In 1715 there was an ill-fated Jacobite Rebellion in Scotland led by James Stuart, The Old Pretender, aimed at deposing the Hanoverian king. Following its defeat, in an attempt to prevent another similar event, restrictive Scottish legislation, including a Disarming Act, was passed[19]. This forbade inhabitants of certain parts of the country from owning *any broadsword, target* [a Highland shield], *poynard, whingar, durk* [edged weapons], *side pistol, gun, or other warlike weapons.* Exceptions were made for members of the landed gentry and officers, who were allowed to own two firelocks, two pairs of pistols and two swords. Judging by the armament that was still around some thirty years later, at the time of Bonnie Prince Charlie's 1745 Jacobite uprising, the Act appears not to have been very effective. Following the defeat of the Scots at the Battle of Culloden in 1746, the Government set about destroying the Highland culture; the Act of Proscription included the Dress Act, which forbade the wearing of the tartan, banned the use of the Gaelic language and insisted that weapons were to be surrendered.

Scottish culture rather fell from favour after this, but matters underwent a marked change largely as the results of the work of novelist Sir Walter Scott (1771–1832). The strong Scottish background in his extremely popular books soon generated a new interest in Scotland and its traditions. Scott was invited to dine with King George IV (1820–1830) and at the event he suggested that a royal visit to Scotland would be very popular. The idea was taken up and great plans were made for a trip in August 1822. Various parades and events were organized, many based on a rather romantic concept of Highland life, clans, tartans and their history. As a result of Scott's novels and the King's visit, all things Scottish suddenly became very popular and much sought after by those anxious to be in fashion. There was a demand for costume Scottish weapons and numbers of decorative, rather than practical, pistols were made around this period.

In the mid-eighteenth century the Scottish pistol made a surprise appearance as part of the official arms of the British Army. After the Battle of Culloden in 1746, although punitive legislation had been introduced in Scotland, recruiting for Scottish regiments was begun. Various units were formed and, in sympathy with tradition, some were armed with basket-hilted Scottish broadswords. In 1757 tradition was strengthened when two new Highland Battalions, commanded by Colonel Archibald Montgomery and Colonel Simon Fraser, were equipped with flintlock pistols, unusual for foot soldiers. Montgomery paid for them but in 1757 was reimbursed by the Board of Ordnance. The concession was extended to two other Scottish officers.

There were two types of Scottish pistol issued, neither of which was of remarkable quality, and the Board of Ordnance is known to have queried the price paid. One model supplied by Isaac Bissell, a Birmingham gunmaker, was of all-metal construction with a butt terminating with an inward-curving ram's-horn finial with a central touch-hole cleaner. The stock tapered and finished an inch or so from the muzzle. The signed lock had a conventional cock and the traditional pillar and ball trigger, and there was a five-inch long belt hook. The circular barrel was eight inches long and engraved with 'H R H', identifying the weapon as belonging to the Royal Highland Regiment

A second type differed in some details, with a gunmetal stock and, in place of the ram's horn butt, one with a kidney shape and lacking the touch-hole pricker. They were supplied by the maker John Waters but purchased from a silversmith in The Strand, London, at ten shillings and sixpence a pair. The colonels had asked for the stocks to be of wood but the Ordnance turned them down saying that they would be too vulnerable to damage[20].

Balkan Pistols

The history of the Balkans is, to say the least, complex and violent with varied cultures and races competing and supporting or opposing one another at different periods, and this cultural mix is reflected in the arms of the area. The pistols exhibit Turkish, Greek and Italian influences and the arms industry was fragmented, with local areas making pistols with peculiar features. As a result, the positive identification of any pistol from one area is very difficult and often the subject of conjecture.

One type of pistol which may, with some confidence, be labelled as Balkan is the so-called 'rat-tailed pistol'. The stock, often sheathed in a decorative brass or silver casing, has a narrow, thin, slightly down-curved butt terminating in a globose pommel with an extended point. One item apparently lacking from many pistols from this area is a ramrod. The stock is often far too slim to accommodate one beneath the barrel, as in the set-up on so many European pistols. The Turks and many Balkans carried the ramrod, the 'suma', as a separate item, normally suspended from the belt. Many have an elaborately pierced finial.

Although not strictly a Balkan model, the so-called 'Cossack pistol' is worthy of note. It has a Turkish-style lock and lacks a fitted ramrod but is distinguished by its ball-shaped pommel.

The locks on Balkan pistols may well have been made in Europe, although many have a type of Turkish Miquelet lock, with the shape of the cock resembling the Spanish square-jaw form. Turkey was for a long period the dominant force in the Balkans, and Turkish

Two Albanian Miquelet pistols, dating from the nineteenth century, with wooden stocks encased with engraved brass and decorated silver panels. Their narrow tapering butts have been likened to 'rat tails'. (Thomas Del Mar Ltd)

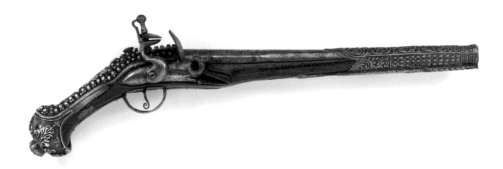

Turkish or Balkan flintlock pistol with silver-mounted barrel and stock decorated with raised patternwork, dating from the nineteenth century. The stock has a typical large pommel and a slim iron ramrod. (Thomas Del Mar Ltd)

Cossack or Caucasian Miquelet lock pistol, nineteenth century. The tapered barrel is decorated overall with scrolling gold foliage and is secured to the leather-covered stock by three bands with niello (blackened silver) work. The globose pommel is of marine ivory and has a lanyard ring. (Thomas Del Mar Ltd)

long guns were widespread in the area. They are well made but the manufacture of pistols was apparently less appealing.

One type of firearm popular among in the Balkans was a miniature blunderbuss, sometimes known as a 'knee blunderbuss', which seems to have been peculiar to this area of Europe and the Near East. It usually has a flintlock and, basically, is a scaled-down version of the conventional weapon, with a much shorter butt. The woodwork is often decorated with applied wirework. The short barrel is remarkable for its extremely wide muzzle, made in the belief that a round of shot would spread further. The design seems to offer no great advantage but, judging by the number that survive, it was reasonably commonly used.

Recent research by Robert Elgood has cast much light on the Balkan/Turkish arms world, establishing guidelines to identifying some of the prime arms-manufacturing centres.

Asian Pistols

Since the vast majority of Indian and Japanese firearms used a matchlock mechanism, pistols of native construction are rare. The Japanese culture did produce some miniature muskets although they cannot be considered pistols in the true sense of the word, meaning that they could safely be carried on the person. Some decorative pistols were made in the arsenal at Lucknow and a French influence can be seen in some examples. The famous Tipu Sultan killed at Seringapatan in 1799 delighted in some pistols made for him in Mysore and featuring the tiger motif he favoured. Another pair of pistols made for him are of interest, in that they were fitted with left- and right-hand locks.

British influence in India meant that many famous gunmakers were called up to supply decorative firearms for presentation pieces to various rulers during the eighteenth and nineteenth centuries. These were often heavily decorated with gold inlay.

Multi-Shot Pistols

An obvious limitation with the vast majority of early firearms was that they gave the user one chance only. Fire a shot and miss the target, and the gun became just a piece of metal and wood until it was reloaded. One obvious remedy was to carry two pistols but that was not always possible or desirable. Another equally obvious answer was to make a gun that, once loaded, was able to fire more than one shot.

Starting with the earliest matchlock weapons, the gunsmith tackled this problem by fitting at least two barrels on one stock. With the hand-held match more than two barrels could be easily fired in sequence. Early examples of metal handguns with three barrels are well known, as was the practice of combining a handgun with another weapon. The Royal Armouries has one such piece, usually described as 'Henry VIII's Walking Staff', a frightening weapon that comprises a 'Holy Water Sprinkler', a club with a spiked head, into which are fitted

Flintlock holster pistol with top-mounted spring bayonet and pivoting ramrod. It bears no maker's name. The barrel is inscribed 'Nottingham Police' and the lock bears the coat of arms of Nottingham. It is most unusual to find British police-marked weapons fitted with an attached bayonet. (Thomas Del Mar Ltd)

Percussion pistol by Ketland made about 1790 and later converted to percussion but retaining the top sliding safety catch. The rather long turn-off barrel is fitted with a spring bayonet. (Thomas Del Mar Ltd)

three matchlock barrels. Its name, it seems, is one of association rather than fact. As with so many of these composite weapons, it is a matter of conjecture as to which weapon is considered to be the prime one since the matchlock gun was primarily a missile weapon, whilst the club is essentially for close combat.

Engravings of the early sixteenth-century Arsenal of Maximilian clearly show three- and four-barrel matchlocks. Sometimes the barrels are arranged side by side but on at least one example the barrels are fitted in cylinder format. Another four-barrel gun has the barrels fitted at each end of a plank of wood; as the front pair was fired, the plank was rotated to bring the second pair in line for firing.

As early as c1540, makers toyed with the concept of a revolver, and a three-barrel matchlock pistol is preserved in Venice. A three-barrel wheel-lock pistol firing darts can be dated to the reign of the Emperor Charles V (1519–1558). The advent of the wheel-lock system, with its fixed ignition system, made possible a variety of multi-barrel and combination weapons, but also introduced mechanical problems. Two barrels could be mounted one above the other and each could be fitted with its own lock, but this made the handgun heavier and bulkier. More ingenious systems used one

lock with two dogsheads adjusted to serve separate wheels.

The combining of a wheel-lock pistol with another weapon was explored and such combination weapons were put together, but their rarity suggests that demand was limited. The dagger/pistol, mace/pistol even sword/pistol were certainly made, but there is little or no literary evidence as to their actual use. It is possible that they may have been little more than the equivalent of a modern 'must-have' fashion accessory.

Another combination weapon that enjoyed popularity in the eighteenth century was the pistol with a spring bayonet. The short bayonet blade was most frequently fitted beneath the barrel and usually hinged below the muzzle. It was folded back against the pressure of a strong spring and held in place by a sliding trigger guard, which engaged with the point of the blade. When the guard was slid back, the bayonet snapped forward and locked in place. Such pistols survive in quantity, suggesting that they were not uncommon but again, as yet, no contemporary literary reference of their use is known.

The mechanically simpler flintlock system opened the way to a wide range of multi-barrel weapons. A side-by-side arrangement of barrels with separate locks was an obvious line of development and such pistols appear quite early in the seventeenth century. A

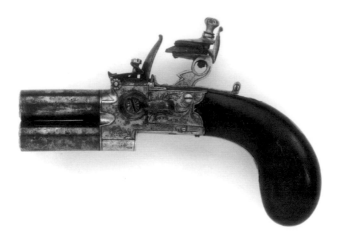

Double-barrelled over-and-under flintlock pistol by Welch of Banbury with Birmingham proof mark, circa 1820. The barrel to be fired is selected by rotating the circular tap-action block. For safety it has a folding trigger and a top sliding catch, which locks the frizzen and cock. (Thomas Del Mar Ltd)

better solution would be to use one lock to fire both barrels in turn and this was achieved in a variety of ways. One slightly complex but popular system was the tap-action. Two barrels were mounted, one above the other, the upper one having a conventional pan and frizzen. The lower barrel was adjacent to a flat disc, which could be rotated through ninety degrees. To fire the top barrel the block was turned so that its edge blocked off the bottom of the top pan and there was no connection. In this position the top barrel could be primed and fired. If the block was rotated, a recess on its circumference now lined up with the top pan, so connecting the lower barrel with the pan. If primed, the second barrel could now be fired. The action had to be cocked for each shot. These turn-off flintlock pistols have survived in quantity so it is reasonable to suppose they were seen as practical weapons. Sometimes, two pairs of barrels were mounted side by side, giving a four-shot firing sequence.

Far rarer (understandably so) was the superimposed load pistol. There were several ways of achieving multiple shots from one barrel. One system used a barrel with several touch holes spaced along its length. The first charge of powder and bullet went into the breech and the charge was located by the first touch hole. A firm pad was then pushed down to block off the bullet and powder. With another charge, the bullet went down the barrel to sit on top of the wad, adjacent to another touch hole. This charge was, in turn, sealed off with a wad and this process was repeated for the required number of loads. A long plate extended along the side of the stock and the actual flintlock could be slid along the plate. The lock was now located by the touch hole nearest the muzzle and the shot fired. The intention was that the wad would prevent any flash from penetrating and setting of the second charge. If this was satisfactory then the lock could be disengaged and slid back to position number two, and the process was repeated until all shots had been fired. The lock obviously had to be cocked for each shot and in practical terms the time and motion needed to fire all the shots soon mounted up, and that was assuming that the inter-charge wads prevented a creep-back of the flame. If they did not, then all charges would fire more or less together, with a spectacularly disastrous result. Failure to check the sequence of shots could also lead to disaster.

A variant on the wad system was the 'Roman Candle gun', in which each bullet was drilled with a hole that was filled with powder. The bullets were loaded on top of each other with the holes lined up. When the first shot was fired in the conventional manner the theory was that the flame generated by the charge ignited the next in line, so instituting a sequence of shots. Unless it was very carefully loaded, the result was an odd burst of fire or a firework display.

There were attempts to make snaphaunce revolvers and one by a London maker, John Dafte c1680, had six barrels and was remarkably advanced as the barrels were rotated as the pistol was cocked. Examples are very rare, which suggests that the practical problems in constructing such a weapon were such that few gunmakers attempted it. Flintlock revolvers were made but retaining the priming *in situ* whilst rotating the cylinder was a difficult challenge; one or two makers did succeed, but such weapons are uncommon.

During the later part of the eighteenth century, the duck-foot pistol was allegedly intended for use in situations when one person was faced with a mob. The four or more barrels were set to cover a cone of fire and all were linked to one box lock so that all barrels would fire together. The implied threat of several barrels might hold a crowd at bay more than the fear of more than one target being hit by the single discharge. According to tradition, these were produced for the benefit of naval officers faced by a mutinous crew, but there seems to be little literary proof for the story. A few specimens

with six barrels are known but four is the more common type.

One main problem with the development of the repeating flintlock pistol was that any proposed mechanisms would have to feed powder, ball and priming for each shot – not an easy matter to achieve mechanically. There were successful designs but they were, of necessity, rather complicated and consequently liable to malfunction. One quite successful system is usually credited to a Michele Lorenzoni of Florence in the mid-seventeenth century. There were three magazines: a small priming magazine was attached to the lock whilst the butt housed one magazine of powder and one of balls. There was a cylindrical breech plug, which could be revolved, and with the muzzle pointing upwards a lever was used to rotate the block and line up two cavities with the twin magazines. Reversing the gun allowed a charge of powder and a ball to fall into the appropriate positions ready for firing. The lever was turned back and this action primed the pan and cocked the action.

A not dissimilar action was designed by members of the Kalthoff gunmakers in the seventeenth century. This system also used a powder magazine set inside the butt and a ball magazine under the barrel. The transfer of powder and ball was made by a horizontal rotation of the trigger guard. However, it was not until the advent of the metal-cased cartridge that multi-shot pistols became a practical reality.

CHAPTER 4

The Advent of Percussion

~ ~

By the end of the eighteenth century the flint-lock had reached its peak and any further major developments seemed unlikely. It had been in service for two centuries or more and was generally reliable and efficient, but it was not without its problems. There was a particular phenomenon known as the hang-fire, which, in most instances, was not important but was an irritation for the hunter and something that had to be considered when taking aim. When the shooter set his sights on the target and gently pressed the trigger, it set in motion a series of events, each of which occupied only a very short period of time. First the sear was activated and then the tumbler turned, the mainspring exerted pressure and the cock had to swing forward to generate the sparks, dragging the flint down the face of the frizzen. The sparks then had to fall into the priming and ignite it. The priming had to catch fire and the flame had then to pass through the touch hole and ignite the main charge, which would burn, thus generating the gas that would build up the pressure. Each of these actions occupied a very brief but finite time. Added together, each tiny delay would create a small but appreciable period between the pressing of

the trigger and the actual firing of the shot. Brief though it was, that moment would allow the quarry to move enough to be out of shot, or the aim to vary. In either case, the shooter was likely to be off target. It was possible for the marksman to compensate for the time delay by making some adjustment, perhaps by aiming slightly ahead of the target, but it was always a matter of guesswork.

For the hunter there was another irritation caused by the action of the lock: in the normal sequence of actions, the frizzen opened shortly ahead of the shot being fired. This meant that the flash and the puff of smoke from the priming preceded the firing of the shot by a brief moment. This was often just enough to startle the quarry into moving away.

On a more practical level, the lock was also very vulnerable to damp, rainy or windy conditions, which could result in a number of misfires, and a disappointing hunt or a lower than expected score.

In the majority of cases the hang-fire and priming flash were no more than minor annoyances but they were more irritating to keen, dedicated shooters, since they often led to a missed quarry. One shooter was deter-mined to see if it was possible to reduce or solve the problems, and fortunately he was well qualified to tackle the subject.

Forsyth's System

Alexander John Forsyth was born in December 1769, at Belhelvie, a small parish in Aberdeenshire in north-east Scotland, the son of a minister of the Presbyterian Church. He attended Aberdeen University and graduated as Master of Arts in 1786, being well read in chemistry, but he was always destined for the church. When his father died, in 1791, Forsyth succeeded him as minister[21]. He was a well-loved member of the church, devoted to good works, but he had always been a keen hunter, and was still able to find time for the sport. He is reported to have been particularly irritated by the warning given to the quarry by the flash of the priming in the pan preceding the shot. He tried hiding the flash by fitting a cover over the lock but soon realized there had to be a better method.

He decided to see if he could reduce the time lag between pressing the trigger, the give-away flash and the hang-fire. Using his knowledge of chemistry, he conducted some experiments to see if he could speed up the action by enhancing the priming with so-called detonating powders such as potassium chlorate. The properties of these impact-sensitive chemicals had been known for centuries – they had been mentioned by Samuel Pepys in his diary – but they seem to have been largely ignored by gunmakers and shooters. Forsyth tried mixing them with the normal priming powder, to speed up the burning, but the results were not encouraging. He knew that the detonating powders exploded when struck a blow but he also discovered that, even when surrounded by gunpowder, but not in physical contact, the flash of the detonating powder failed to ignite the adjacent gunpowder. However, if the two powders were in actual physical contact, a blow to the detonating compound generated a swift and immediate reaction with the gunpowder. Here, Forsyth saw the possibility of a simple firing mechanism for the future. If it were possible to place a small amount of

Trade label from the London shop of Alexander Forsyth demonstrating his scent-bottle lock. It shows the two positions utilized to prime the pistol.

this detonating powder in close proximity to the gunpowder in the breech of a gun, and then strike it a blow, it should fire the shot without needing many parts of the flintlock mechanism, such as the frizzen, flint or a pan, although some form of hammer to replace the cock would be necessary.

Simple and obvious as this solution was in theory, it proved to be less so in practice, and several systems were found to be unsuitable and, indeed, positively dangerous. After further experiments, including one in which Forsyth's detonating mechanism was rather like a cartridge and was sited inside the breech, he finally came up with a simpler system. A pinch of detonator was placed by the touch hole and a snaphaunce-type arm with a hammer or solid block at the tip swung down to hit the detonator. The system seemed to work and Forsyth had a gun made to his design and hunted with it for some months to ensure that it was practical. Eventually, he felt confident that his scheme was sound.

Presumably, Forsyth must have recognized the potential of his new system, for in 1806 he undertook the long journey to London in order to demonstrate the system to some friends and contacts. Through them, it was seen by the Master General of the Ordnance, Lord Moira, who was responsible for the arming of Britain's troops. He was sufficiently impressed and presumably saw a future for the system for he invited Forsyth to take up residence at the Tower of London and work in secret on it. Leave of absence from his ministry in Belhelvie was granted to Forsyth, with the Government agreeing to pay for his replacement, and promising his return to Scotland when his time in London was over.

Whilst the basic idea of using a detonator was now seen to be quite sound, Lord Moira sensibly set Forsyth certain objectives of a practical nature; if the system was to be used by the military it had be safe, easy to operate and, most importantly, reliable. Forsyth set about the task and, despite an apparent lack of co-operation from the Tower workmen, he produced a lock only to find that the mercurial detonating compound he was using was too powerful and tended to split metal parts. Other detonating powders also proved to be too strong or too dangerous and, following several accidents, there was a marked reluctance on the part of manufacturers to make them.

The results of Forsyth's first efforts were not encouraging and were seen as disappointing; indeed, the Board of Ordnance even defined them as a failure. Despite this, however, Forsyth was asked to continue his work on the system. Shortly afterwards there was a change in the political set-up, with Lord Moira leaving the Board of Ordnance. His successor, John Pitt, First Earl of Chatham, was apparently unimpressed with the system and, in effect, dismissed Forsyth, telling him to remove his 'rubbish' from the Tower.

Forsyth was able to remain in London when he received some payment from the Government for his work, but more importantly he now felt confident enough to apply for a patent for the system. This was granted on 11 April 1807 and the following year, with the help of others in a partnership, he opened a shop in Piccadilly, Central London. He later sold his share of the business and returned to his church duties in Belhelvie, and it was not until 1834 that he received further payment from the Government. He was eventually granted the substantial sum of £1,000 for his discovery, but only after some prolonged legal wrangling. He died in 1843, before the financial matter was finally settled. During his lifetime there were several attempts to breach the patent but it held fast.

The lock patented by Forsyth did work, but it was rather complex and consequently expensive to make and maintain. The basic problem facing Forsyth was how to deposit a very small amount of the fulminate detonator by the touch hole in such a way that it could be struck by the external hammer. At the centre of his lock plate was a hollow, two-section metal container known, because of its shape, as the 'scent bottle'. This could be rotated around a fixed central block, which housed a semi-circular gutter leading directly to the touch hole. Fulminate was stored in the lower section of the scent bottle, which was connected to the upper section via a small channel. To charge the touch hole the container was rotated, allowing a few grains of the detonating powder to drop through into the touch-hole channel. Returned to the upright position, the upper part of the scent bottle housed a spring-loaded plunger that now sat above the detonator. If the plunger was struck by the descending hammer it would descend and detonate the powder and so fire the charge. Despite its complexity, the scent-bottle system did have one great advantage, for a firearm with a conventional flintlock could be converted to operate the new mechanism with a minimum of modification.

The main problem with Forsyth's lock was the ingenious but rather complex scent bottle and what was needed was a simpler system of setting the detonator grains at the touch hole. Forsyth's patent was very comprehensive and he was able to take action against several gunmakers who tried to use similar systems. One of the first attempts to solve the scent bottle problem came from Collinson Hall, who came up with a simple paper cap. It comprised two small circular discs of waxed paper, which held, between them, at the centre, a small amount of detonating powder. The cap was pushed into the recessed nose of a hammer, which was sited to hit a small cone or nipple screwed into the breech of the gun. The nipple served as a touch hole connected to the main charge and so fired the shot. The system worked but it was a little fiddly and the hammer nose was liable to become fouled.

In 1816, Manton, one of the leading London gunmakers, devised a similar lock, which used small pellets of detonator set in the head of the hammer. In 1818 he produced a tube lock that used a small copper tube filled with the detonator compound and held in place on the pan by a simple cover. The tube was pushed into the touch hole while the projecting end rested on a small adjacent, flat platform. Hit by the head of a hammer, it worked well but there was one serious problem. As the detonator powder exploded it tended to send fragments from the copper tube flying in many directions, often into the face of the shooter. Manton patented a modified hammer in 1834 with a hooded section that cured this problem but by then a better system had become available, and his idea was out of date. In France a system using a roll of caps with blobs of detonator was proposed; this idea was to resurface on a carbine in service during the American Civil War.

The Percussion Cap

The failed systems all pointed the way to the final and most convenient solution, which proved to be a percussion cap. This was a small, copper thimble with corrugated sides and a layer of detonating compound deposited on the inside of the closed end. The flintlock could be easily modified to use this device; the pan was removed from the lock plate and the space was usually filled, the frizzen and frizzen bracket were similarly disposed of, and finally the cock with its flint was replaced by a cock or hammer terminating in a solid recessed nose. The last modification was to drill out the touch

Cased pair of officer's percussion pistols by Edward of London Wall, about 1830. The octagonal browned barrels are fitted with swivel ramrods and have platinum plug touch holes. The butts have small base traps and the accessories include a three-way powder flask, a wad cutter and cleaning rod. (Thomas Del Mar Ltd)

hole and insert a small metal drum to which was fitted, at right-angles, a coned nipple. Both were drilled with a channel connecting it with the breech. This was the simplest method and many pistols were converted in this way; if a new barrel was fitted, it incorporated an integral nipple.

The pistol was loaded in the normal manner and a percussion cap placed on the nipple. The corrugations allowed just sufficient spread and grip to hold the cap in place. The pistol could now be carried at the half cock or set with a safety device. To fire a shot the hammer was pulled back, the trigger was pressed and the hammer swung forward to compress the crown of the cap against the tip of the nipple to generate the flash and fire the shot. The recessed hammer head partially enclosed the cap and so prevented pieces of the copper casing being blown about. The system was more positive than that of a flintlock and offered a more certain detonation.

The cap could be manufactured in any size and many makers developed their own brand but the majority were supplied by two British manufacturers. The larger was Eley, which had a cartridge factory in London for many years and in the 1860s was offering no less than eight different percussion caps. The firm also manufactured cartridges of many types, marketing them via a board that displayed a selection of cartridges tastefully arranged in patterns. The other main British supplier of caps was the firm of Kynoch, founded in Birmingham in 1862 and later amalgamated with other ammunition manufacturers. Caps intended for long arms were usually larger and for the military there was the top-hat version, which had a flat segmented rim.

The manufacture of caps was complex and risky and full details are given in an instruction manual for the Madras Artillery, dated 1847, which was largely a reprint of an earlier version[22]. It lists some thirteen machines or processes required. The body of the cap was cut from copper sheets four feet long by two feet wide and .016 inches thick. The detonating compound was composed of fulminate of mercury, chlorate of potash, saltpetre, sulphur and pounded green glass. The instructions for mixing warn emphatically that the greatest care is necessary, especially after the fulminate has been added, as the least blow is liable to cause an explosion.

Strangely enough, despite the importance of the design of the percussion cap, or perhaps because of it, no certain conclusion has ever been reached as to who first thought of it. There were, needless to say, a number who claimed that distinction, including Colonel Hawker, a famous shooter, as well as well-known London gunmakers such as Egg and Purdey, but all have their detractors. It is generally thought that the man with the best possible claim to this honour is probably Joshua Shaw, a Lincolnshire man who had emigrated to America in 1817. He was certainly granted a patent for a percussion cap in 1822 in the USA and claimed to have been working on it well before this date.

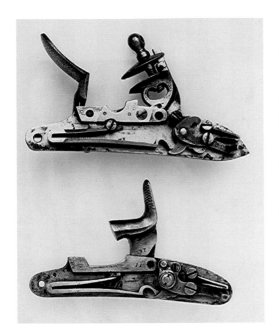

One virtue of the conversion of flintlock pistols to the percussion cap was that the locks required virtually no internal change. The main mechanism only required a hammer being substituted for the cock. The removal of the pan and frizzen was a little more involved.

Like so many revolutionary ideas the detonator system was greeted by shooters and gunmakers with a mixture of enthusiasm and opposition, and heated arguments for and against it were voiced. Various trials and competitions were held to determine the truth or otherwise of the various claims and denials. The famous nineteenth-century shooter Colonel Hawker, writing in 1830 about the percussion system, admitted that he had 'like all other modern shooters, been rather over-rating its merits than otherwise'[23]. What should be borne in mind is that nearly all the discussion on the merits or otherwise of the new percussion system was based on hunting considerations, and in many cases the points were largely irrelevant as far as handguns were concerned.

Although there may be doubt as to its true inventor, there is no question as to the importance of the percussion cap, for it opened up the way to a series of guns that would have been extremely difficult to make prior to its introduction. Despite the fact that Forsyth was well ahead in developing the percussion system, his efforts were regarded with little appreciation and the Board of Ordnance, in particular, appears to have been rather loath to make use of it. The Royal Navy adopted the percussion lock for its firearms but the Army resisted it and it was not until 1834 that an official Ordnance comparative test was held at Woolwich. Six flintlock muskets and six percussion ones each fired 6,000

Cased pair of over- and under-percussion pistols by Parker Field circa 1850. Each pistol has two locks operated by separate triggers; they also have the pivoted ramrod.

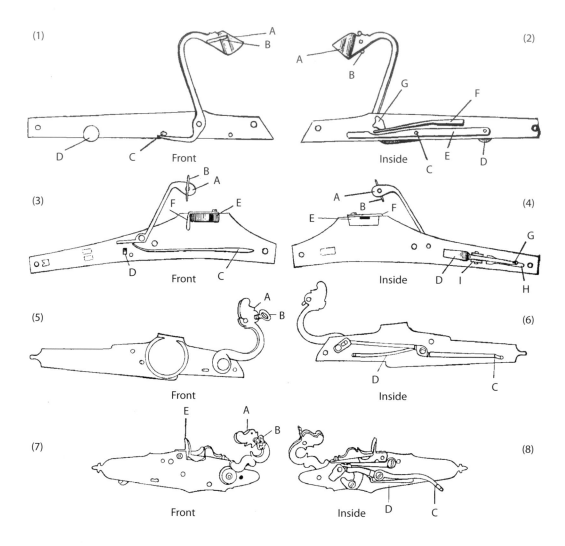

Gun-lock mechanisms. (1, 2) Snap matchlock. A piece of smouldering slow-match is held in the jaws (A) which are operated by a screw (B). The match-holder is held back in the cocked position (as shown) by the sear (C) attached to the springy sear-lever (E). Pressure on the trigger-button (D) withdraws the sear allowing the match-holder to tip forward into the pan under the action of the mainspring (F) against the tumbler (G). (3, 4) Snap matchlock. This operates in a similar manner except that the mainspring (C) is mounted on the front of the lock plate and the sear-lever is designed to be operated by a trigger of modern type pivoted in the stock of the gun. This acts against the hooked end (G) of the sear-lever which is pivoted at (I). The spring at (H) serves to return the sear and trigger to their original position on release. (5, 6) Sear matchlock. The sear-lever is linked at (C) to a long lever-trigger resembling that of a crossbow. Upward pressure on this causes the opposite end of the sear-lever to move downwards against the action of the mainspring (D) so moving the tumbler attached to the spindle of the match-holder and tipping the latter into the pan. When the trigger is released the mainspring returns the match-holder to its original position. (7, 8) Trigger matchlock. This operates in a similar manner to the last but the sear-lever is shaped so that it can be operated by a trigger of modern type. The sliding pan-cover is operated manually, the horizontal spring above the sear-lever serving to secure it in the open or closed position.

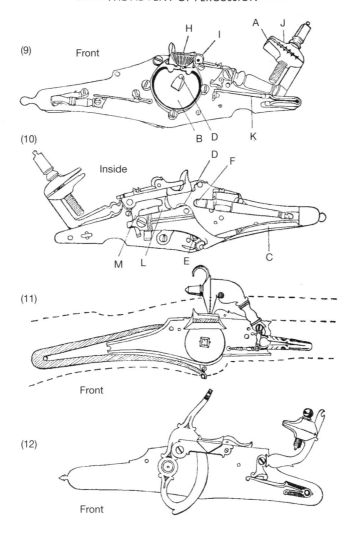

Gun-lock mechanisms. (9, 10) Wheel-lock. A spanner is fitted on the squared end (D) of the wheel-spindle and the wheel (B) is turned in a clockwise direction, winding up a short steel chain (E) which connects the spindle with the free end of the mainspring. When the wheel has been turned through three-quarters of a revolution a sear (F) engages in a recess in its inner face, so securing it. After the gun has been loaded and the pan (H) primed in the usual way, the sliding pan-cover (I) is closed and the cock (J) is moved down until a piece of pyrites held in its jaws (A) rests on the cover; the cock is held in this position by a spring (K). Pressure on the trigger, which is pivoted separately in the stock, brings it into contact with the end of the sear-lever, causing it to move laterally and free the wheel. This last begins to rotate rapidly under the action of the mainspring, and at the same time a cam forming part of the spindle strikes against a steel arm (L) linking the pan-cover to a pivot on the lock-plate. The movement of the arm opens the cover allowing the pyrites to come into contact with the rotating wheel, so striking a shower of sparks and igniting the priming. A spring (M) serves to hold the pan-cover in either the open or the closed position. Note that the mainspring is permanently attached to the inside of the lock plate. (11) Wheel-lock of French type. This works in exactly the same way as the last, but the mainspring, instead of being attached to the lock plate, rests loose in a cavity in the stock (shown by dotted lines), being held only by a transverse pin through its apex. The inner end of the wheel-spindle is supported in a hole in a bearing plate on the opposite side of the stock to the lock. (12). Segment-lock. This operates in a similar manner to the wheel-lock except that the wheel is replaced by a steel striker shaped like a segment of a circle.

rounds. The results were pretty conclusive, with percussion having fewer misfires, greater accuracy and lower recoil. In 1836 percussion muskets were issued for trial by members of the Guards Regiments and in 1839 the 1st Battalion Rifle Brigade was issued with percussion rifles. In 1840 the Black Watch were issued with flintlock muskets that had been converted to the new percussion lock but it was not until the 1840s that the British Army was completely armed with percussion weapons. The emphasis on long arms may seem excessive but hand-guns were seen by many to be vastly inferior weapons.

Whilst the hunters and military forces might agonize over the new percussion system, there was less controversy about its use in pistols. Converted to percussion a pistol was far less bulky, the frizzen and pan were gone, and in place of a sometimes bulky cock there was an elegant hammer. By the 1840s percussion pistols of all types, including top-quality duelling pistols, were in full production and, although there were a number of stubborn shooters who remained convinced that flint was best, their numbers were diminishing. A round tin of percussion caps became a usual fitting in most pistol cases. Repeating pistols were a particularly attractive field for experimentation and some bizarre designs were patented but seldom passed beyond this legal requirement. Double-barrel handguns were now much easier to make and side-by-side and over-and-under styles were made with twin locks.

The percussion cap saw the increased production of one very unusual type of pistol in which the hammer was fitted below, rather than above, the breech. A few flintlocks with this underneath fitting are known and, despite the fact that the priming would obviously fall out of the pan, it seems that they

The main suppliers of percussion caps in Britain were the firms of Eley, based in London, and Kynoch, based in Birmingham. Some gunmakers did offer their own named brand.

did indeed fire. Various advantages were claimed for this style: it provided a clear sight line when target shooting, it was of a very simple construction and its narrow outline made it easy to tuck down a boot out of sight. Evidently these points were not widely accepted for this under-hammer or bootleg system never really caught on and examples are not common. Most of those surviving are of American manufacture and there are also some rifles fitted with this system[24].

The simplicity of the percussion lock permitted makers to experiment with ideas for handguns and there were some ingenious

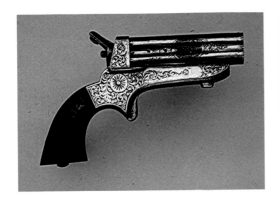

Sharps four-barrelled pistol; each barrel fired in turn by a rotating hammer. It was developed in the mid-nineteenth century by Christian Sharps and was produced mainly in two calibres of .22 and .32 using rimfire cartridges.

as well as rather impractical designs. Since the detonator could be struck from any angle, the blow could be delivered in any manner appropriate to the design and some gun-makers explored the idea of mounting the lock inside the stock and dispensing with the external hammer. The first such mechanisms appeared as early as 1829 but there does not appear to have been much demand for them and examples are rare.

One type of handgun that was to benefit from the adoption of the percussion system was the pocket pistol, and arms centres such as Birmingham and Liège began to produce cheap pistols in quantity. The compact nature of the mechanism enabled the gunmaker to produce a small, neat pistol that could be tucked into a waistcoat pocket, or hidden in a purse or a book. One American gunmaker, Henry Deringer (1786–1868) (like Forsyth, the son of a Presbyterian minister), identified a market for a small but more powerful pocket pistol. From his Philadelphia factory he began manufacturing one style that soon enjoyed universal acceptance. First appearing in the 1830s, it had a number of recognizable

features: the round, rifled barrel was short with a flat top and most had a blade front sight, which was largely superfluous since the pistol was seen as a self-defence weapon to be used at close range. The bore could be as much as nearly half an inch (1.25cm).

The stock, which was made of walnut, was in the shape of a bird's head and was fitted with a back action lock, which meant that the long V-shaped mainspring was mounted to the rear of the hammer rather than in front, as it would have been on a conventional lock. This system was commonly used when there was limited space in the stock to accommodate the lock. Any furniture on Deringer's pistols was usually of German silver. Apparently the pistols were normally sold in pairs and were especially popular with gentlemen of the Southern United States.

Deringer appears never to have patented his design and soon copies were being produced using variations of his name – 'Derringer' with a double 'r' was often used. The pistol gained notoriety and wide publicity when John Wilkes Booth used one to assassinate President Abraham Lincoln in 1865. The name was increasingly used to refer generally to a type of small pocket pistol rather than those made by Deringer himself.

Another pistol intended for self-defence was the later four-barrelled cartridge pistol by Sharps, popular in the 1870s. The head of the hammer rotated as it was cocked, bringing the striking surface in line with each barrel in turn. To remove the empty cases the barrel block slid forward, allowing them to fall out, and new rounds were loaded in the same way.

Percussion Revolvers

The percussion system was adapted to fit all types of handgun but there few changes to the pistol itself, although the new-found freedom

Double-barrelled, over-and-under percussion pistol made by a top London maker, Samuel Nock. Each barrel has its own lock operated by separate triggers and both are served by the swivel ramrod. The walnut butt is finely chequered and there is a trap at the base. (Thomas Del Mar Ltd)

of design led to many experimental firearms. Some were successful and some less so, but one area that was definitely revolutionized was that of the repeating pistol. Multi-barrel flintlocks had been made in quantity, with two, three, four and more barrels, but the need for a reliable, simple priming system had complicated the design. There had been many attempts to produce practical flintlock revolvers and some were quite successful, but the weapons were bulky, awkward to carry and at best unreliable. Multi-barrel percussion pistols were common; the simplest was the double-barrelled side-by-side with twin locks, while another variant had the barrels mounted one above the other, but again with twin locks. Four-barrelled weapons with rotatable pairs of barrels were another system – four appeared to the practical maximum.

Around the 1830s and 40s there was a new and important development in firearms technology when the 'pepperbox' or 'pepperpot' revolver appeared. Its name was derived from the end view of the barrel block, which, with its five or six muzzles, resembled a pepper shaker. The weapon comprised a tubular metal block of some kind, which housed a number of barrels that were individually loaded with powder and ball. The breech end of each was fitted with a nipple, over which was set a percussion cap which

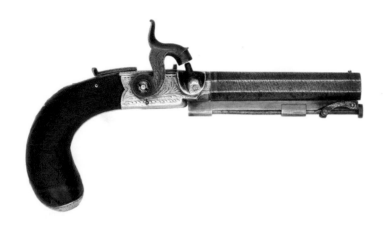

Percussion pistol by Van Wort Son & Co., Birmingham, circa 1840, with an octagonal barrel with a top sliding safety catch. The butt is a rather unusual shape and the pistol has a blued steel belt hook. The maker was an American who emigrated to England and later became a supplier of powder flasks to Samuel Colt. (Thomas Del Mar Ltd)

could be struck by a hammer to fire the shot. This block was rotated, either manually or mechanically, bringing, in turn, each loaded tube or chamber into a firing position with the nipple beneath the hammer. The idea was not new – twelve-shot pistols had been made as early as the sixteenth century, with the block being rotated by hand to line up barrels and chamber. Fitted with a match-lock mechanism, it was reasonably effective, although match and flint revolvers all faced one great challenge: how to hold the priming powder in place as the block was turned. If a pan cover was used, it had to be moved clear of the pan, either manually or mechanically, before the shot could be fired.

Flintlock revolvers were produced during the seventeenth and eighteenth centuries but, judging by the number of examples that have survived, they were not made in quantity. One of the most successful was almost certainly designed by an American, Elisha Haydon Collier, who patented it in 1818. His original patent allowed for mechanical rotation of the cylinders but so far no surviving example of his revolver using this system has been found, and it would appear that he abandoned the idea. His manually rotated revolvers are among the most successful flintlock ones and a number have survived. In 1819 Collier's revolver was examined by a British Committee set up to consider its use by the Army but, although the committee approved of the weapon, it concluded that it was too complicated for general use. Collier's system was used on a range of weapons, including pistols, rifles, shotguns and even a blunderbuss, which were all available either as a flintlock or percussion version.

Although Collier revolvers were made using both flintlock and percussion systems, it was obvious to the gunmaking trade that the percussion system was simpler and far less difficult to manufacture. The new trend was pointed out by an unusual example made by an Edward Budding, who had been granted a patent for a lawnmower in 1830, and was, according to the evidence available, the same man who made the new-style pepperbox revolver. It was a delightfully simple pistol with a long, hooked wooden stock secured by three large screws. There were five barrels arranged in a block and these were rotated by hand to bring each in line with an internal hammer. The barrel block was detachable for loading and the nipples and caps were entirely enclosed within the frame. The striker was spring-operated by a trigger-like lever hanging down below the centre of the pistol. This was pulled back, putting a spring under tension, and then engaged with a notch to hold it back. To fire, the lever was given a nudge and it flew forward to strike a cap and discharge a shot. It is known that Budding made at least one other model, which has a traditional trigger and guard.

From the 1830s on, the production of pepperbox-type revolvers increased rapidly

Transitional revolver with rifled barrel and signed 'Smith John Street London', but proved in Birmingham. The action is enclosed within a German silver mount. Mid-nineteenth century. (Thomas Del Mar Ltd)

So-called transition revolvers marked the change from percussion pepperbox revolvers to the more usual percussion revolver with a single barrel. This example is typical of the numerous cheap versions on the market.

Good cased percussion pepperbox revolver by Parker Field of Holborn, mid nineteenth century. Complete with powder flask and other accessories but lacking the bullet mould.

and, whilst the cap was soon to dominate the market, some pistols did experiment with percussion pellets and tubes. The Massachusetts Arms Company produced one handgun that used a paper strip with small percussion pellets spread along its length. A roll was put into a recess on the side of the frame and, each time the pistol was cocked, an arm pushed the tape along to place a pellet in position ready to be struck by the hammer.

Soon, gunmakers were offering a five- or six-barrel pepperbox pistol, most with mechanical rotation and a double-action trigger mechanism. The barrels were formed in one block, with the nipples set at right-angles at the rear. The hammer was now in the form of a bar located on top of the frame, with the head in line with the nipple of the top barrel. Pressure on the trigger operated the lock mechanism and turned the barrel block and lifted the bar until the barrel was correctly positioned when the bar was released and fell to strike the cap and nipple. Allowing the trigger to return to its normal position reset the mechanism, ready for the next shot.

On many of the pistols the frame was extended to form a partial shield over the caps, to reduce the chance of a flash from one nipple setting off the others, although this did occasionally occur. The butt was commonly plain except for some fine hatching and, at the top of the cylinder, many had a sliding safety bar, which could be pushed forward to lock the bar hammer and prevent accidents. A variant form dispensed with the bar hammer, had the nipples located at the rear of the barrels and a striker that was mounted internally. Another variety, known usually as 'Coopers', dispensed with the bar and used a hammer with a ring trigger mounted beneath the barrel. Whilst many of these percussion pepperboxes were basic, the well-known makers sold good-quality cased sets with pistol, powder flask, bullet mould and a tin of caps. Since the pepperbox had no attached ramrod, the cased sets included a separate one.

The pepperbox was a popular gun and was produced in quantity in most countries, although the highest demand seems to have been in the USA and Britain. They were simple, effective weapons but they could be rather barrel-heavy and consequently, perhaps, a little awkward to carry around in a pocket. It is probably no coincidence that personal holsters became more common at about the same time. The pepperbox was generally a self-defence weapon and as such did not achieve any great fame. It was carried by the leader of the Mormons, Joseph Smith, when he was killed by a group of Mormon-hating people of Missouri in June 1844. He had a pepperbox revolver by the famous American maker Ethan Allen with him when the mob attacked the jailhouse in which he was being held. It was a six-shot .36 calibre pistol but, according to accounts, when the mob broke down the door, although Smith tried to fire six times only three shots were forthcoming.

The next step in the emergence of the conventional revolver was soon adopted by many makers. The logical process was to reduce the length of the barrel block, turning the barrels into chambers and substituting one longer barrel, which could be used by each chamber in turn. This was the so-called 'transitional revolver' and many appeared on the market around the middle of the nineteenth century. Some makers, such as the well-known E. Baker, famed for his rifle, went a step further and removed the bar hammer, substituting a spurred one that could be cocked by hand. These transition weapons were not the most efficient. On most, the junction of the barrel and the mouth of the chamber was not as close and tight as it should have been, and there was a loss of pressure from the gaps, with consequent poor performance.

Samuel Colt

Unbeknown to most British and Continental gunmakers great strides in revolver design were taking place in America under the control of one of the best-known names in the world of firearms. Samuel Colt or, as he rather liked to be addressed, Colonel Colt, was to have an enormous effect on the market, despite the fact that in the early days he enjoyed little success and his business looked as if it might sink without trace.

Colt was born on 19 July 1814 in the town of Hartford in the small state of Connecticut on the east coast of America, into a large family headed by his father, an ex-farmer turned businessman. At the age of eleven Samuel was working on a farm but still managed to attend school, where, it is

Contemporary engraving of Samuel Colt (1814–1862), whose name became almost synonymous with the revolver. Although he had for some time called himself 'Colonel', he was only commissioned for about a month and never saw active service. The Civil War with its heavy demand for weapons made him a rich man and his firm still exists today.

alleged, he first developed an interest in fire-arms. Aged fifteen, he went to work at his father's factory, a move that gave him access to mechanical facilities, which offered him greater chances to study and experiment. He was an inventive individual, and is reputed to have made some form of anti-ship mine, which he exploded remotely using a battery that he had also designed.

A crucial change came about in his life when his father sent him to sea, and he was away for several years. According to his own account, it was whilst on the high seas that he began to develop an idea that was to bring him fame and fortune. He had carved a wooden model of a mechanism that would rotate a pistol cylinder and then lock it in place, an operation that would occur every time the hammer was cocked. From a historical viewpoint he had done little that had not been done previously on other revolvers of the era. What was perhaps different was that he had produced an efficient system that he could patent and, once this was achieved, it meant that no one else could copy his design unless he granted permission.

Following his return to the USA, Colt made a couple of pistols based on his design.

The Paterson Belt five-shot revolver, with varying lengths of barrel. Produced from around 1838 to 1840, it was never a great commercial success, but it was the first of a line of top-class percussion revolvers. It was made in only two calibres, .31 and .34.

The results were hardly encouraging, and his father declined to finance him in any further work. Undeterred, the young man set out to earn some money and became a travelling showman, demonstrating the strange effects of nitrous oxide. This gas was used as an anaesthetic and had one interesting side-effect: people who inhaled it tended to become very relaxed and were inclined to giggle, earning it the name of 'laughing gas'.

When he was ready and able to afford it, he sailed for England in 1835, and made an application to claim his patent. Whilst awaiting the result he visited London gunmakers and places of interest, including the Tower of London, where he closely examined some of the repeating firearms in the firearms collection. In December he applied for and was duly granted a British patent for his system. Returning home he did the same in America, receiving patents in February and August 1836 and, with his system now legally protected, he set up a company to produce the pistols. The Colt Patent Arms Manufacturing Company was established at Paterson, New Jersey, in March, with substantial capital backing.

Contrary to Colt's hopes and expectations, the revolver was not well received and there was no great demand for the weapon. Despite the fact that he sought, and received, a written letter of recommendation from the American President himself, sales were very disappointing. It was pretty obvious that the business was in danger of collapse. In the end, closure of the factory was delayed by a sudden demand for guns created by the outbreak of the Second Seminole War in 1838. The conflict resulted from the attempt to evict the native Seminoles from their home in the Everglade areas of Florida. Some Colt pistols and revolving muskets saw service during this war and proved to be popular with the troops, although they did suffer from various technical problems.

Despite this boost in sales and Colt's efforts to remedy the faults, orders continued to diminish and in 1843 the Paterson factory finally closed down.

Far from giving up, Colt persevered. He did reasonably well in other areas, but success in the firearms market seemed to evade him, until 1847, when another war brought him salvation. The state of Texas in the southwestern part of America was politically chaotic: the area was under a rather loose and less than effective Mexican rule, and American citizens had, for a long time, been allowed to settle in small communities on Mexican territory. The number of Americans had increased and they had begun to demand some say in the governing of the state. The Mexican government tried to take firmer control of the situation and then attempted to impose restrictions on the settlers, who naturally opposed them. Matters became so difficult that eventually the Americans living in Texas united and declared themselves to be an independent republic. Talks between the Americans and the Mexicans failed and in 1846 the Mexican government declared war on the settlers.

An attempt was made to crush the new Texan state, which led eventually in 1836 to the Battle of the Alamo in San Antonio, Texas. The American defenders took up positions in an old Mission building and held out against the efforts of the army of the Mexican dictator, Santa Anna, to capture the building. Eventually the Mission was over-run and legends about the battle in late March and early April have become part of US history. Despite this reverse, the Texans fought on, finally establishing an independent republic.

Among the combatants in the Mexican War was Samuel Walker (1817–1847), an ex-Captain of the Texas Rangers and now commanding a US Mounted Rifle Regiment. He had witnessed the effectiveness of Colt's revolvers during his service in the Seminole Wars and Colt now offered him a good financial deal on his revolvers, encouraging Walker to place an order for one thousand. Unfortunately, Colt no longer owned a factory and had, in effect, to sub-contract the manufacture of the order to Eli Whitney Blake, an established arms manufacturer. The order was placed on condition that the revolvers were delivered on time – if they were not, there would be no repeat orders. Despite sundry problems Colt delivered and the weapons saw service with the Rangers and various other units. Even more importantly, as a result of his wartime service, Walker had collaborated with Colt on the design of his revolver and encouraged him to make one or two changes in the design. The result was the Paterson Colt, the first of a long line of revolvers. Although it was an improvement on previous models, it was by no means a total success. A number blew up and some troops complained of its weight but, when it was in action, there was only praise for it.

Several versions of this five-shot revolver were made, with varying barrel lengths and calibres; the Number 5 or Belt model was of .36 calibre and the cylinder was engraved with a stagecoach hold-up scene. The revolver had a drop-down trigger and some were made with a pivoted loading lever mounted beneath the barrel but others had a separate loading rod[25].

In 1847 The Colt Walker Revolver made its appearance and it was this revolver that really set the pattern for so many subsequent models. One of its most noticeable features was its weight – over four and half pounds (about 2kg), which was amazingly heavy for a revolver. The weight was the result of a six-chamber cylinder and a nine-inch barrel. It was also of .44 calibre, which meant that it required a large powder charge which, in turn, meant stronger metal

The .36 1851 Colt Navy Percussion revolver, probably the most popular of the range of Colt's percussion revolvers. It was six-shot and the cylinder was engraved with a naval scene.

components had to be used in order to handle the increased power. The pistol was composed of two sections held together with a crossbar at their junction, a feature of most of Colt's early revolvers. The front section was composed of the nine-inch barrel, part round and part octagonal in section, with an attached loading lever mounted beneath. The other section was made up of the character-istic butt, trigger and mechanism, as well as a central spindle or arbor around which the cylinder rotated. The cylinder was engraved with a scene of combat between Rangers and Indians.

Changes in design led to the Dragoon Colt, a .44 revolver with a shorter barrel, of seven and a half inches, which sold well. It also underwent various design modifications and three different versions were produced. Like all of Colt's early models, this revolver was single action only, requiring the action to be cocked manually using the thumb.

There was much discussion, especially among the military men, as to the rela-tive virtues of the two firing systems. It was argued that single action made for slower, more accurate shooting, thus conserving ammunition, whilst double action encour-aged wild, wasted shooting. However, double action could be faster than single in an emer-gency.

There was a half-cock position for the hammer that allowed the cylinder to be rotated for loading, and pressure on the trigger had no effect. If the hammer was pulled back into the full-cock position, cyl-inder and barrel were in line and pressing the trigger fired the shot. The location of the trigger within the trigger guard normally indicates whether the weapon is single or double action. Since a double-action mecha-nism requires a longer pull, the trigger is set well forward inside the trigger guard.

In 1849 Colt was back in England, where there was much discussion about and plan-ning for the forthcoming Great Exhibition of 1851. This highly prestigious event was to be held in London's Hyde Park from May to October, and was intended to demonstrate to the world Britain's great engineering and cultural power. Representatives from many countries would be displaying their prod-ucts and shrewd businessman Samuel Colt foresaw a great opportunity for making contacts and increasing business, and imme-diately booked space. When the Exhibition opened Colt had mounted more than four hundred firearms on his stand, the largest such display in the exhibition. It attracted much attention and he, as a skilled public relations man, missed no chance to publicize his product. The name Colt was often seen in the newspapers and the man himself frequently engaged in public debate, including on one occasion when the doyen of English revolver production, Robert Adams, was present. Knowing the value of the personal touch, Colt also presented cased revolvers to government officials and to anybody he thought might prove to be a useful contact. By the time the exhibition closed, some six million people had visited it.

Apart from displaying his goods Colt was also allowed to sell some revolvers. *The Times* newspaper of 28 October 1851 lists people who had availed themselves of the sanction of the Government authority that allowed them to obtain samples of foreign firearms displayed in the Great Exhibition. This list includes numerous British officers about to leave for foreign service, who were taking several of Colt's revolvers, in many cases for friends, as well as for personal use. All these sales helped spread word of Colt revolvers across the world, but at first there was little official Government interest in his products. In June the Royal Navy asked the Board of Ordnance, the central supply body, to purchase some Dragoon pistols;

four were sent to be tested at the naval base at Portsmouth and four went to the Tower of London.

Eventually, Colt was given a contract for 4,000 Navy Model revolvers, which were of .36 calibre and consequently much lighter than the Dragoon. This was later followed by equally large orders for Army Models in .44 calibre. His early sales and experience in Britain appear to have convinced him that there was a huge European market opening up for his products and he decided to set up a factory in London to manufacture and assemble his revolvers. By 1852 he had acquired the lease on an old brick building in London, near the River Thames, in the area known as Pimlico, and by January 1853 his factory was in production.

This bold and rather unpopular action startled the gunmakers of Britain who, until now, had shown little interest or initiative in producing revolvers. They saw their trade being taken away by a brash Yankee and Colt's success piqued their interest, stimulating a flood of percussion revolvers. There was some personal hostility towards Colt, and many claims and counter-claims were

The odd one out of Colt revolvers – the Side Hammer 1855 revolver. Intended as a five-shot pocket weapon, it was never popular and suffered from sundry mechanical problems.

made about the quality and effectiveness of the different revolvers. Tests were organized to demonstrate which were better, British or American, but they were mostly inconclusive, although each manufacturer naturally claimed victory. In addition to his factory Colt also opened a shop in the fashionable area of London at 14 Pall Mall. It was from this address that he published a note in the newspapers warning purchasers of firearms to be wary of cheap weapons, which were being advertised at several shops as being 'on Colt's principle, at 30/– each'.

Despite any high hopes that Colt may have had for his London factory, it was not such a great success and was closed in 1856. He did, however, maintain his London shop[26].

There were setbacks, but demand for Colt's revolvers soared, with many countries equipping military units with them and many public services such as police forces also adopting them. Colt's success later enabled him to build an American factory, The Colt's Patent Fire-Arms Manufacturing Company, at Hartford, Connecticut. This was followed by the building of a larger factory and of a grand house that he called 'Armsmear'. The result of his success was a burst of revolver production greater than ever before. One of the reasons for this commercial success was his use of machinery to manufacture the weapons; one of his most important claims was that all parts of his revolvers were interchangeable from one pistol to another, without any requiring any adjustments. Around the 1850s and 1860s, a whole range of new revolvers appeared on the market, generating much debate. Shooting competitions took place to determine which was the best weapon but the differences were, in fact, fairly minor.

Demand for revolvers was particularly high in the middle of the nineteenth century. British officers purchased Colt revolvers on

their way to the Crimean War (1854–1856), the Indian Mutiny of 1857 and for use in other outposts of the Empire. In America the California Gold Rush, the American Civil War (1861–1865), Indian Wars and the opening of the Frontier all ensured a continuing demand. Colt was commissioned as a Colonel in the State forces. He saw no action and was discharged after a month, but he cherished the rank none the less and used it to impress the public. By the time he died, in 1862, he had built up an enormous business and with it a considerable fortune. He had proved himself to be a tough businessman who looked after his workers but would tolerate no slacking. Even after his demise, the Colt factory and business expanded and, indeed, continues today.

For Britain, the Crimean War (1854–1856) naturally generated much debate about the use of revolvers by the troops, and the cavalry in particular, and *The Times* columns often contained letters urging their adoption. Despite the generally good publicity that Colt received, there was one discordant note. On 19 December 1854, a correspondent wrote to *The Times* claiming that Samuel Colt had been to St Petersburg and was planning to supply the Russians, the enemy in the Crimean War, with large numbers of his revolvers. The weapons were apparently to be made in Liège, in Belgium. This letter prompted a reply from Colt on 28 December, stating that as a result of this letter he was being unfairly condemned by various journals. He denied that he had supplied any arms or machinery to the Russians and reminded the readers of his offer to the British Government, to make arms at a lower cost than that paid to other makers. He added, 'It is not my fault if all my facilities are not now devoted to the British Government.'

From the mid-nineteenth century, a stream of new models flowed from Colt's

Colt Pocket percussion revolver 1849 model .31 calibre, with New York address and matching numbers throughout. (Thomas Del Mar Ltd)

American and London factories. Some of the London ones were assembled from parts imported from the USA and others were manufactured entirely in London. All had the address of their factory engraved along the top of the barrel. Another feature of Colt's products was that each part of the revolver was stamped with the same number and this made it clear if any part had been changed.

The number of different models continued to grow:

- 1848 The Pocket revolver was introduced, available with either five or six chambers and with various barrel lengths, calibre .31, the cylinder engraved with a hold-up scene
- 1849 A London-made five-shot version appeared
- 1851 The Navy model. Six-shot, .36 calibre, probably the most popular of all Colt's percussion models. Seven-inch, part-round part-hexagonal barrel, cylinder engraved with a ship scene. Produced in New York and London
- 1855 A departure from the usual style with a side-mounted hammer for easier maintenance and a solid, one-piece frame; five shots in either .28 or .31 calibre. Never a popular seller
- 1860 The Army model. Six-shot, .44 calibre with a different style of loading lever with a

toothed or cog connection. As popular as the Navy Model
- 1861 Navy revolver with some details the same as the 1851 Navy but with a round barrel and creeping, cogged loading lever
- 1862 Police model, five-shot, .36 calibre, barrels of various length
- 1862 Pocket model, .36 calibre and similar shape to 1851 model

All Colt revolvers could be supplied cased with accessories such as a bullet mould, a tin of caps (often Colt's own brand), a cleaning rod and a combined turnscrew and nipple key. Most of the cases were of oak or mahogany, with green or blue baize-lined compartments. The factory would also engrave a revolver, fit an ivory grip or otherwise modify the weapon to the customer's instructions. Some of Colt's revolvers were available with a detachable stock that could easily be fitted to the butt, making the revolver into a carbine. Some versions of Colt's revolvers were manufactured in Belgium.

So successful was Colt in his marketing techniques that there is today an entrenched belief that his pistols alone were carried and used in the development of the Wild West. It is a myth unintentionally endorsed by the cinema. Examination of shipping records of arms sales between 1868 and 1886, from one

Percussion revolver made by Deane Adams and Deane, circa 1850. Note the lack of a spur on the hammer so that it was almost impossible to cock the action other than by pressure on the trigger. The base of the butt is hollowed to form a small compartment for spare caps or nipple. (Thomas Del Mar Ltd)

big shipping firm in New York, shows that his pistols make up a very small proportion of the orders[27]. Colt pistols, especially the Army and Navy models, figure in the list as do Remington revolvers, whilst the English Adams revolver barely appears. It is unwise to attempt to draw any firm conclusions from these figures alone, but they certainly suggest that the cinema's representation of the Colt revolver being the only weapon in use in the Wild West may be wide of the mark. It should also be borne in mind that Colt's prices were comparatively high and cheaper surplus weapons, especially after the US Civil War, were plentiful. Certainly, for the period around 1850–60 Colt was the leading manufacturer, but with the advent of the metal cartridge there was a surge of new models from various makers.

British Percussion Revolvers

Around the middle of the century some of the main competitors for the percussion revolver market were British. Colt's arrival on the scene stimulated a number of gunmakers to explore the design of the new pistol. Some indication of the tremendous growth in production can be seen from the number of barrels, listed as being for revolvers, passing through the London Proof House. In the period 1844–1848, there were seldom more than just over a hundred; in 1851, the figure rose to 954 and in 1852 it jumped to 6,121. In Birmingham, by 1857 the number was 35,593[28]!

At the Great Exhibition of 1851 a number of countries had displayed a selection of firearms, with the French and Spanish makers noted particularly for their beautifully decorated guns. One English firm Deane, Adams & Deane, offered in their display a percussion revolver as one of a number of items connected with firearms. The enormous interest generated by Colt's revolvers spread to the weapon offered by Deane, Adams & Deane, which was a percussion revolver patented in 1851 and very different from the Colt pattern. It was generally reckoned to be better made – the Colt had a two-part frame, but the Adams was on a single, solid frame. Colts were single action only and the Adams revolver was self-cocking, in other words, it could be cocked simply by squeezing the trigger, giving it, at least to military eyes, a slight edge by being that much quicker in action. The hammer or cock had no spur so it could not be cocked manually, and it was a five-shot weapon against Colt's six. In one arranged competitive shoot, the Adams was matched against a Dragoon, a much heavier and a larger-calibre pistol. Although Adams

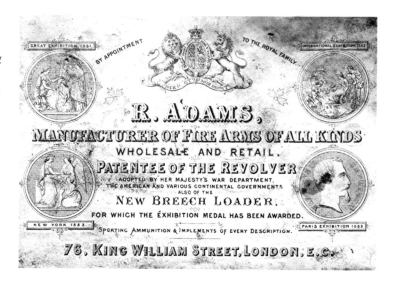

Typical trade label from the lid of a cased percussion revolver, supplied by R. Adams, one of Britain's leading manufacturers. This example post-dates 1862, the maker's last model.

claimed victory, there was apparently very little difference between the performances of the two pistols.

The Deane, Adams & Deane revolver was made in various calibres and barrel lengths and was reckoned to be a very reliable weapon but in February 1855 its suitability for military service was greatly enhanced. A Lieutenant Beaumont of the Royal Engineers filed a patent transforming the single-action Adams into a double-action weapon. Some modification of the internal mechanism was required, but the obvious difference was the fitting of a spur to the cock. This now allowed the option of using the trigger or the thumb to pull back the hammer and cock the weapon.

Colt's loading levers were mounted beneath the barrel but Adams and Beaumont Adams revolvers have a side-mounted rammer, one model with the lever fitted beside the barrel and the other with it curved and sitting beside the butt. The earlier models had the side-mounted, or Adams rammer, and the later ones have the barrel-mounted type. A more complicated barrel-mounted system loader was patented by Joseph Brazier later in 1855.

By now there was a marked increase in the enthusiasm of British gunmakers for the new percussion revolvers and several new names appear in the listings. The well-established Deane, Adams & Deane firm was dissolved in 1856. The new London Armoury Company started straight away under the leadership of Robert Adams and a factory was set up in Henry Street, London. Robert Adams left the company in 1859 and opened a shop in prestigious Pall Mall in the West End of London, and the company was wound up in 1867.

Among the revolvers made by the London Armoury Company was one patented in 1858 by James Kerr. Compared with the rather sleek looks of the Colt and Adams, the Kerr looks bulky. It has a side-mounted hammer, was produced in both single- and double-action models, was fitted with an under-barrel rammer, had five chambers and was available in various calibres and different barrel lengths. Its selling point was that the mechanism was side-mounted, giving easy access should a mechanical problem occur.

The number of different percussion revolvers in production increased steadily. One patented by William Harding in 1858 had some superficial resemblances to the Colt design and comprised a two-piece frame although the locking system varied considerably. It also used a double-action trigger mechanism. The loading lever was also barrel-mounted but operated on a different system. Another revolver, designed by Joseph Lang, had a feature that ensured that cylinder chamber and barrel were closely united when the shot was fired, to ensure minimum gas leakage, so helping to increase the power. Another elegant model, from Daw, had a hooded hammer designed to prevent pieces of the metal percussion cap being blown over the shooter.

In the 1860s the name of Webley begins to appear among the gun-trade listings and this company, started by brothers Philip and James was to dominate British gunmaking for many, many years. The Webleys were from Birmingham, a town noted for its metal-working, but at this period making little contribution to the gun trade. That situation was to change immeasurably. Both brothers seem to have come to prominence almost by accident. Neither was originally concerned with revolver manufacture but from the 1850s they became increasingly involved. Philip began to take a serious interest in developing the gun trade, started employing machinery to make of parts for the revolver and in 1853 patented a self-cocking revolver. Whether this development had any direct bearing is uncertain, but Colt closed his London factory in 1857 and around this time Philip Webley began to expand his production to include all manner of arms and accessories.

The firm produced a range of percussion revolvers and pepperboxes, as well as the so-called transition revolvers, most of which were built on a two-part frame and were single action. The loading rammer was mounted along the side of the barrel. One of Webley's best-known early revolvers was the Longspur model, made between 1853 and

1899. Its main feature was a very long, rearward-pointing spur on the hammer. Three basic models were produced, all with a two-part frame. In addition to the guns, the firm manufactured a range of metal-worked items such as handcuffs, leg irons and swords.

Many of the English percussion revolvers were sold individually or as a cased set, usually in an oak box, with bullet mould, turnscrew, a tin of caps and often a tin of lubricating grease to use when loading the chambers. Like the Colts, the inside of the lid usually has a maker's label extolling his virtues or giving instructions on the handling of the revolver.

By the 1850s and 60s the selection of available percussion revolvers was more than adequate and, although there were numerous patents for extra details and strange variations, development was basically at an end. One revolver of the period explored new ideas with a double-barrelled set-up – one a conventional pistol barrel and the other a short, large-bore shotgun barrel. The idea was patented in 1856 by a doctor, Jean Alexander LeMat, serving on the staff of the Governor of Louisiana, USA. The main section was a more or less conventional revolver but with a nine-chamber cylinder revolving around the second barrel, which

Contemporary illustration of a Le Mat revolver clearly showing the two barrels mounted one above the other, and the adjustable hammer when set to fire the shotgun round.

was a big .63 calibre. The hammer had a nose that could be adjusted so as to fire either the revolver or the central shotgun barrel. Three hundred were made in New Orleans and later some 2,200 were made in France, and in 1864 manufacture was transferred to Birmingham. The LeMat revolver saw some service in the US Civil War but its appeal was limited.

In 1859 another unusual idea was patented by J. Walch. It was in fact an up-to-date version of an idea dating back to the fifteenth century: a double revolver housed on one frame. The elongated cylinder housed twin chambers, each with two charges and each with two nipples and caps. The frame of the smaller-calibre weapon housed one hammer whilst the Navy model had two hammers mounted side by side. The chambers were loaded with special bullets composed of two halves separated by a wad of oil and soap. The idea was that, when the bullet was loaded into the chamber and pressed home, the wad was compressed to form an isolating layer between the two parts. The nipples were linked to the separate sections of the bullet and as the trigger was pressed the hammer struck the front nipple and fired that shot. The trigger was cocked and the cylinder rotated to bring the next front bullet in line with the barrel. This sequence was repeated for each of the five or six chambers. The rear bullets were fired in the same manner, using the second hammer. The Walch revolver was rather complex and it is likely that the separating wad sometimes failed to isolate the rear section, leading to an unexpected volley of shots. Production costs must surely have been high and only a small number have survived, suggesting that it was never in great demand. Three models were made, two in .31 calibre and one in .36 calibre.

Another name that was to feature significantly in the trade in percussion revolvers was William Tranter, who held a number of English revolver patents. His double-trigger models are probably the best known. There was always debate on the benefits of the two systems of shooting a revolver – single- or double-action – but Tranter sought to combine both systems, in an attempt to achieve the best possible result. His double-trigger revolvers had a solid frame and a very long double curved trigger. This extended through a slot in the trigger guard and when the lower section was pressed it rotated the cylinder and cocked the action but did not fire the shot. The section enclosed inside the trigger guard was then pressed and this fired the shot. The shooter could thus take aim, hold it and, when certain of his target, fire the shot, and he could then immediately cock the action ready for a second shot.

A similar, double-trigger Tranter action was revived in the 1880s when a six-shot .45 revolver was made by George Kynoch, who had previously been one of the main manufacturers of percussion caps. Only a limited number of these hammerless revolvers were produced and a later version had both triggers enclosed within a trigger guard. A variety of models were made and collectors classify them by the type of rammer. The First Model had a separate rammer, which many would not rate as an excellent idea since it could so easily be lost. The Second Model had a separate rammer that could be clipped to the frame, whilst on the Third Model the pivoted rammer was permanently attached.

The 1850s and 60s witnessed a steady stream of different percussion revolvers but changes were afoot that were to render them old-fashioned and obsolete, by removing the necessity for percussion caps and loading levers.

CHAPTER 5

Breech-Loading

~ ~ ~

From the first discovery of gunpowder, most firearms were loaded via the muzzle. It was a slow, tedious business, and the goal of many inventors was to devise a system whereby powder and ball could be loaded in at the breech end. This was particularly appealing to hunters and troops for, although it was not impossible, it was certainly difficult to load a rifle or sporting gun unless the shooter was standing up and holding the barrel vertically. If the barrel was horizontal, ramming home the bullet with the ramrod was awkward, but it could be done. However, getting the powder charge into the breech was very difficult. Paper cartridges made it simpler but still involved some juggling.

Early Systems

The first practical system of breech-loading was used on cannon, when the breech end of the barrel was left open. A metal cylinder of correct size, with a touch hole, was charged with powder and ball and dropped in at the breech end. It was secured in position, often by jamming it in place with wooden wedges, and the gun could then be fired, and the empty chamber removed and replaced by a loaded one. The system worked but was hardly ideal as the gas leakage at the junction of barrel and chamber could be severe. As they had to withstand the full power of the charges, the chambers were heavy. There is no doubt that this system was in use from a very early date and on one or two smaller cannon the chamber was threaded so that it could be screwed into the barrel.

A similar system was adapted for use with muskets, and examples from the armoury of Henry VIII have a metal flap that lifts to expose a space, into which was dropped a charged metal tube. Although the locks of these weapons are missing, judging by their date they must have been wheel locks. Henry also had some small matchlock breech-loading pistols, which were centrally mounted into metal shields used by his bodyguards.

It is surprising that, despite this early sixteenth-century use of cartridge-like chambers, few makers seem to have attempted to develop simple breech-loading handguns. The first positive steps took place in France in 1704, when a threaded plug system was tried by an engineer named de la Chaumette. However it was not widely adopted or expanded and one of the best systems was devised much later, in 1776, by Patrick Ferguson, a Captain of the British Army. Ferguson's solution was to gain access to the breech by means of a coarse, threaded screw plug attached to the trigger guard. As it was rotated it caused the metal plug to drop, giving direct access to the breech, into which first ball and then powder could be loaded. Captain Ferguson gave an impressive demonstration of his rifle. He loaded it whilst lying prone on the ground and even in the middle of a rainstorm was able to attain an impressive rate of fire. A limited number of Ferguson rifles were issued to troops but there was no wide acceptance or great enthusiasm for the new idea. Once again the virtue of aimed fire was not seen as a priority since using troops to fire coordinated volley firing was the accepted military system. Ferguson was killed in action during the American War of Independence.

In the late seventeenth and eighteenth centuries some pistols, most commonly pocket models, were produced with a simple breech-loading system. The barrel was composed of two sections: the front section was threaded at the end and the back section comprised the breech with its touch hole. The front section was unscrewed, allowing the shooter to deposit powder and ball directly into the breech. The front section was then screwed firmly back into place. The front part of the barrel was often secured to the pistol by some form of metal link since it was obviously very vulnerable. This section frequently has a small down-projecting lug near the end, which engages with a circular key when it is passed down over the barrel. This meant that the shooter could easily get a firm grip when seating the barrel, ensuring that a tight fit was made between barrel and breech. Another method of ensuring a tight-fitting junction of both sections of the barrel was to cut small V-shaped notches around

An extremely rare Colt cap dispenser dating from around 1840 for use with one of Colt's earliest models, the Paterson percussion revolver. It is of brass with blued steel fittings. (Thomas Del Mar Ltd)

the muzzle into which a tapered, square-ended key was pushed to engage with these slots. These notches are sometimes mistaken for rifling. These simple but effective methods were used on pistols until the mid-nineteenth century.

Variations on the theme of using detachable barrels were tried but they were rather unreliable and there was always a chance of the barrel working loose. Another approach to the problem was the use of a tipping block in which the breech was a separate section which could be pulled back and tilted up so

Top left: Percussion revolver nipple key with spare nipples held in compartments at the end of the arms; simpler and later nipple key; wad cutter; cap dispenser, two-ended screwdriver or turnscrews, to use contemporary terms; nipple primer; cap dispenser; powder primer for nipples of percussion pistol or revolver; cap dispenser.

that powder and ball could be loaded and the block re-sited. However most systems were intended for use on long arms and the pistol was rather neglected; in any case the future of breech-loading pistols lay with cartridges rather than with mechanical systems.

The stimulus for developing breech-loading handguns was the appearance of the percussion revolver. The percussion cap had simplified and speeded up loading but, as each chamber had to be primed and the cap was rather small, sometimes it could be difficult to place the cap on the percussion nipple, especially with cold fingers or in adverse weather conditions. This difficulty led to the development of some quick cap-locating devices known as 'cappers' or 'caps'. Most comprised a flat container that held a quantity of caps and these, under the gentle pressure of a spring, were pushed, individually, into a small, open-sided aperture. This was placed over the nipple, thus locating the cap, and the container was then pulled away, leaving the cap *in situ*.

The cappers were simple, efficient and certainly speeded up loading but with the revolver each chamber had to be charged

with powder and ball, and this could be too time-consuming in an emergency. Some percussion revolvers were sold with a spare cylinder, which could be pre-loaded and carried in readiness. In action, the fired cylinder was removed and replaced by the spare ready-loaded one. It was not ideal but it could be faster than normal reloading. A few cylindrical powder flasks were made with multiple nozzles suitably located to match the chambers of the revolver cylinder. The system was only feasible if there was direct access to the cylinder, so that all cylinders could be charged with one action.

Self-Contained Cartridges

The next improvement for revolvers was the introduction of self-contained cartridges. The idea was not new – the military had long been using them in their muskets and rifles. A paper tube of appropriate size was fashioned by rolling it around a wooden former, twisting one end closed and filling it with powder, and inserting a ball at the open end, which was also then twisted closed. To charge the musket the soldier tore off one end with his teeth, charged the pan and then poured the rest of the powder down the barrel, followed by the ball and paper. A supply of these cartridges could be stored in pouches, enabling the soldier to maintain a reasonable rate of firing of about three rounds a minute.

In the mid-nineteenth century the idea was extended to revolver ammunition and smaller cartridges were fashioned with cases of waxed paper or similar materials. These were often chemically treated, to initiate rapid burning. To ensure swift ignition of the powder by the flash from the cap on some cartridges it was felt advisable to split the paper case, thus exposing the powder. For this purpose, a small tag was attached to the body of some of the cartridges. When loading a chamber, the tag was pulled, tearing open the cartridge. The cartridge was pushed into the chamber and the revolver's pivoted loading lever was used to press the bullet well down on the powder in the chamber. It might also slightly expand the bullet, resulting in a close fit and ensuring a minimum leakage of gas.

Even with this improvement there was still the problem that two separate loading steps were needed: first the cartridge, then the cap. Tentative steps to incorporate the percussion cap into the body of the cartridge case were taken as early as the beginning of the nineteenth century. The

Pages from an early twentieth-century sale catalogue showing the number of cheap pistols and revolvers available with very few legal restrictions on ownership.

Lang percussion revolver retailed by Parker Field & Sons circa 1850. It is fitted with a special spring- loaded side-mounted rammer patented by Parker Field. (Thomas Del Mar Ltd)

most successful system was probably that designed by a Swiss, Johannes Samuel Pauly (1766–1820?), who, as early as 1812, had devised a brass cartridge case with a centrally base-mounted primer. The base of his case was formed of soft brass and at the centre was a pellet of his detonating mixture, which was struck by the firing rod. The weakness of the system was that this pellet was vulnerable. It could, and did, fall out and it was also likely to be struck accidentally. When the system worked, the soft base of the cartridge was expanded by the gas from the burning gunpowder, which meant that there was a very tight seal at the base of the breech. This reduced the obturation or gas leakage to an absolute minimum, ensuring maximum power. The Pauly gun was made with either a drop-down barrel or a lifting breech for inserting the cartridge and was far ahead of other contemporary firearms. He offered the idea to the French military but, despite impressive results in test shoots, they rejected it. Two years later Pauly was in England taking out a patent for a new compressed ignition system but, as in France, his advanced ideas were rejected by the British. Handguns would have to wait several more years before they became breech-loaders.

Another most important step was taken in the nineteenth century, with the placing of the detonator in close proximity to the powder. The French seem to have had an affinity with the idea and in 1826 Galy-Cazalat patented a paper cartridge with the percussion cap fitted in the base of the case. Obturation was poor, with an excessive leakage of gas, and the idea gained little support. In 1829 Clement Pottet was granted a patent for a cartridge with a paper body fitted with a detachable base housing the detonator. In 1855 he had

Percussion cap dispenser with the top plate removed to show the spiral spring that feeds caps individually to the end of the tube.

Six-shot pinfire pepperbox revolver with Birmingham proof marks, circa 1865. It is fitted with a folding trigger. (Thomas Del Mar Ltd)

Two pinfire revolvers bearing Liège proof marks and dating from 1860–70. They are six-shot and, as they lack trigger guards, their triggers can be folded back to reduce the chances of any accidental shots. Cheap pistols like these were produced in quantity in Liège. (Thomas Del Mar Ltd)

another patent with an improved base, which had the percussion cap at its centre and was in effect the modern shotgun case.

The next step was taken by Augustus Demondion, who patented a gun designed to use a cartridge with a tube of detonator that was struck by the hammer. Again, obturation proved poor. It was becoming more and more apparent that paper alone was not a terribly good sealing material.

A father and son pointed the way next and in 1835 the father, Casimir Lefaucheux, received a patent for the new family of cartridges. These cartridges had a circular metal base with a short metal wall to which was attached a paper body. Set into this base was a percussion cap with one end pressing against the base of the wall. A thin metal rod passed through the wall and one end touched the cap whilst the other projected outside the cartridge case, which was then filled with powder. A bullet was fitted into the open end. This, then, was the new pinfire cartridge.

Guns intended for use with this system had a small hole appropriately positioned at the breech or, on a revolver, in the chamber, so that when the cartridge was in place, the tip of the rod stood out above the surface. The

revolver or gun lock had a hammer with a solid head, which, on pressing the trigger, swung forward to strike the pin, which was pushed down to hit the cap and detonate it, so firing the shot. The system proved popular and went on to be developed by Lefaucheux's son Eugene. Pinfire weapons continued to enjoy some popularity until the 1880s and 1890s.

The pinfire system was a great success, especially with hunters for it was now easy to break the gun, remove the fired base and drop a cartridge into the breech or chamber. Pinfire revolvers were manufactured in quantity by most European countries, especially Belgium, and the output included a number of revolvers with cylinders holding many rounds (up to twenty plus in some extreme cases). Although the high capacity of such weapons may appear, at first glance, to have been a significant benefit, this was not in fact the case. The weight of a revolver holding twenty rounds was considerable and carrying one on duty or taking aim was less than pleasant.

The next improvement to the pinfire system was to replace the paper case with a metal one, making the system even more popular. Pinfire revolvers saw service on both sides in the American Civil War (1861–1865).

Although the pinfire action was an improvement on earlier systems it was not without its problems, the main one being the projecting rod, which was vulnerable to loss and accidental knocks. What was wanted was a better method of locating the detonator inside the metal case. Several attempts were made but none proved to be quite right. One earlier system had experimented with the detonator set in cylindrical form around the base of the case, and it was an improvement on this idea that was to provide the answer. Many contributed to the solution, but two men may rightly claim the main honour.

Horace Smith (1808–1893) was a mechanic skilled in several trades who came, like Samuel Colt, from Connecticut, USA. He took out several patents dealing with firearms but his fame really dates from his union with Daniel Wesson (1825–1906), a gunsmith by trade. They were both involved with the Volcanic Arms Company; Wesson left in 1856 and a year later joined up with Smith. In 1866 the Volcanic Company manufactured a repeating pistol, The Volcanic, patented in 1866 by Walter Hunt. It was, in effect, basically a small version of the Winchester rifle. The special bullets had the detonator fitted in the base and were housed in a spring-loaded tubular magazine fitted beneath the barrel and filled with rounds from the front end. The action was operated by means of a toggle lever, a double-ringed lever that also served as a trigger guard. Lowering this lever caused

The Volcanic, the forerunner to the Winchester. The cartridges were loaded into the lower tube and were lifted into the breech by operating the trigger guard. It was developed by Smith & Wesson in the 1850s and later taken up by Winchester.

an internal breech block to extract a bullet from the magazine and a forward movement of the lever lifted the cartridge into position in the breech and pushed it in place.

Oliver Winchester (1810–1880), originally a maker of shirts, bought some shares in the Volcanic Company and eventually took it over when it went bankrupt in 1857. In 1866 it was renamed the Winchester Repeating Arms Company and began production of what is probably one of the world's best-known rifles, the lever-action Winchester, which has featured in almost every Western film made. A variety of versions were produced in differing calibres and sizes.

When Smith and Wesson left the company, they set up their own firm in Springfield to manufacture a small .22 revolver. They had one great advantage in that they were the owners of the rights to a patent granted to a Rollin White in 1855. The importance of this patent seems to have been overlooked by Colt and other gunmakers; on the face of it, it seemed hardly exciting as it merely covered the right to drill a chamber right through the length of the revolver cylinder. The patent stated that this was for the purpose of breech-loading, an idea that was not yet widely accepted at the time as really practical. It also stated that no breech-loading pistol could be made without the approval of and a payment to the owner of the patent. Once the virtues and advantages of breech-loading had been properly appreciated, there were attempts by some gunmakers to circumvent the patent, which led to some legal action. In the end, the patent was held valid until it expired in 1869.

Valuable as their work in firearms was, it is in the field of ammunition that Smith & Wesson made their greatest contribution. The pinfire cartridge enabled quick loading of the revolver as the cartridge was dropped into the chamber, but there was a minor problem as the case had to be correctly positioned to ensure that the rod was in the right place. What was needed was some way to dispose of the pin and of enclosing the detonator completely inside the case in such a way that it was unlikely to be knocked or displaced. The way forward had been unknowingly charted some time before when another Frenchman, C. Houllier, worked on a cartridge with the detonator encircling the base of the case. Smith & Wesson took up this idea and covered the entire inside base of their metal cartridge case with detonating compound. However, they soon realized that this was wasteful and sought a more economical use of the detonator.

In order to be detonated, the chemical had to be struck between two hard surfaces and Smith & Wesson designed a metal cartridge case that had a small, hollow rim encircling the base. This rim was filled with the detonator and, when the case was inserted into the chamber, this rim rested on the face of the cylinder, one solid surface. If the rim could be struck by the hammer this was the second hard surface and the detonator would explode. They patented their design in 1860 and it proved to work sufficiently well for them to manufacture a small .22 revolver specially designed to accept the cartridge. The modern breech-loading revolver had

arrived. Revolvers designed to take these cartridges are sometimes recognizable by the hammer, which often has on the face a central ridge of the same width as the cartridge case, so ensuring that both sides of the rim were struck.

Cartridges could now be made self-contained, with powder, ball and cap all incorporated into one unit, but there was a limit to their use. This rim firing was a big step forward but it was found that development was somewhat held back by one factor: the thickness of the metal case. In order to withstand the pressure generated by the enclosed charge of powder and prevent fracture, the metal case needed to be of a certain thickness. If the charge of powder was increased, the thickness of the case also had to be increased or it would split under the greater pressure. This imposed a limit on the size of the bullet that could be used with the rimfire cartridge. There came a point at which, in order to discharge a large-calibre bullet, the case needed to have a very substantial wall indeed. If the case wall was too thick, the hammer was not able to dent it to explode the detonator.

This limit to case thickness and bullet size generally restricted the rimfire cartridges to smaller calibres. Today, most rimfire ammunition is largely restricted to .22 calibre firearms, which are commonly used for target shooting or vermin control. One answer to this problem was obviously to locate the detonator in a position that was away from the case wall. Pauly had provided the answer years previously with his centre-fire system. New designs meant that the shooting world was about to take a great step forward. The introduction of the modern metal self-contained cartridges would change and expand the entire shooting scene.

Various patents sought to provide a system where the percussion cap or detonator was stimulated at the centre of a metal base. It was the work of an American, Colonel Hiram Berdan (1824–1893), that triumphed in 1866. He had fought in the Civil War and was a noted marksman who had developed a method of making brass cartridge cases by drawing them from a block of metal. Centrally placed in the base of his cartridge case was a slightly recessed depression, into which was fitted firmly and safely a small primer. If the firearm had a hammer with a central protrusion this would hit the primer and fire the shot.

It is a remarkable coincidence that in the same year, 1866, an Englishman, a Captain Edward Boxer (1823–1898), Superintendent at Woolwich Royal Laboratory, was working along similar lines. His given task had been to develop a cartridge for the new breech-loading Snider rifle, which was used by the British Army from 1866 to 1901. His final design was a cartridge that had a case fashioned of sheet brass and a base with the primer set at the centre. As with Berdan's system, all that was required to fire the cartridge was for the hammer to hit the centrally mounted primer. The only real difference between the two systems was in the method of locating the primer in the base; Boxer's was the simpler. His original design was modified and solid brass cases were found to be much stronger and less likely to split than the original sheet brass cases.

The new round worked well for the Snider rifle and of course demonstrated that it would be just as suitable for any other weapon capable of accepting a breech-loading round. Although the design was acknowledged to be brilliant, Boxer upset the authorities by taking out a private patent for the system. His commercial involvement was considered to be inappropriate for a serving officer in the British Army, and he resigned his commission some three years later.

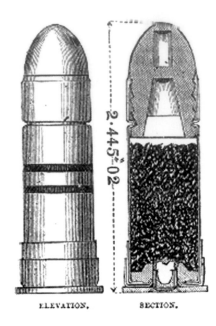

ELEVATION.   SECTION.

Although this round is for the Snider rifle of the 1880s, it shows clearly how a round was assembled.

This new style of cartridge introduced a series of problems for manufacturers as it meant that muzzle-loading firearms would have to be converted to breech-loading. In the case of revolvers, the solution was simply to drill the chamber through the cylinder and adapt the hammer. The path was now open for a whole range of new and converted breech-loading pistols and revolvers, except for one obstacle: the Rollin White patent held by Smith & Wesson. This effectively prevented any maker from boring through the revolver cylinder to accept the new cartridge unless permission was given and payment made.

The Smith & Wesson small-calibre revolver using their cartridge was popular but had its limitations. Its small calibre, .22, meant that its penetrative power was low, but increasing the calibre would introduce the case-thickness problem. In addition, extraction of fired cases was rather tedious. To remove a fired cartridge case from the cylinder it was necessary to press a catch on the revolver frame, which allowed the pivoted barrel to be lowered and the cylinder lifted clear of the frame. Each case was then ejected in turn by pushing the chambers in turn down over a rod, fitted below the cylinder, which ejected the case.

Extraction of fired cases from the revolver cylinder was a problem from the beginning and in earlier models it tended to be a slow process. A great improvement was achieved by making the process automatic. If the revolver was made on a two-part frame and a catch was pressed, the revolver barrel, with cylinder attached, could be depressed. At the same time, a rod that ran centrally through the cylinder was pushed up by a simple arrangement of internal cams and levers. This rod was fitted at the cylinder end with a plate, which sat flush in a shallow recess in the face of the cylinder. The plate was cut with a number of semi-circular spaces corresponding with the chambers. As the plate was raised it engaged with the rims of the cartridge cases and lifted them out of the chambers to fall clear. After a set movement the plate and rod snapped back into place, allowing new rounds to be inserted.

On some models the ejector rod had to be pushed out manually but on others it was

Loading a Smith & Wesson revolver with a swing-out cylinder, using one pattern of strip speed-loader enabling six rounds to be inserted into the cylinder by one action.

The cylinder and hammer of a Smith & Wesson rimfire revolver showing the specially shaped hammer designed to ensure a firm blow on the rim to ensure detonation.

.357 MILITARY & POLICE REVOLVER
MODEL No. 13

PARTS LIST • INSTRUCTIONS FOR USE • MAINTENANCE
SPECIFICATIONS

SPECIFICATIONS

Caliber	.357 S&W Special	Sights	Fixed, ½-inch serrated ramp front, square notch rear.
Number of Shots	6	Frame	Square butt
Barrel	4 inches	Stocks	Checked walnut Service with S&W monograms
Length Over All	With 4-inch barrel, 9¼ inches	Finish	S&W Blue
Weight	With 4-inch barrel, 34 ounces	Ammunition	.357 S&W Magnum, .38 S&W Special Hi-Speed .38 S&W Special .38 S&W Special Midrange

Smith & Wesson
a BANGOR PUNTA Company

2100 Roosevelt Avenue
Springfield, Massachusetts 01101 USA
Telephone (413) 781-8300
TELEX 95-5465. CABLE-WESSON SPM

Leaflet issued with Smith & Wesson .357 Magnum Model 13 revolver. The catch is for the cylinder release.

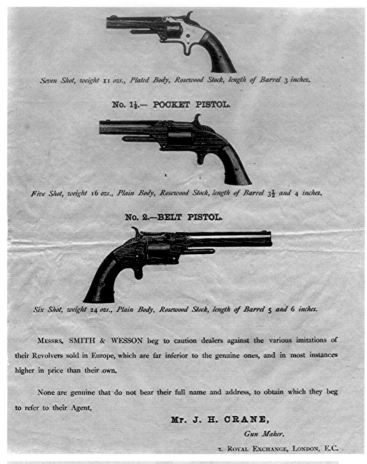

Seven Shot, weight 11 ozs., Plated Body, Rosewood Stock, length of Barrel 3 inches.

No. 1½.— POCKET PISTOL.

Five Shot, weight 16 ozs., Plain Body, Rosewood Stock, length of Barrel 3½ and 4 inches.

No. 2.—BELT PISTOL.

Six Shot, weight 24 ozs., Plain Body, Rosewood Stock, length of Barrel 5 and 6 inches.

MESSRS. SMITH & WESSON beg to caution dealers against the various imitations of their Revolvers sold in Europe, which are far inferior to the genuine ones, and in most instances higher in price than their own.

None are genuine that do not bear their full name and address, to obtain which they beg to refer to their Agent,

Mr. J. H. CRANE,

Gun Maker.

2, ROYAL EXCHANGE, LONDON, E.C.

The development of the rimfire system by Smith & Wesson led to a number of copies appearing on the market. This original leaflet distributed by their London agent is an attempt to warn purchasers to look for the full address as a guarantee that the revolver is a genuine Smith & Wesson.

A Latch for locking barrel and breech when closed.
B Stem of extractor.
D Extractor for extracting shells.
C Ratchet wheel operating extractor.
H Pawl, holding and releasing wheel C.
n Tubular centre-pin on which cylinder revolves.

Contemporary illustration showing the internal details of a Smith & Wesson Russian Model revolver. The action of lowering the barrel activates the ratchet, which raises the extractor arm to eject empty cases.

done automatically. In many of the early cartridge revolvers, the empty fired case is pushed from the chamber by means of a spring-mounted rod fitted on the outside of the barrel or on the frame, as in the Colt Single-Action Army revolver. The cylinder has to be rotated to bring each chamber in line with the ejector rod and loading gate.

On some solid-frame revolvers the cylinder was mounted on a frame that was

Webley nickel-plated No. 5 .38 revolver with a two and a half inch barrel. It is only proved for use with black powder as modern cartridges would be too powerful and possibly damage the frame. The ejector rod pivots sideways and is then pushed through the chambers to eject the empty cases.

released by a catch and allowed the cylinder to be pushed sideways clear of the main frame. The extraction rod was pushed back and the cases ejected.

Colt Single-Action Army Model and Similar Items

Breech-loading was a great step forward but it presented gunmakers and shops with a significant problem – they now held stocks of percussion revolvers that were old-fashioned and poor sellers. The obvious solution was to convert these percussion weapons to cartridge-loading, but it had to be done in such a way that there was no infringement of the Rollin White patent. In 1868 Colt came up with the Thuer conversion, which involved fitting a disc at the rear of the cylinder, but it was, at best, only partially successful. In 1871 the firm went over to the Richards system, which involved modifications to the revolver, with new parts and extra fittings. There were numerous other ingenious attempts to circumvent the restriction imposed by the patent but none succeeded and the makers

had to wait, giving Smith & Wesson a virtual monopoly on breech-loading revolvers, until 1869, when the patent expired. In 1873, once the patent had expired, Colt produced probably the most famous of all its items, the Single-Action Army Model revolver. Mechanically it was the same as Colt's percussion models but it now incorporated the essential bored-through cylinder.

This revolver was to be made in a wide range of models of different calibres, with varying barrel lengths, and is probably the most easily recognized revolver ever. It has appeared in Western films and plays and has gained a reputation as being, along with the Winchester rifle, the 'Gun that Won the West'. In fact, the Western connection is a little over-blown, but it could probably claim to be 'One of the Guns that Won the West'. It was certainly a revolver favoured by many of the legendary characters of the Wild West, including Wild Bill Hickok and Buffalo Bill.

It is a single-action weapon, the hammer being cocked with the thumb. Case extraction is by means of a spring-loaded rod, mounted low on the side of the barrel, and loading and ejection are by way of a gate to the right rear of the cylinder. To load the cartridge, the gate swings out and the lock is set to half-cock, allowing the cylinder to rotate freely, bringing each chamber in turn in line with the rod and gate. The ejector rod is pushed into the chamber to expel the empty case and then the new one can be loaded. When fully charged with six cartridges, the hammer is very gently lowered on to the cartridge at the top of the cylinder, although some shooters prefer to leave this chamber below the hammer empty, to avoid the risk of an accidental discharge.

Colt expanded its range of revolvers on offer with variations based on the Single-Action original. In 1888 a version fitted with a different-shaped butt was offered as the

Colt Single-Action Army revolver system for ejecting empty cases. The loading gate was swung open and the spring-loaded ejector rod pushed through the cylinder to engage with the case and push it clear.

A .357 Smith and Wesson revolver with a swing-out cylinder allowing ejection of empty cases by one push of the ejector rod which, when the cylinder is pushed back into the frame, is housed beneath the barrel.

Target Model and another target version was the Bisley Model named after the famous British shooting centre. The butts on these models were designed to offer a firmer, more

comfortable secure grip, suitable for dedicated target shooting, and the sights were also supposed to give a better sight picture in order to improve accuracy. In 1877, Colt introduced the Lightning Model, special because it was the first Colt product to use double-action. Samuel Colt had earlier publicly decried the double-action system, claiming that greater pressure was needed to cock and fire the revolver and that this made it difficult to hold the aim. However, more and more revolvers on the market were using a double-action mechanism, so Colt presumably felt bound to produce its own version. It was not one of Colt's most popular pistols, but one infamous Western gunfighter, John Wesley Hardin, was known to carry one. Hardin was believed to have killed as many as forty-four men in personal combat. When he was finally shot down by a Sheriff in El Paso, Texas, in August 1895 he was found to have at least one, and possibly two (accounts vary), double-action Colt revolvers on his person.

On the whole, Colt stuck to well-established basic patterns for his revolvers, changing them little, while some manufacturers such as Smith & Wesson were more innovative. The majority of revolvers of the period had spurred hammers so that they could be cocked manually, but there was always some risk of the hammer being caught on clothing or a holster, resulting in an accidental discharge. Smith & Wesson tackled this problem by producing a hammerless revolver. In effect, the hammer was mounted internally and safety was ensured by an ingenious device in the form of a ridge, which stood proud and extended along the back of the butt. When at rest it prevented the action from working, but if the revolver was gripped, ready for action, the bar was depressed and the trigger could then be used.

Smith & Wesson .44 first model revolver with patent dates of 1880. It has a double-action mechanism and walnut grips. (Thomas Del Mar Ltd)

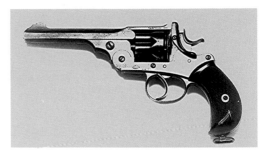

The Webley W.G. revolver 1889 Model, with bird's-head butt. It fired a .455/.476 calibre round and had a simultaneous ejection system, which operated when the barrel was released by the large catch and lowered.

The Single-Action Army Model was the basic pattern for numerous and variously named revolvers produced by Colt, but the factory also offered a self-defence pistol

H. & R. Hammerless
No. 40-45

.22 and .32 Caliber

No revolver so perfectly meets the requirements for a satisfactory pocket arm as well as the Hammerless Model.

The H. & R. Hammerless is entirely safe to carry, is not subject to jams, and may be fired until empty without drawing it from the pocket. Empty shells are ejected automatically when the revolver is opened for reloading, and correct alignment is maintained by an independent cylinder stop.

This revolver can be supplied with "Checked Walnut Target Grip" at an extra cost.

AMMUNITION

.22 caliber arm shoots the .22 Short, Long, and Long Rifle cartridges. The .32 caliber, the .32 S. & W. cartridge.

SPECIFICATIONS

Length of barrel.....2, 3, 4, 5, and 6 inch
Number of shots.....22 caliber 7, .32 caliber 5
Weight.............Either caliber 13 oz.
Finish.............Either nickel or blue

HARRINGTON & RICHARDSON ARMS CO., WORCESTER, MASS.

Page from catalogue of revolvers by Harrington advertising their safety hammerless revolver.

marketed as a 'Derringer'. Using this name avoided any chance of legal problems that might have arisen if they had used 'Deringer' (the name of the original designer). Colt produced a series of these small self-defence weapons: the majority of early models used a .41 rimfire cartridge, but in the 1950s and 60s a .22 short rimfire model was made.

The firm went from strength to strength, offering an extensive range of firearms that included rifles, sporting pistols and self-loading pistols. It was involved with machine guns and remains today at the forefront of arms production.

Whilst Colt may have dominated the pistols market in terms of publicity, a number of other American firearms manufacturers were producing perfectly good weapons in quantity. Probably the closest rival to Colt was the firm of Remington, which made a number of revolvers with a superficial resemblance to the Colt. The firm was started in 1812 by Eliphalet Remington (1793–1861), who, like Colt, was fascinated by guns at an early age and by 1828 was making complete weapons. In 1845 he became a government supplier of rifles and then in 1857 was manufacturing small pocket revolvers, establishing a firm that was noted for the rugged construction

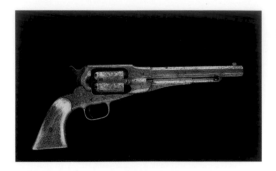

A .36 Remington New Model Navy Percussion revolver circa 1863–78. It has been embellished with scrolled engraving and the wooden butt plates have been replaced by stag horn. (Thomas Del Mar Ltd)

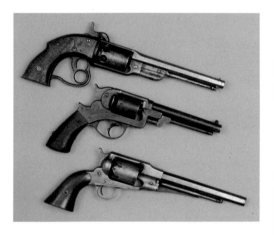

Top: Savage and North 2nd Model Navy Revolver, circa 1861–62. The ring trigger worked in a similar fashion to the Tranter double trigger. Middle: Star revolver with double-action and the barrel pivoted to allow the cylinder to be removed. Bottom: Remington New Model Army revolver of .44 calibre.

There are many more pistols that cannot be mentioned here, and many well-known firearms manufacturers that are closely associated with various countries. There is also a useful geographic listing in Hogg's *Illustrated Encyclopedia of Firearms* (London 1978)[29]:

Belgium	Bayard, Bernadelli, Browning, Colt
France	Velo dog, MAB Modèle A & D, MAS
Germany	Arminus, Decker, Rohm, Adler, Dreyse, Erma, Haenel, Heckler & Koch, Jager, Ortgies, Roth-Sauer, Sauer, Walther
Italy	Beretta, Bernadelli, Frommer
Japan	Nambu
Poland	Radom
Soviet Union	Nagant
Spain	Ruby, Astra, Llama, Star
Switzerland	Sig Sauer

of its products. The advent of war inevitably brought Remington much business.

Although Remington's main area of manufacture was in rifles, it did produce some percussion revolvers in the 1860s, and in 1874 it made its most famous revolver, the .44 New Model Army. It was not dissimilar in appearance to the Colt Single-Action Army,

with a very look-alike butt. The big difference in appearance was the ejector rod situated below the barrel and housed in a long, narrow, triangular fitting. Possibly because the firm lacked the publicity drive of its rival, this revolver, despite its good qualities, was always a poor second to Colt and production faded away in the late 1880s. Remington produced a number of revolvers including a large Model 1871, as well as some Derringer pocket pistols and some vest-pocket models. They rather moved away from the revolver market but ventured into semi-automatic pistols in the 1920–30 period, having become one of the prime suppliers of cane gun from circa 1858 to 1888, available both as a percussion and cartridge model.

Besides Colt, Smith & Wesson, and Remington, there were many American firms, such as Harrington and Richardson, Savage, Bacon, Allen & Wheelock, and others, who produced a number of revolvers ranging from cheap and cheerful to good-quality firearms[30].

British Production

In 1853, British gunmaker Webley was exploring solid-frame, double-action revolvers. When the Smith & Wesson cartridges became available, the firm began production of its rimfire models, which were similar in appearance to the Smith & Wesson revolvers. Like other gunmakers, Webley quickly changed to centre-fire cartridge guns and even produced one model that was capable of using either percussion caps or centre-fire cartridges; all that was needed was a change of cylinder.

In the late 1860s, Webley put into production a limited number of one of the largest-bore pistols ever made, a .577 centre-fire revolver. It had a short barrel and a cylinder that was little more than a cluster of six short tubes with a back plate to hold the fairly massive cartridges. Traditionally this weapon was requested by the military, based on claims that the normal .45 round was not powerful enough to stop the charging fanatics who were sometimes encountered during skirmishes on the frontiers of the Empire.

Many of the larger-calibre revolvers have two triangular plates fitted to the frame, one on each side just ahead of the cylinder. These holster guides were designed to prevent the cylinder snagging on the sides of the leather holster as the weapon was inserted.

Webley went from strength to strength as it introduced new models; the different-style revolvers included a small-calibre pocket model that was fairly standard, with a three- or four-inch barrel and a six-shot cylinder. It is remarkable for it is one of a very small number of revolvers of any make fitted with a safety catch.

The Birmingham Small Arms Company, founded in 1861, was another producer of handguns. It was primarily involved in rifle production but in 1919 began work on a self-loading pistol. It was a strange time to consider such a project – the war was over and there were many surplus weapons available – and, unsurprisingly, it came to nothing. It is of interest because it was to be produced in .40 calibre, a size that was seldom considered at that time.

Webley moved into the arming of various British Police Forces, starting with the Royal Irish Constabulary when it was established in 1868. The RIC revolvers were supplied in .442, .380 and .32 calibres, and with barrels of varying lengths. The first model was replaced in 1883 by a five-shot revolver known as the Bulldog. This was also available in a variety of calibres and with various minor differences of detail.

During the early 1880s London was shocked by a number of violent incidents involving the Metropolitan Police and there was an unusual public outcry demanding more arms for the police. The Home Secretary bowed to the demand and, as a result, the officers in the so-called Exterior Divisions, based on the outskirts of London, were balloted on the question of whether they should be armed. In September 1883, the result was announced: 58 had voted in favour while 41 per cent were opposed. Since the ballot had been so close, it was decided that the matter should be left to the discretion of individual officers. In October of that year, 931 officers in the Exterior Divisions were granted permission to carry a revolver on duty. The approved model was a Webley revolver with a six-shot cylinder of .450 calibre, henceforward known as the Webley MP Model. It was not until 1936 that this concession was withdrawn.

Webley also became involved with training the police forces in the use of a revolver, suggesting to the authorities that each officer would need to fire several hundred rounds before he could be considered reasonably efficient. Of course, Webley was making a charge for this service and, in April 1885, the cost-conscious Commissioner in Charge authorized the firing of just six rounds a year[31]. The fact that the Metropolitan Police Force, the largest in the UK, had adopted a Webley revolver as its official weapon gave Webley sales a boost. Other British forces soon followed the same path, as did some overseas units.

On 29 March 1884, *The Field, The Country Gentleman's Newspaper* reported on a trial shooting of 'an improved army revolver, made by Messrs Webley', which had been carried out at Nunhead Rifle Range. Mr H. Webley himself demonstrated the revolver, claiming that it could shoot more than a hundred rounds without the action being cleaned, and fifty rounds at twelve and twenty-five yards without cleaning out the barrel. *The Field* printed targets showing the hits; as far as accuracy was concerned, the results were fairly average, but the revolver functioned well without any cleaning. Interestingly there was some discussion about problems encountered with double action, or trigger action, as it was called in the report. The action of the revolver was described as 'remarkably smooth'.

The same article included a letter concerned with powder charges and recoil, the writer complaining that, after firing a number of .455 rounds from a Colt revolver, his elbow was injured. The letter recounts how a six-foot member of the writer's staff had his elbow and wrist 'lamed for several hours' after shooting the Colt, with its 'heavy recoil from a larger charge than is commonly used in England'.

In 1886 Webley made a whole range of big .455, .476 calibre hinged-frame revolvers, marketed under the name of Government Revolver, and all fitted with a simultaneous ejection system. The butt was slightly unusual, in that it was a bird's-head shape, but it could also be supplied with the conventional shape.

The other supplier of British Government revolvers was the Royal Small Arms Factory, based at Enfield near London. It was primarily involved in designing, testing and manufacturing rifles, however, due to a shortage of commercial suppliers, it was suddenly requested in 1879 to manufacture a revolver. In a remarkably short time, designs were prepared and approved, and the revolver was put into production as Pistol, Revolver, Breech-Loading, Enfield Mark I. It was a six-shot weapon using a slightly unusual calibre (.476), with an extraction system that was also rather different. At the rear of the cylinder was a fixed plate that engaged with the face of the cylinder; when the cartridges were loaded, the rims rested on the plate. Once the shots had been fired a top catch was released, which allowed the barrel to drop down. The plate stayed in place and so withdrew the empty cases from the chambers, allowing them to fall away. If one cartridge remained unfired, its length, with the bullet in place, was too long to allow it to fall.

One revolver that went into mass production in the late nineteenth century was the Gasser, which is interesting because it is immediately recognizable by its size. Designed by Austrian Leopold Gasser, it fired an 11mm round, and was manufactured in quantity and supplied to the Balkans,

Official Webley leaflet advertising its Metropolitan Police model, adopted in 1883 and demonstrated by Henry Webley himself. It remained the official police weapon until 1911, when it was replaced by the Webley self-loader.

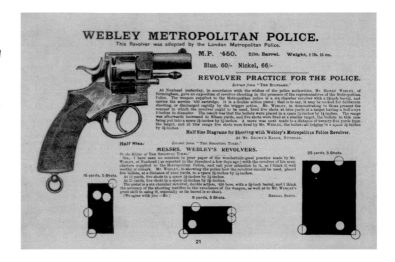

especially Montenegro. According to tradition, every male Macedonian was by law required to possess a revolver. The tradition has a further twist – allegedly, the King of Macedonia had a financial interest in the factory, although the Scottish verdict of 'not proven' is probably the most appropriate in his case. There were two versions, the second, using a break-frame auto-ejection system, was adopted by the Austro-Hungarian Army until it was replaced by a self-loader in 1908.

Following the First World War there was a period of relative quiet in the development of handguns. A gradual increase in pistol shooting and in the number of clubs led to an interest in ballistics, techniques and competition shooting, which probably reached a peak in the 1980s and early 90s. In Britain, annual shoots at Bisley attracted entrants from all over the country and, indeed, the world. With this growth in interest there was a surge in experimentation in pistols and ammunition, with unusual rounds being tested and new-style competitions, and a corresponding increase in black-powder shooting. In Britain there was a reasonable relationship between the police in their capacity as licensing officers and shooters. There were some incidents

when prejudice and perhaps a lack of expertise on the part of officers, or an over-zealous approach by shooters, led to confrontation, but in general the relationship between the two parties was one that worked.

Self-Loading and Semi-Automatic Pistols

By the later part of the nineteenth century the cartridge revolver was available in so many shapes, sizes and calibres that it had probably reached its pinnacle of performance. Many European countries had developed their own national models and the general lack of legal restrictions meant that there were large numbers of firearms in circulation. In 1885 *The Times* newspaper was reporting that the carrying of revolvers in France, Ireland and England was commonplace. According to the article, in the issue of 25 January 1885, the habit had originated in America and had crossed the Atlantic to Europe[32].

The next step along the line of technical development was in the direction of self-loading pistols – in effect, a form of repeating firearm. Gunmakers had toyed with every type of ignition – match, flint, percussion and pinfire – but each had presented some special

WEBLEY EXTRACTING REVOLVER

TO OPEN.—Hold revolver in right hand and press right thumb on the serrated lever of the barrel catch. Hold barrel with left hand, place the left thumb against the top of the barrel catch and press the thumbs towards each other. At the same time depress barrel with the left hand. It is dangerous to cock hammer before opening revolver.

TO CLOSE.—Having loaded the cylinder do not bring the barrel up to the action with the possibility of displacing the cartridges but bring the action up to the barrel and cylinder. **NEVER CLOSE REVOLVER WITH HAMMER COCKED.**

TO EXTRACT—Follow the procedure described for opening the revolver, but this time the cylinder should be facing downwards so that the empty cases fall to the ground.

DIRECTIONS FOR DISMOUNTING CYLINDER.

Remove cam lever fixing screw, open Revolver to full extent, push round cam lever, remove cylinder. No further stripping is necessary for cleaning purposes.

DIRECTIONS FOR REMOUNTING CYLINDER.

Care must be taken to clean thoroughly all the parts and to ensure that no dirt or grit be left inside cylinder or on the axis. The parts should be slightly oiled to ensure perfectly free movement

Replace cylinder on its axis, observing that the cam lever is pressed against the tooth of the cylinder cam. Replace cam lever fixing screw.

CAUTION—AUTOMATIC PISTOL CARTRIDGES MUST NOT BE USED IN THIS REVOLVER. DO NOT SNAP THE HAMMER WITHOUT CARTRIDGES IN THE CYLINDER.

CLEANING—Directly after firing, clean inside of barrel and cylinder with "Webley" Oil.
Use stiff bristle brush and work the brush backwards and forwards about ten times.
Wipe out residue with clean flannelette patch and thoroughly dry.
Oil the Barrel and Cylinder with a slack fitting patch soaked with "Webley" Oil.
"Webley" Oil may also be used for lubricating the action and wiping over the external portion of the revolver. Even when the revolver is not in use it is advisable to examine and oil every two or three months.

WEBLEY & SCOTT LTD.

Revolvers sighted and tested for accuracy with :
I.C.I. ·38 S. & W. Cartridge, 145 grain LEAD bullet.
I.C.I. ·32 S. & W. Long Cartridge, 98 grain LEAD bullet.
I.C.I. ·22 Long Rifle Cartridge.

BIRMINGHAM 4

C.62

PRINTED IN ENGLAND

Instruction sheet pasted on the inside of the lid of a case for a Webley WG revolver.

problems. It was really the advent of the centre-fire, metal, breech-loading cartridge that opened the way to practical, reliable, repeating firearms.

Even with the self-contained cartridge the challenges facing a designer of a practical self-loading gun fell into five main categories:

1. storing the supply of cartridges (and selecting the type of cartridge);
2. transferring a round from the storage to the breech ready for firing;
3. firing the round;
4. removing the fired case; and
5. transferring another round from the store to the breech, ready to start the cycle again.

For best results the entire sequence needed to be self-perpetuating and independent of any outside input.

There were only two practical initiating power sources of energy available for the required movements: springs and the cartridge (the main source). Both had to be prime initiators, which not only had to expel the missile but also, by various means, activate any necessary movement. The rounds had to be stored near the action, safe and easily accessible. In the majority of cases the storage would take the form of a magazine, which was usually flat, although it was sometimes another shape, to suit a particular weapon. When empty, the magazine needed to be suitable for quick and easy replacement. Most modern magazines have an internal spring that puts the rounds under pressure and ensures that the top round is ready to be moved into the firing position.

There are good reasons for crediting the American Sir Hiram Maxim (1840–1916) with being the pioneer pointing the way to semi-automatic or self-loading pistols. Maxim was blessed with an inventive mind and at his workshop in London's Hatton Garden he used the recoil of the cartridge in a rifle to operate the loading mechanism of the same weapon. It was one of the first steps along the path to developing pistols that were capable of doing the same. As is usually the case, once the principle of self-loading had been demonstrated, many others followed in Maxim's footsteps The end result of his pioneering experiments was the eventual appearance of the Maxim or Vickers machine gun, in 1884.

Any self-loading pistol involves moving parts, which require a motive force, and in the handgun that can normally come only from springs and the potential power of the cartridge. When the shot is fired, the propellant generates a high volume of gas and recoil. It was the recoil that was first utilized by Maxim to operate his self-loading system. Another, unusual use of the recoil featured in one successful design, the self-cocking revolver, designed by an officer in the Indian Army, George Fosbery (1834?–1907). He had seen action and had been awarded Britain's highest decoration for bravery, the Victoria Cross, when taking a leading part in capturing a rebel post during a local rebellion in 1863.

Fosbery was interested in the mechanics of firearms and held some patents but his most successful venture was the creation of his self-cocking revolver. He started with a Colt Single-Action Army revolver and transformed it into a two-part weapon. The major part was made up of the barrel, cylinder and upper frame. The lower section was composed of the butt, trigger and mechanism. The cylinder had a deep zigzag channel cut into the surface, which engaged with a stud mounted on the frame.

The six chambers were loaded with cartridges, the hammer cocked and the trigger pressed. The shot generated recoil, which drove the top section of the pistol backwards. The interlocking stud and channel steered the cylinder along a path, which rotated it to bring the next chamber into the firing position. The same rearward movement activated a trigger mechanism that cocked the action so that the next shot could be fired very quickly. There were several modifications patented and the revolver was produced with barrel lengths of four, six and seven and half inches and in .455 and .38 calibre. In another unusual feature, apart from its self-cocking action, it was fitted with a safety catch, like the Webley revolver. This was necessary since the revolver was intended to be carried in the fully cocked position.

Shooters using this model for the first time found it rather unfamiliar – as the shots were fired, there was a substantial amount of metal moving backwards and forwards, and this took a little getting used to. It was eventually patented in 1906, proving to be a very accurate weapon and being manufactured by Webley and Scott until 1915[33]. Despite highly complimentary reports and impressive demonstrations by top shooters, the self-cocking revolver never gained wide acceptance. The comparatively small production numbers have ensured that it is now highly prized by collectors.

Probably inspired by Maxim's work, by the 1890s a number of gunmakers were now experimenting with the concept of a self-loading pistol. One of the earliest experimental pistols was the Steyr, made in Austria in 1892. It was based on the recoil principle, but the action depended on a very small movement of the primer in the cartridge case. Since ammunition manufacture was not as efficient as it might have been, such small movements were not always reliable and the system was never going to be widely accepted. It had a box magazine holding six rounds situated in front of the trigger guard. Despite its problems it can legitimately be called the first effective self-loading pistol.

Next to appear was the Bittner, which had a ring trigger and was based on a bolt action operated by movement of the trigger.

Several versions were manufactured but none was really effective and production ceased in 1904. These pioneering pistols never achieved any great success but each highlighted some point that perhaps helped another gunmaker to tackle the problems. In 1893 came the pistol that was to become transformed into one of the most valued self-loading pistols in the world – the Borchardt pistol. Its inventor was Hugo Borchardt (1850–1921), a German who emigrated to the USA, and gained considerable experience in the US arms industry of America, working for both Colt and Winchester. After returning to Europe, he worked for a while in Hungary but, after a brief return trip to the USA, he settled back in Berlin and began work on his pistol.

The Borchardt pistol was patented in 1893 and remained in production from 1894 to 1899, during which time some 3,000 were made. Not many have survived and these few are highly regarded by collectors. The design of the pistol was very clever and introduced features still in use today, first solving the problem of where to locate the flat rectangular magazine. Borchardt housed it inside the butt, and this is still done today on most semi-automatic pistols. A toggle arm, hinged at the centre, is rigid when lying flat in line with the

Cut-away diagram showing the internal spring housing of the Borchardt self-loading pistol and the butt magazine containing the rather large cartridges.

barrel, and at one end is the bolt that houses the firing pin. When the trigger is pressed the pin strikes the primer and fires the cartridge, the recoil forces the arm backwards and a small arm engages with a groove in the case, pulling it clear of the breech and ejecting it. The two-section block continues backwards until, at a fixed point, it is lifted slightly, allowing it to divide so that it is no longer rigid and the bolt section can continue moving back.

During this time the moving block has been compressing a large, curved leaf-spring attached at the rear of the pistol and housed in an oval-shaped compartment. As the power of the recoil diminishes and falls away, the spring takes charge and pushes the block forwards. The arm now becomes straight and rigid again. On its journey forward it scoops up the top cartridge from the magazine and pushes it forward into the breech, where all action ceases. The block with firing pin is now under tension but locked in place and pressing the trigger frees it to strike the primer and set the whole sequence in motion again. The action is repeated each time the trigger is pressed

The Borchardt self-loading pistol, the forerunner of the Luger. The housing for the mainspring at the rear gave the pistol a rather top-heavy appearance but it proved to be an effective weapon.

until the last cartridge in the magazine has been loaded and fired.

The system on the Borchardt pistol worked and was quite robust, but there was one complication in that it fired a specially designed cartridge of 7.65 mm calibre with a case that was necked down and had no rim, making extraction a little difficult. The pistol had a long barrel, of around eight inches, which aided accuracy, and was usually supplied with a carbine stock that could be attached to the butt.

The Borchardt pistol could rightly be called the first really practical, self-loading, semi-automatic pistol, but it was not perfect. The large, oval spring housing gave it an awkward, rather unbalanced look and the cartridge was not without its problems, but Borchardt was fortunate to encounter another practical gunmaker, who was able to help him face these challenges. Georg Luger (1849–1923) had served with the Austro-Hungarian Army, so he had practical experience as well as a mechanical interest in firearms. After a spell as a railway engineer, he became involved in designing rifles and by luck joined the Berlin firm of Ludwig Löwe, which also employed Borchardt. In 1896, the firm changed its name and became Deutsche Waffen- und Munitionsfabriken, or DWM for short.

The two men began working together and Luger offered some practical suggestions on how to improve Borchardt's design. These were soon incorporated into the construction of the pistol. Apparently, Borchardt was not always enthusiastic about some of Luger's ideas but Luger's modifications gradually transformed the pistol into a more robust and practical weapon. The Swiss Army showed some interest and finally adopted it as its official pistol in 1900. In 1901 it was christened the Parabellum pistol, the name coming from the telegraphic address of DWM. Other

The action of the Luger mechanism at the point when the block is fully retarded. The empty case has been ejected and the block is about to move forward to pick up a round from the magazine.

Top: Artillery model with long barrel and adjustable rear sight, and fitted with a snail-drum magazine. Bottom: Standard model next to a simple lever mechanism needed when loading the snail-drum magazines; the rounds require a degree of pressure to drive them home when the magazine is nearly full.

countries followed the Swiss lead, with the German Navy declaring its interest in 1904 and the German Army doing the same in 1908.

The Parabellum had undergone several changes and one of the basic modifications was the use of a new calibre round, as the neck of the case was straightened and a bullet of 9mm inserted. The basic concept of the toggle arm and return spring was retained, but the system operated in a slightly different manner. The toggle now had two finger grips part of the way along it and, as the block was blown back, the toggle rode up a small ramp to allow it to bend, extract the case and complete the movement to load a new round. The finger grips also meant that the loading/unloading sequence could be initiated without firing a round.

To facilitate loading the magazine was still housed in the butt, which was now set at an angle rather than being straight, as it had been in Borchardt's pistol. It could be removed from the butt by pressing a release stud mounted behind the trigger guard. This type of magazine, with the cartridges stacked one on top of the other, is very safe as it removes any possibility of the primer being struck by accident. The butt grips were of wood, with fine chequering helping to ensure a firm hold.

The Parabellum, or Luger as it became known, was to prove an outstanding success, being adopted by various armies, police forces and civilian bodies. By 1908 what might be called the 'standard' pistol was in production, in 9mm calibre, with a four-inch barrel, chequered wooden grips and a magazine with an eight-round capacity. The earlier models had a safety catch set in the rear of the butt, rather like that used by Smith & Wesson, which would allow action only when depressed as the butt was held ready for firing. This device was omitted on later models and a more conventional safety catch was mounted at the rear of the frame on the left-hand side. A simple wooden stock was available to fit on to the base of the butt. The Luger was, however, a reasonably complex and expensive pistol to make and the Swiss Army designed their own simpler, cheaper version, which remained in production until 1947. Germany followed and in 1938 the Walther P38 replaced the Luger.

The Luger was so successful that demand outstripped the supply capability of Ludwig Löwe in Berlin and some pistols had to be made at the arsenal at Erfurt. A new version known as the Artillery Model was introduced in 1917. It differed from the original in that it had an eight-inch barrel and, since it was intended for long-range shooting, an adjustable back sight. The holster for the 1908 Luger housed a spare magazine and a small loading tool fitted in a flap in the top, fold-over section. For the Artillery Model there was a special holster that carried the carbine stock as well. One additional option was a snail-drum magazine, which could hold thirty-two rounds of 9mm cartridges.

Under the terms of the peace treaty at the end of the First World War, production of the Luger by DWM was forbidden, but some were made by the firm of Krieghoff. In 1932, DWM recommenced production. At the same time, a British arms company, Vickers, supplied many thousands of Luger pistols to the Netherlands, although it is unclear as to how they obtained the parts. Production of the Luger was undertaken by various firms and it is still available in somewhat simplified form. Mauser, another famous firm, also became involved and produced some customized versions of the Luger. These were carbine versions with an extra long barrel, a shotgun-style fore end and adjustable rear sights.

The Borchardt/Luger pistol was so successful that gunmaker after gunmaker sought to produce their own semi-automatic pistol and the number of models on the market increased considerably. One very successful competitor was the firm of Mauser, founded by brothers Paul and Wilhelm. Their prime interest was in rifles, and their models were highly valued and used by armies around the world.

They decided to expand their interests and in 1877 the firm made a single-shot pistol, followed in 1878 by a revolver with a zigzag groove cut in the cylinder surface, not unlike the Fosbery. This system rotated the cylinder but did not cock the action. It was a break revolver and the barrel was lifted and the empty cases ejected by a ring-trigger device. The German Army decided that it was too expensive and too complex and rejected it, preferring, in 1870, a rather clumsy, old-fashioned, six-shot, solid-frame revolver. To eject the empty cases the cylinder had to be removed from the arbour and a rod used to push out the cases. The Reichsrevolver, its official designation, was issued in two styles in 1879 as the Trooper or Cavalry model, and in 1883 as the Officer's model. Despite its antiquated design and action, it remained in service until replaced by the Parabellum in 1908.

In 1896 thanks to some design work by Federie, the Mauser factory Superintendent, the firm produced a winner, popular with many groups but never officially adopted by any army. The model that proved to be the most popular was known as the Broomhandle or Model 96, the name derived from the rather slim tubular butt. It was beautifully made and has acquired a certain cult status. It fired a 7.63mm round, and ten rounds were housed in a box magazine below the barrel, ahead of the trigger guard. The manufacturing was of a very high standard and, with no bolts, screws or nuts, the action could be disassembled and reassembled using only a cartridge and a small screwdriver. However, it was not a task to be tackled lightly for it was a somewhat tricky process.

The mechanism works on a reciprocating bolt action with an external hammer, which gives a nasty nip to the web of skin between thumb and first finger if the shooter fails to have a proper grip on the butt. It is normally loaded from a clip, which is inserted into the top of the magazine when the bolt is pulled back. The basic design was left unaltered for the whole of the Broomhandle's working life, but several patterns were manufactured, including one with a shorter than usual barrel. This model was exported to Russia and acquired the title of Bolo, from its association with Bolshevik Russia. In response to demand from Germany, a version chambered to accept the 9mm Parabellum cartridge was put into production. This version is easily recognized for it has the figure '9' carved into the butt and is coloured red.

In response to a request from Spanish arms manufacturers, a special selective-fire version, the Schnell Feuer, was produced in the 1930s. It had a selector plate fitted on the left side of the frame. With the selector in one position, it fired single shots, while in the second position it would go fully automatic, firing as long as there were rounds in the magazine and the trigger was pressed. Unfortunately, any handgun firing on a fully automatic setting is extremely difficult to control and is often just a waster of ammunition. Like the Parabellum Luger, the Mauser 96 had a stock that was easily fitted on to the butt, but in this case it also served as a hollow wooden holster for the pistol. A special leather harness to hold the holster, cleaning rod and sundry odd spares was available. In another similarity with the Luger, the 96 could be supplied as a carbine with the basic pistol and permanently attached butt and a fore end like a shotgun.

An 1896 9mm Bolo Mauser self-loading pistol, the butt marked with a red painted '9'. It is with a wooden holster and leather harness fitted with cleaning rod, magazine pouched for carrying the pistol.

The 96 was by no means the only pistol made by Mauser. In 1910 the company introduced a pocket pistol in 6.35mm calibre, followed in 1914 by a larger-calibre version in 7.65mm. In 1918 came another, rather chunky-looking, pistol, the *Westentaschenpistole*, also in 6.35mm, and in 1938 the basic shape was updated to the HSc model, which unusually for a semi-automatic pistol, was a double-action model. The firing mechanism could be cocked by the trigger action alone, so that the pistol could be carried with a round in the chamber and the first shot could be quickly fired without having to do any more than squeeze the trigger. Another pistol, Model 38H, made by

Sauer & Sohn, was also double-action, and was manufactured in quantity during the First World War.

In the USA, Colt was still producing a wide range of revolvers but developments in Europe would have naturally turned their attention to semi-automatic pistols. The firm was greatly helped by one of the most prolific and talented firearms designers (if not *the* most), John Moses Browning (1855–1926). Moses came from a firearms background – his father was a competent gunmaker as well as a friend of the future President Abraham Lincoln. A keen supporter of the Mormon faith, Moses senior fathered twenty-two children, including John. He later gave up his interest in firearms,

An 1896 Mauser self-loading pistol. The magazine is situated in front of the trigger and the rounds were loaded in from above. The narrow tubular butt led to the 'Broomhandle' nickname.

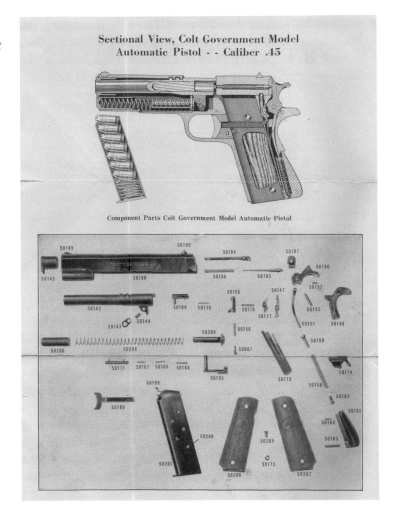

Page from a Colt catalogue showing a disassembled 1911A1 self-loading pistol

despite having invented as least two rather unusual repeating rifles. According to anecdote, John Moses was absorbed by firearms as early as the tender age of six.

In 1878, John Moses invented a single-shot rifle, for which he received several thousand dollars from the Winchester Repeating Arms Company. He was associated with the firm for nearly twenty years and designed in 1885, among many other guns, the Winchester lever-action shotgun. They parted company in 1902 over a question of payment. By 1890 Moses had perfected a gas-operated machine gun as well as an automatic shotgun. During his lifetime he took out more than 120 patents on almost every type of firearm, from pistols, rifles and shotguns to machine guns, and most of the main firearms manufacturers of the USA and, later, Belgium used his designs.

Colt became involved with his work on semi-automatic pistols and in 1895 he patented a .38 semi-automatic pistol. This was succeeded by several other models and later followed by other patents, all of which were assigned to the Colt company.

In 1898 the Colt company had put together a pistol of Browning's design, which it submitted to the Government to be considered as the main Army issue pistol. By 1900, it had a .38 calibre pistol in production, with a six-inch barrel and a magazine of seven rounds housed in the butt. To load the first round the top slide was pulled back and then allowed forward to pick up a cartridge and load it into the breech. It was a feature that was found on Colt self-loaders and other models. Two years later, a Sporting version was produced, although it was basically the same weapon; there was also a Military Model, with longer barrel and a magazine holding eight rounds of a more powerful .38 cartridge.

Other pistols included a small pocket version with a .25 cartridge. In 1905 the firm tackled its first pistol using a .45 cartridge. Apparently, both US and British Army experts had decided that a .38 round did not have sufficient stopping power when tackling a crazed, fearless opponent and felt that .45 would be better.

In 1911 one of the most popular pistols ever, the Colt Model 1911, was adopted by the US Army; it was to remain in service for many decades. In 1907 a competition was organized to compare the Colt 1905 with a pistol made by the Savage Arms Company, a New York firm set up in 1894 by a remarkable character called Arthur William Savage. Both pistols were of .45 calibre and tests to determine reliability, time taken to strip and reassemble, reliability and accuracy were all carried out. It was the considered opinion of the board that the Colt Model should be accepted for use by US Forces. Interestingly one conclusion of those firing the weapon was that firing 500 rounds with the Colt was the equivalent of firing 2,000 with the Savage.

The design of the 1911 was to remain unchanged until 1923, when a number of minor modifications were made. The trigger was narrowed, the rear of the butt was given a more curved appearance and the butt safety grip was changed slightly. This pattern of pistol was known officially as the 1911A1 and remained the official US military pistol until it was replaced in the 1970s by a Beretta pistol.

Versions of the 1911 were made in Norway, Mexico and Argentina. During the First World War the demand was such that Colt alone was unable to meet it and some pistols were made by other firms such as Remington and Singer, whose name will be found on the frame. The 1911 was a solid, reliable pistol and was sold in a variety of patterns, including a .22 version. There was also a conversion kit, which allowed the same pistol to be used for either calibre by swapping barrels. In 1929, a .38 version was put on the market and in 1927 Colt ventured into target pistols with the .22 Woodsman[34].

Browning was not yet finished and in 1927 his latest 9mm pistol patent was granted, to become the Model 1935 or the Hi-Power. In 1935, the Belgian firm of Fabrique National d'Armes de Guerre produced this very successful model, the Browning High-Power 9mm GP35. It was widely adopted by the armed forces of several countries and saw extensive service during the Second World War. In 1940, the factory at Herstal in Belgium was captured by the Germans, but 200,000 High-Power pistols were then manufactured in Canada by Inglis. All this work on pistols was only part of Browning's output. He also did considerable work on rifles and shotguns as well as making the light machine gun, the Browning Automatic rifle, used extensively by US forces during the Second World War.

Whilst Colt may have been the dominant pistol and revolver manufacturer in North America, it was by no means the only one. The number of smaller suppliers included Savage, Manhattan, Harrington & Richardson, Iver Johnson and others.

In Britain a remarkable pistol was produced, which, although it had something special, never went into mass production. This rarest of all self-loaders was designed by Hugh Gabbett-Fairfax, a man of enthusiasm and drive but a little out of touch with practical gunmaking. In 1895 he patented a self-loading pistol under the name of the Mars, which used an unusually long recoil and an equally unusual rotary magazine. As far as is known, only one example was ever made before the inventor changed the design and the magazine was then housed in the butt. The inventor offered the design to Webley; they declined to take it, but agreed to manufacture it for him. Gabbett-Fairfax liked the idea and in 1901 set up a company, Mars Automatic Firearms Syndicate, to market his pistol. Unfortunately, Webley evidently decided the project was not a viable one and withdrew. Gabbett-Fairfax found another company to take on the job and submitted examples of the pistol for Army approval, which was not forthcoming. Gabbett-Fairfax's company closed in 1903. Another was tried, but that also failed, in 1907.

It is not known for sure exactly how many Mars pistols were made, but it is fairly certain that it was fewer than a hundred. The design had few really innovative features and was soon superseded by the new range of self-loaders that was becoming available. It was produced in several calibres, all of which used high-powered cartridges – according to reports, few who fired the pistol once were keen to do so again.

Despite the non-starter of a project with Gabbett-Fairfax's self-loading pistol, the firm of Webley (since 1907, called Webley & Scott) soon began to explore the market for this type of weapon. In 1902, the Commander-in-Chief of the British Army took the initiative and demanded a report comparing the new self-loading pistols with the trusty revolver.

The remarkable Mars self-loader, designed by H.W. Gabbett-Fairfax. It was very powerful but awkward in design and never really satisfactory in either .36 or .45 calibre.

He wanted quick action but little was done immediately. A report from an official body known as the Small Arms Committee discussed the different effects of lead revolver bullets and metal-coated missiles from self-loaders. It raised thirteen points[35] to consider when examining self-loaders and suggested the tests that should be carried out when determining suitability.

In 1903, Webley & Scott was in a position to test an experimental 9mm pistol and by the following year a .455 model was ready, together with a modified cartridge, to be offered for testing by the Army and Navy. The final assessment of the pistol was not at all favourable and it more or less disappeared, but much had been learned. The firm, under Director William Whiting, who was fast becoming a leading light of design, turned to consider a smaller-calibre weapon. Model 1905, a .32 or 6.35mm pistol, was put into production and lasted until 1909. As a result of experience, various modifications to the model were made but this same style of pistol continued in production until 1940.

In the early twentieth century it was not at all difficult for the ordinary citizen to

At first glance this is obviously a Colt 1911A1 self-loader, however a closer look reveals that is a Star self-loader made in Argentina, South America.

purchase a pistol and many people felt that it was right and proper to carry a gun for self-protection. When selecting a pistol intended for self-defence, power and accuracy were considered to be of minor importance. Of greater concern was the way in which the weapon might be carried – it needed to be small enough to fit in a jacket pocket or in a lady's purse. To meet this market Webley

& Scott went for a pistol that was basically a smaller version of the 1905 Model, and in 1907 offered a miniature version of the pistol. There were some internal design changes but basically it was the same pistol, with a shorter barrel, a smaller butt and reduced magazine capacity. It proved popular and sold well.

During the early part of the twentieth century London witnessed an unusually high number of firearm incidents. In January 1909 a botched robbery led to a cross-London chase, with the police armed with their Webley revolvers and borrowed shotguns. The sadly farcical incident was probably the reason why, in March 1909, a group of police and army officers visited a London gun-maker to test-fire a number of self-loading pistols. They came down in favour of a Colt No. 3 pistol, presumably the seven-shot .38 pistol, but apparently no further action was taken and the matter was dropped.

In April 1910 one incident began with three City of London Police officers being murdered and finished with an armed siege of a house in Sidney Street, East London.

Top: .22 target pistol with long barrel for accurate shooting and single-shot only. Middle: Standard .22 version with shorter barrel. Bottom: Standard .32/7.65 self-loader as adopted by many police forces.

Official attention was drawn to the fact that the police had still been equipped with six-shot revolvers whereas the terrorist had been using self-loading pistols. It was, accordingly, felt that the police armament might be examined, with a view to adopting a similar weapon. This time an official committee was created, with terms of reference set down, and a wide range of pistols were test-fired and subjected to various tests for reliability. Interestingly, one feature that the committee was told to consider was the stopping power of each round.

The committee came to the conclusion that the .32 Webley & Scott self-loading pistol was the most appropriate for the police, although there was some debate as to the suitability of the calibre since most foreign police forces opted for a larger-calibre round. Official orders were placed and, as with the revolver, the pistol's adoption by the Metropolitan Police encouraged other forces to follow suit, and it sold well. Rejecting the previously miserly approach to familiarization shooting, due consideration was given to training and practice and a .22 version of the pistol was available. Official police ranges were established and competitive shooting was encouraged. The pistol served the force well and, although a number of minor modifications were made during its working life, it was not until 1960 that the force disposed of its last stock and replaced it with the Mark IV .38 revolver[36].

The number of self-loading pistols on the market during the early part of the twentieth century continued to grow and Browning's patents figured prominently as he improved and modified his designs. An Eley Brothers Catalogue of 1912 lists seventy-two different cartridges, the great majority for handguns of various makes. Although there is a long list of self-loading pistols available, this has not stopped experimentation and new models coming on to the market. Some are little more than up-dated versions of current models but some explore new areas of shooting, and power is one field that has attracted some attention.

In 1970, the Auto-Mag self-loader was mainly noted for the round that it fired – a 7.62 rifle cartridge used by NATO forces, which was cut down and fitted with a .44 Magnum bullet. It was extremely powerful, developing a muzzle velocity of 1640 feet per second compared to just over 800 feet per second for a Colt 1911A1. Commercial ammunition was not available, which meant that shooters had to load their own – not a really serious drawback but certainly an inconvenience. Despite its great power it was not a commercial success but it is sometimes used for long-range pistol shooting and hunting.

At the other end of the size scale is the Austrian Kolibri semi-automatic pistol, the smallest functional handgun ever made. The theory was that it was so small that any lady might carry it in her purse, handbag or pocket without any bother. It carried six tiny 2.7mm or 3mm cartridges in a butt magazine and the barrel was smooth-bored. The stopping power of such a weapon was so small as to be virtually useless except, possibly, if it was fired at the face. Muzzle velocity was about the same as that of an air pistol.

In 1980, in the race for a new USA handgun a remarkable new self-loading pistol emerged as the winner. The Glock 17, made in Austria, incorporated several new ideas, such as a trigger-mounted safety catch and polymer body. The commonest model is the Glock 17, so named because the butt magazine holds seventeen 9mm rounds, and is available in several other calibres and variant forms. It is a pistol that is cheap to maintain and repair. It is also lightweight, and some police firearms officers found it difficult to adjust to the feel of the Glock after using a heavier revolver or self-loader. So successful has it been that it

On the 9mm Glock Model 17, the small catch behind the trigger is the magazine release. Much of the pistol is fashioned from plastic, making it very lightweight.

The Glock 9mm self-loading pistol as supplied, with its plastic box, cleaning rod, loading tool and spare magazine. The success of the original model led to the pistol being produced in different calibres. Note the safety catch set in the trigger.

has been adopted as the official side arm of numerous police forces and armed services across the world. A larger magazine holding thirty-two rounds of 9mm ammunition and a fully automatic model are available.

There has been and there continues to be some debate over which is the better handgun, self-loader or revolver. Size and shape favour the self-loader, which is easier to conceal thereby recommending it for covert use, whereas the revolver cylinder is more difficult to hide. The self-loader is much better in terms of firepower, with magazines holding between ten and twenty rounds, and reloading is simpler and quicker than on a revolver. For military use this high firepower may well be an advantage, but for law enforcement it is less so – statistics show that in fire-fight situations very few shots are fired. The empty magazine can be ejected at the same time as a full magazine is made ready to replace it. Even with speed loaders,

revolver reloading is bound to be slower. One big advantage of the revolver lies in its ability to be fired in the event of a misfire. Should the cartridge fail, then it is simply a matter of pressing the trigger and turning the cylinder to line up the next round. If a misfire occurs on a self-loader, the slide has to be pulled back to extract the round and then allowed to go forward to feed in the next round – a more complicated remedy than with the revolver. There is also the potential problem of a jam, which is greater in the more mechanically complex self-loading system.

In fact, there is no single answer to the question of which is the better, and purpose is probably a main factor in the choice. Over the past few years there has been, in most countries, a noticeable change-over from revolver to self-loader among law enforcement armament. This would suggest that experience has shown that self-loaders are better but, whichever type of handgun is used, practice and experience are more important than design.

CHAPTER 6

Curious, Disguised and Combination Pistols

∾ ∾

Designers and engineers have always had a desire to improve on existing models, and this was certainly the case with the handgun. As soon as the *hand gonne* had appeared, it was inevitable that gunmakers would seek ways to make it a more effective weapon. The first and most obvious move was to increase the number of barrels, but that was about the limit of innovation for the matchlock. With the appearance of the wheel-lock mechanism, the opportunities were multiplied and the obvious approach was to combine it with another weapon. Wheel-lock pistols were united with daggers, axes, maces, crossbows and swords, but it is uncertain whether this gave any advantage to the owner, apart from a sense of ownership. If there was one that might have been effective in an emergency, it was probably the sword- or dagger-pistol. This type of double-purpose weapon was the most common and was used with flint, percussion and cartridge systems.

Hunting swords were sometimes combined with a firearm and it is quite likely that these could have been useful to deliver the *coup de grâce* to a quarry. In this situation, there is possibly a case for the attached pistol, since a wounded animal might well make an unexpected attack. Not all the combined pistol-edged weapons were hunting swords and few examples of military swords with pistol fittings are known, but they seem never to have been considered seriously as a standard issue. The barrel and mechanism were usually fitted just below the hilt and the trigger was situated somewhere within the hilt/knuckle bow or basket guard. Occasionally, a maker would fit two

Combined wheel-lock pistol and dagger mid-16th century.

German mid-eighteenth century hunting sword. The blade, double-edged at the point, is fitted on one side with a flintlock pistol. The hilt/butt has bone plaques, a lion-head brass pommel and side plates. The lock has a folding trigger and, like all combination weapons, raises the question of how effective such a weapon would be. (Thomas Del Mar Ltd)

pistols, one on either side of the blade. It would seem obvious that the barrels should point in the direction of the blade but there is one known example in which the pistol is fitted to a large blade and points in the opposite direction, towards the owner. The purpose of such a fitting is unclear and, since the hilt has the flintlock exposed, it would have been difficult just to hold the weapon![37]

The most commonly encountered bladed pistol is likely to be a version of the penknife pistol. This is frequently just a conventional pocket knife with a barrel, usually percussion, fitted on the back of the body with a simple hammer mechanism attached. Many will be found to house a diminutive bullet mould and a pair of tweezers slotted in the side panels. There are variations of the basic model and some may well be fitted with up to three folding blades. Many were made by the firm of Unwin and Rodgers, which was associated with the famous Bowie knife. As a

Penknife pistol similar to those produced by the firm of Unwin and Rodgers in the mid-nineteenth century. It has two blades, a folding trigger and side panels of stag horn. The short barrel is of German silver. (Thomas Del Mar Ltd)

serious weapon these knife pistols amount to very little, but as a last-minute self-defence device they may have had some value.

The Great War of 1914–18 was one in which hand-to-hand combat with trench-raiding parties from both German and Allied forces was a common feature. Silence was most important on such ventures and fire-arms were a last resort, but some raiders did carry revolvers. From 1916, many had an extra weapon that was patented in that year. Designed by a serving British Army officer, Arthur Pritchard, a Lieutenant in the Royal Berkshire Regiment, it was made by the well-known gunmaker Greener. The Pritchard revolver bayonet reverted to an idea of the pistols of earlier periods and was designed to convert an empty Webley revolver into a lethal stabbing weapon. Using eight-and-a-quarter-inch blades cut down from the bayonets of the old French Gras rifle, it had a specially shaped hilt and guard that fitted over and locked on to the barrel of the revolver. It was housed in a cut-down scabbard, also from the Gras rifle. It was never an official issue and remained a private purchase item. So far, no report of one being used has been traced but in the desperate world of trench warfare it was probably seen as a practical weapon.

Like many other handguns, the Webley Mark VI revolver could also be supplied with an attachable shoulder stock in the hopes of converting it into a carbine. The butt was of wood and the fitting commonly of brass. There is no doubt that a detachable stock would have enabled more accurate shooting, but it did mean that, once fitted, the revolver was no longer a handy self-defence weapon as the stock would have made it too clumsy.

The percussion cap and, even more so, the cartridge meant that the firing mechanism of the gun could be made very compact indeed, which meant in turn it could be incorporated into a large number of devices. Although they are not strictly speaking handguns, worthy of mention are the popular walking-stick guns that were favoured on opposite sides of the law, both by the poacher and by the gentleman taking a casual stroll in his grounds. In its late nineteenth-century catalogues, the firm of Remington offered several models, percussion and cartridge, suggesting that, as they were rifled, they could be used with shot as well as rifle cartridges. Some walking sticks were made with a pistol fitted to the hand grip and some French models were fitted with four small barrels with a central spiked blade. The armament was housed inside the body of the cane and was withdrawn by a twist and pull movement.

The small .22 Short Rifle cartridge made it very easy to fit locks into a number of devices such as pens, keys and pipes, and many disguised weapons were made in the latter part of the nineteenth and early twentieth centuries. Some were more ambitious and, because of the size of the object, were equipped with pinfire or cartridge revolvers. A few umbrellas were fitted in this way, but perhaps more surprising was the fitting of a small pinfire revolver into the end of the handlebar of a pedal cycle. It is sad to report that this type of concealed firearm has been used by criminals in the USA, and adapted to the handlebars of a motor cycle. Apparently, the French and the Belgians were particularly troubled by dogs when out cycling and this sort of weapon was

A revolver bayonet designed to be fitted to the barrel of the official Army .45 revolvers. The blade was fashioned from obsolete French weapons. There is little evidence that the item ever saw much use during the First World War.

The Colt 1860 Army model revolver could be supplied with an attachable stock; the butt strap had to be altered to accept the stock. One very rare stock was fashioned to serve as a canteen.

offered as a way of dealing with the menace. A more conventional special 'Velo-dog' revolver from 1894 was also on offer, firing a low-powered 5mm cartridge; the weapon apparently could be loaded with balls of something non-lethal if the cyclist was not feeling aggressive. Modern versions of these combined weapons are still produced and a Chinese-made dagger with attached .22 barrels is known. Using these weapons is not easy and trying to aim such a knife is difficult. Presumably, since their use is obviously intended to be covert, this is not seen as important.

Despite the ingenuity of the various devices, mostly produced late in the nineteenth century, it seems that they were never best-sellers but they do play an interesting role in the history of the handgun. Around the same period, a number of concealed weapons

A brass truncheon incorporating a percussion pistol, patented by John Day and dating from about 1823. It is rare and must have been an impractical weapon – too solid for safe use as a truncheon and hardly an efficient pistol. The eagle-head pommel is complete with inset glass eyes. (Thomas Del Mar Ltd)

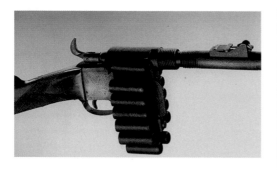

Patented in 1855, Treeby took the idea of a cartridge-loading system and created a series of metal cylinders linked in a chain, which were, one by one, brought into the firing position by the percussion lock. The idea was fine but impractical and never achieved any acceptance.

The flintlock could be put to peaceful use, as in this tinder lighter in which the lock generated sparks to light kindling and, in turn, a candle. There were various patterns and this is a top example.

were offered to an apprehensive public and one that seems to have been popular was the Squeezer type. The disc-like body held the cartridges and on one side was a short barrel, whilst at the opposite side was the trigger, which was a curved bar; the pistol was held in the clenched fist with the barrel projecting between the fingers and a shot was fired by squeezing the fist-operated trigger mechanism. Releasing the pressure re-cocked the pistol. There were a number of variations on this design.

Another fist pistol was known as 'My Friend' and this was basically a small pepperbox with a flat metal butt with a hole. The revolver was held in the fist with the little finger passing through the hole so that it was now a knuckle-duster, but, should the situation progress beyond fisticuffs, the hand was turned to point the pistol and, if necessary, fire it.

For the very nervous person who wanted several back-up systems, the French Apache pistol was one option. Patented in France by L. Dolne, this was a three-tier defence. At the lowest level of aggression there was a knuckle-duster, which was hinged; when folded back, it exposed a small, pinfire pepperbox held within the fist. If the fusillade of shots failed to resolve the problem, then a spring-operated bayonet was in reserve.

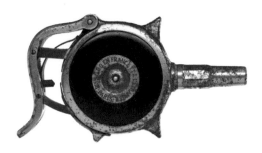

Palm pistol, ten-shot 5mm calibre, named 'Le Protector' and patented in 1883 by J. Turbiaux. It was held in the hand with the barrel protruding between the fingers, and fired by squeezing the hand. (Thomas Del Mar Ltd)

Tradition has it that the combination weapon acquired its name from the thugs of Paris who were supposed to favour it. There are known to have been several versions of the weapon and, since they are not too uncommon, they presumably sold reasonably well.

O. Frankenau obtained a patent, Number 3375, in 1877 for a small arm to be combined with 'purses, portemonaries, memorandum books, cigar cases & c'. Despite the range of possible combinations, the only one made in quantity seems to have been a pistol/purse. The purse was in two sections, one side containing a pinfire pepperbox, the muzzle pointing out on one side but hidden by a moveable plate, and the pistol having a drop-down trigger at the base. The other section was a conventional purse to hold the money. Any thief was due for a nasty surprise as the victim handed over the purse, the cover was pushed clear, the trigger dropped down and he got more than he bargained for.

As a group, knife pistols are the most common. Some, like the penknife, were intended not to be obvious but others, such as the version with the spring bayonet fitting, made no attempt to hide the blade. A few

handguns were made with the blade as an integral part and the best known of these is probably the Elgin cutlass pistol. This was essentially a normal percussion pistol but mounted below the barrel was a broad-bladed Bowie-type knife. Little is known about George Elgin, who patented the device in 1837. A number were purchased by the US Navy for a proposed expedition to the South Seas, but there were no large orders. Some of these pistols were made with a bar running from the base of the butt to the trigger guards, intended to serve as a knuckle bow to protect the owner's hand from an opponent's blade. Samuel Colt toyed with the idea but presumably decided that it had little to recommend it, for none seems to have been produced commercially. A specially shaped sheath to fit the weapon was available.

Circumstances sometimes called for the development of a handgun for a special purpose and this happened during the Second World War (1939–45). Germany had by the end of 1940 over-run most of Europe. Whilst the official armies may have been defeated, there were still many brave people anxious and willing to fight against the occupying forces. At first, much of the resistance was isolated, scattered and poorly organized, but Britain and the USA united the units into more effective networks. Secret lines of communication were established and the groups demanded arms to strengthen their resistance. Requests for weapons had to be balanced against those of the regular forces and some thought was given to mass production of simple but effective handguns. The result was the Liberator, which was a crude and basic single-shot .45 pistol, fashioned, not from precisely machined parts, but from stamped metal sheets. It had a short barrel and was loaded by pulling back the hammer and turning a breech plate to give access. When fired, the plate had to be turned and

The trigger was attached to a string, which was threaded through the clothing, and its end held in one hand. To fire the weapon, the wearer had only raise his arm or in any other way pull on the string to deliver the shot.

The Third Reich possibly considered the ideas worth exploring for there is at least one example in existence. It is a large belt buckle with the inevitable swastika-bearing eagle, which, when two side levers were pressed, snapped open to reveal four short-barrelled pistols that could be fired separately or together.

Possibly the most ambitious – some might say ridiculous – combination weapon was a device sold at auction in Toronto in 1935. It was found originally in Bordeaux in France in 1917, the work of an amateur armourer who offered it to the French Government. To his lasting regret, it was rejected. It was an *en suite* set of pistols, the main item being a steel breastplate fitted in rows with basic cartridge pistols, nineteen in all. They were hinged and could have the barrels lowered for loading and then returned to a firing position. They were fired in batteries of four or five by a series of buttons and, as if this were not enough, they were accompanied by stirrups that incorporated pairs of pistols. The entire apparatus weighed 35 pounds (about 14kg).

Much lighter and more deadly are some of the disguised firearms now being produced. One of the latest reported is a 'mobile phone' that is, in reality, a multi-shot .22 pistol. During the Second World War the Special Operations Executive (SOE) and other secret agents had a fountain pen that was a single-shot .22 pistol. Today there seems to be no ordinary domestic item that cannot be converted or transformed into a crude but lethal handgun. Bicycle pumps, lipsticks, pipes, torch, even a screwdriver are all recorded as having been converted to fire at least one shot.

Frankenau's purse, circa 1870. It houses a .22 pinfire revolver, the muzzle just projecting from the side.

the empty case pushed out with a rod, pencil, stick, or something similar. The hollow butt held spare rounds. This cheap but lethal pistol was mass-produced and dropped in quantity to the resistance forces. Its accuracy was minimal but, since it was intended to be an assassination or last-resort weapon used at close range, this was of no importance.

Crude though the Liberator was, it was manufactured in quantity and it did see service. There were a few other pistols produced that seem so unusual that it is questionable whether they were ever intended seriously to be used. There was a fist gun (patented in 1947) affixed on the back of a glove, which comprised a barrel using a Smith & Wesson .38 cartridge. It was fired by a trigger set by the side of the barrel and the idea was that, if the gloved hand was clenched into a fist, the firing trigger projected beyond the knuckles. If the fist was then pressed against the victim, it would fire and dispose unobtrusively of the target. Another oddity was the belt pistol, which was a basic percussion pistol fitted to the front of a waist-belt plate.

ᘓ CHAPTER 7 ᘓ

Ammunition and Loading

Powder

From the fourteenth to the nineteenth century, gunpowder was the main chemical propellant available to the gunner and shooter. Over the ages the formula was modified, with different variations of the proportions being tried, but most propellants still depended on the three basics: sulphur, charcoal and saltpetre. In most countries, a gunpowder industry developed and obviously thrived, especially during periods such as the Napoleonic Wars, when demands became excessive. Powder mills were established with well-planned working procedures marred by an occasional, unfortunate, disastrous accident. In Britain one of the main gunpowder mills was at Faversham in Kent, established there in the sixteenth century and taken over by the Government

in 1760. The machines were driven by water-mills and horsepower.

Once the corned system of powder production had been developed it was possible to produce powder of a better quality, with varying sized grains intended for specific purposes. The hand gunner preferred

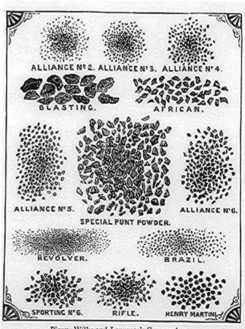

RIGHT: During the 19th century the manufacture of gunpowder was greatly expanded and developed as this advert from one supplier shows. Note the revolver powder is very fine grained for positive and fast burning.

powder that burnt very rapidly. The shorter barrel of the pistol meant that there was less time for the internal pressure of gases to build up before the bullet was expelled from the muzzle. By the nineteenth century, the choice of propellant was very important to the keen shooter and a wide range of powders were available. Gun shops carried the various grades of gunpowder in stock and these were usually designated by a number. The choice was a matter of the individual preference of the shooter. Pistol shooters tended to be less demanding and normally did not require a variety of powders.

Each shooter needed to have a personal supply of powder to hand, so some form of container was necessary. The arquebusier had his large, wooden powder flask but the development of the wheel-lock, with its higher social status, meant that containers became more decorative and embellished. They were fashioned from a variety of materials and in many different shapes, and their decoration was often quite elaborate. A doughnut style was popular and novelties such as a tortoise shell were adapted. These containers and flasks were probably at their most decorative in the sixteenth and early seventeenth centuries.

One popular container was the powder horn, simple and cheap to make from a length of cow horn. In the sixteenth and seventeenth centuries the horn was softened, then flattened and the wide end was closed by a block of wood. The narrow end was fitted with a simple metal pourer with a spring-loaded cut-off plate at its base. These horns were commonly decorated with simple engraved hunting or martial scenes, and are occasionally dated. Many powder horns and flasks were fitted with a belt hook on the back of the body – a metal bar standing proud of the container – that was pushed through the belt as a convenient way to carry the flask.

Late sixteenth-century powder horn fashioned from stag horn and decorated by an engraving of a couple against a rural background. (Thomas Del Mar Ltd)

German powder horn dated 1603 and decorated overall with scrolling foliage encircling a fleur-de-lis. (Thomas Del Mar Ltd)

'Doughnut' powder flask of the late seventeenth century. It has a central bone plug and the entire surface is decorated with small, stained discs of horn brass nails and inlaid wire. (Thomas Del Mar Ltd)

In the eighteenth century there was a change in fashion and the horn was left in its natural shape, with the blocks and pourers being fitted as before. During the late eighteenth and early nineteenth centuries, these horns, popular with hunters, were often decorated by their owners with simple scrimshaw work. Maps, pictures and patriotic sentiments were engraved on the horn with the lines sometimes being blackened. Horns carrying this scrimshaw decoration are highly prized by collectors. Some smaller versions were made for use by the artillerymen to prime their cannons.

The hunter or marksman often preferred to adjust the charge of powder to suit the target and range. As a consequence, many flasks for long guns had quite complicated, adjustable chargers, offering a variety of measures of powder. Since a pistol was effectively a short-range weapon, there was not the same necessity to vary the charge, but some pistol flasks did have an adjustable nozzle, allowing the choice of perhaps three slightly different charges. A correct charge of powder for the pistol could be thrown with a flask using just one hand. The tip of a finger closed off the open end of the nozzle, while the spring-operated cut-off at the base was pushed open and the flask was up-ended. The powder ran into, and filled, the nozzle, the cut-off was closed and the flask righted.

German powder horn dated 1603 and decorated overall with scrolling foliage encircling a fleur-de-lis. (Thomas Del Mar Ltd)

The nozzle now held the correct amount of powder to load the pistol ready to be poured into the barrel.

The development of the pinfire system generally made the powder flask superfluous. Cartridges were now self-contained, with powder, ball and cap all incorporated into one unit. The pinfire cartridge was quite efficient, if somewhat awkward to handle, but it could be a little dangerous as there was always the chance of an accidental hit on the pin. The development of the centre-fire system was a turning point, for the cartridge could now be made in quantity, carried safely and was largely impossible to discharge except when located in the firearms. Powder flasks, bullet moulds, nipple keys and similar accessories were no longer necessary, and largely disappeared from the scene.

Consistency of performance was very important for shooters, especially for target shooters and hunters, so they needed to know just how effective a powder would be in use. Every batch of gunpowder was likely to vary slightly in composition, thereby giving differing results, and this might mean that the point of aim should be adjusted to compensate for the variation. To ensure consistent accuracy, keen shooters would want to assess each batch of powder and to do this, various testing devices, or 'eprouvettes', were used from the sixteenth century onwards. Most worked on the basis of firing a small sample of powder and measuring the generated pressure. Basically most testers used the explosion to push against a spring-loaded plate and the degree of its displacement was then measured. Some tests were simple, with no more than a graduated arm to indicate the

Nineteenth-century Scottish powder horn fashioned from a natural, shaped cow horn and fitted with silver mounts. (Thomas Del Mar Ltd)

amount of movement. Some elaborate ones were designed to permit more accurate assessments. Using the figures obtained as a comparative indicator, the size of the powder charge could be adjusted to obtain the best result.

In the eighteenth and nineteenth centuries, it became increasingly common for gunmakers to supply a pistol neatly housed in a wooden case, and this meant that some form of powder flask became a standard component. The pistol case replaced the older style of packaging, with pistols apparently being sold in small material bags. The majority of cases held a barrel- or pear-shaped metal powder flask, which, in the eighteenth century was most likely to be fairly plain. In the nineteenth century, however, there was a growing fashion for the flask to be stamped

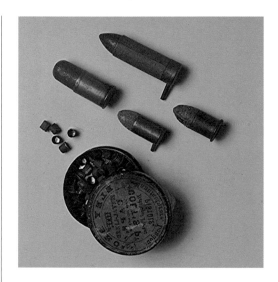

Top: Pinfire, cartridges including early paper case, rimfire and modern centre fire cartridge. Bottom: percussion caps by Eley specifically aimed at use by Colt percussion revolvers

Tools and accessories: wad cutter; Prideaux speed-loader, tin of caps, flintlock bullet mould and revolver bullet mould, three-way powder flask, nipple key with receptacles at tips of the cross arms to hold spare nipples or percussion caps.

with embossed patterns. Some flasks of oval section were modified to hold some spares; at the base of the body was a compartment just big enough to hold a spare flint or two. An internal, tubular compartment, formed as part of the body of the flask, could hold two or three bullets. Mostly made of copper, and occasionally of silver or leather-covered, the powder flasks for use with rifles and sporting guns became increasingly decorative and innovative, while the pistol flask remained fairly plain.

Powder flasks had to be treated with some care for they were full of black powder, which needed only one spark to set it off. One nineteenth-century writer, K. Watt, wrote a rhyming book on shooting and he included a clear warning:

> Your keenest caution let me seek
> Whene'er you choose your powder flask
> See the partition is air-tight
> Or all the powder may ignite
> While loading, if you leave but one
> Insidious spark within the gun.

The interior of the pistol case, which was usually of mahogany or oak, was partitioned by wooden strips and lined with green or blue baize material. Continental casing was

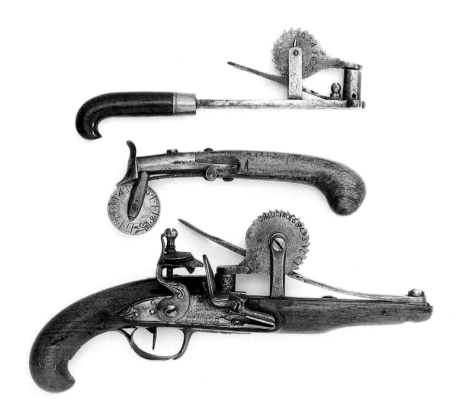

Powder testers or eprouvettes: the top two require the test charge to be ignited by an external heat source, while the bottom one functions by means of a flintlock mechanism. All date from the late eighteenth or early nineteenth century. (Thomas Del Mar Ltd)

Flintlock eprouvette of the early nineteenth century. The lock is of brass and the pressure from the test fire was deflected down to the graduated wheel, which turned to indicate the relative quality of the powder. (Thomas Del Mar Ltd)

generally more elaborate than British or American, with the inside partitioned off into individually contoured sections into which each item fitted snugly in place.

The development of the pistol case gave the gunmaker an opportunity to advertise his business. In the later part of eighteenth century it became common practice to

Typical late eighteenth-century three-way powder flask. A disc at the base unscrews to reveal a small compartment to hold a spare flint, and an internal tubular section holds two or three lead bullets.

stick a trade label on the inside of the lid, announcing the maker's available products and qualities, and to embellish it with decorative engravings. Some trade labels gave instructions for loading the pistol. The cases were usually fitted with a lock and some of the larger ones, such as those holding a pair of duelling pistols, had a folding, recessed handle mounted on the lid. The cases were generally well made, sometimes with brass reinforced corner fittings.

Bullets

The flintlock pistol was available in a wide variety of sizes and shapes, and fired balls ranging in diameter from a few millimetres up to musket bore of approximately three-quarters of an inch. Obviously, a gun is of no use without a missile to project and from the earliest days gunners and shooters had to be able to make their own bullets. Stone cannonballs were chiselled out and iron ones moulded, but the adoption of lead compounds as the prime bullet material made it possible for any individual to cast his own bullets. A fire, an iron pot, a supply of lead compound and a mould to shape the bullet were all that were needed. Soon, a basic type of bullet mould was established. The commonest style of mould had two metal arms hinged at the junction and each arm had a semi-circular cavity of the right measurement so that when the arms were closed they formed a hollow sphere of the correct size.

Most moulds were designed to cast only one or two bullets but others, known as 'gang moulds', were used to cast six or more. The mould was closed and the molten lead was poured into the mould, where it ran down a central channel, linked by small tubes to the cavities. It was left to cool, then the mould was opened and the contents tipped out. Each ball had a small tail, or sprue, left by the short connecting channel in the mould. Most moulds incorporated some form of scissor or blades to cut off the sprue and, after the ball had been given a rub or two, it was smooth and ready for use. From the mid-sixteenth century, moulds were common and this scissors type became more or less standard.

From the mid-nineteenth century the advent of revolvers led to experiments

Full-jacketed .38 and .45 bullets that have been fired, hit something solid and mushroomed, thus passing on maximum energy to the target. This effect is important when the stopping power of a round is vital.

to decide on the best shape for the bullet. Moulds became much more complex and some bullets were cast with a slightly hollowed-out base so that the expanding gas would exert pressure and spread the base to ensure a tighter fit of the bullet in the barrel. By the middle of the century, most revolver bullets were cylindro-conical in shape and many revolver moulds were designed to cast two bullets of slightly different shape, offering the shooter a choice. Many moulds were made of bronze and, in place of the scissors blades, there was a flat cutting blade on the top, which was pivoted and turned to trim the sprue.

Lead balls, mostly shot for hunting, were made in quantity at shot towers, tall, chimney-like buildings with a water tank in the base. A workman at the top would pour molten lead through a sieve into the tower. As it fell, the drops of lead would form spheres and when these hit the water they cooled and set as a solid bullet or shot.

During the twentieth century a great deal of research time was devoted to the question of a bullet's stopping powers. In hunting and, regrettably, in confrontational shooting such as that practised by law enforcement officers, it is necessary to consider the effect on the target of the impact of the bullet. In order to achieve maximum effect, as much of the bullet's potential energy as possible must be transferred to the target, and as quickly as possible. In hunting, a pointed bullet may pass right through a quarry and cause minimum damage, allowing the wounded animal to escape. A bullet with a flat or hollowed-out nose will spread on impact, increasing the area of transfer, and will not penetrate as deeply as a pointed missile. A significant amount of energy will be transferred, and maximum damage will be inflicted. It is therefore more likely to stop and kill the quarry. In the case of law

A favourite form of advertising by manufacturers of caps and cartridges was to assemble as many different rounds as possible and set them out to make patterns. This example came from Kynoch. Mounted in glazed frames, the assemblages were displayed in gunmakers' shops.

enforcement, this type of round will be more likely to stop an offender. The flattened nose has another advantage for police use: should the shot miss the target, and strike any hard surface, the bullet is more likely to spread. This deformation will make it much less likely to bounce or ricochet, and thus the potential for danger to the public is reduced.

Used in target shooting, the wad-cutter is quite cylindrical and makes a very clearly defined circular hole on the target. This reduces the chance of differences of opinion on whether a marking line is cut by the shot or not.

Apart from shape, another factor involved in assessing stopping power is muzzle velocity. Generally, the higher this is, the greater the stopping power, subject to bullet calibre. In any one calibre, different cartridges can offer a wide range of velocities. In .38 Special ammunition, the range of speeds can be from 599 feet per second to 1,023 feet per second;

in .45 Automatic ammunition, the spread is from 799 fps to 1,129 fps, and in .44 Magnum rounds, from 961 fps to 1,406 fps[38].

One line of continuing research involves the hunt for caseless ammunition. A considerable proportion of the weight of cartridges is made up by the metal case, and on the

From left to right: ACP round; plastic-nosed .38 round; disabling round holding small bag of shot; dummy .38 round

Eighteenth-century cartridge pouch with wooden frame holding eighteen paper cartridges for a musket. It has loops to attach it to the belt. (Thomas Del Mar Ltd)

pistol the part of the mechanism that is used to extract the empty case from the breech can cause problems. If a totally consumable round can be developed, this will simplify pistol mechanisms and lighten the round, enabling the soldier or hunter to carry more ammunition, and increasing the rate of fire. So far, the results have not been very encouraging, with corrosion, fouling in the chamber and heat dissipation all presenting challenges.

A wide range of pistol cartridges is commercially available to legitimate shooters but many enthusiasts prefer to make their own. There are simple hand-operated machines that will remove the spent cap from the base of the fired case, straighten and resize the case, load the correct amount of powder and set the bullet into the mouth of the cases. Reloading is one way to reduce the costs of shooting and it also allows a dedicated target shooter to ensure that all his cartridges will be identical. Simple hand tools for reloading

were first introduced with the pinfire system during the later part of the nineteenth century and tools designed for the various cartridges were available. Some ingenious tools incorporated several of the necessary devices into one gadget, whilst other tools were intended to perform one task only.

Although the centre-fire system cartridge of the same calibre is used by revolvers and semi-automatic pistols, these weapons cannot, in general, accept the same cartridges. Cartridges intended for use in a revolver have a rim around the base, like the old rimfire case. When the round is loaded, the rim sits on the face of the cylinder. Cartridge cases for self-loading pistols do not have the rim, but instead there is a shallow groove around the base. Once a cartridge has been fired, obviously the empty case must be extracted from the breech before the next round can be loaded. In a semi-automatic pistol, as the block is thrown back by the recoil, the tip of a small hooked arm engages with the groove, pulling the case clear and throwing it to one side. Whilst it was generally impossible to use self-loading cartridges in a revolver cylinder, there was one way in which this could be done, by using special clips. The special plates were in the shape of a half moon and each was cut with three cusps, which fitted around the cases of the semi-automatic cartridge and in effect became the rim and rested on the face of the cylinder.

Following on from the development of the centre-fire cartridge, the next big step in ammunition design was the introduction of smokeless powder. When gunpowder burns it generates considerable amounts of whiteish, grey smoke, and a battlefield with artillery and massed troops all firing could swiftly become enveloped in a fog. The smoke generated by each shot could also betray the position of a hunter and warn game of the shooter's presence. A propel-

Rounds for a self-loader and a revolver. The self-loader case has a groove at the base to allow the extractor to catch hold and eject the empty case. The revolver round has a rim that will be engaged by the ejector plate of the cylinder.

Special Bullets

Although the majority of bullets are composed of lead or lead-based compounds, there are occasions when some other material is needed. When a less than lethal projectile is wanted, rubber or plastic may be used for bullets instead of the usual solid lead compounds. For police service there is a special round that is designed to inflict a substantial impact on a target, and may well subdue a violent offender, but is not lethal. It is rather like a small beanbag, the contents of which spread out on impact, increasing the diameter several times and reducing penetration, but increasing the shock of impact. The modern handgun armoury now contains a number of similar rounds that are intended to reduce the terrible necessity of lethal fire in confrontations. One round has a plastic head that will cause shock but little more. Another is a cartridge with a light plastic missile that is used for certain practices to emulate real rounds. One specially designed 'maximum impact'-style is the Glaser, a frangible bullet in which the projectile is composed of small pieces of iron. These shatter and spread out on impact, ensuring a rapid, complete transfer of energy to the target.

For spaces such as aircraft[39], where normal rounds could have a disastrous effect, a special version of a 'stun gun' has been produced by the SAS of America Inc. It is a type of airgun with a detachable magazine holding three carbon dioxide-powered rounds, of tear gas, a noise generator, marker paint (which, on impact, leaves a bright fluorescent mark) or beanbag.

During the nineteenth and twentieth centuries a number of experiments were undertaken to develop body armour. Most early trials, especially during the First World War (1914–18), used various forms

lant that would burn with little or no smoke would be a great asset. In 1846, a material known as 'gun cotton' was produced, to do exactly what was wanted. However, it was a little unstable, a little too powerful and very tough on the guns firing it, so it was seldom used. Experimenters sought safer materials and, in 1886, Frenchman Paul Vielle produced a new propellant, Poudre B, which offered several advantages. It was safer than gun cotton, it produced hardly any smoke and it was lighter in weight than gunpowder. The soldier or shooter could carry more rounds with Poudre B than he could with gunpowder.

In Britain, Henry Noble's cordite achieved the same result with much less drawback and soon all the armies of the world, hunters and shooters were using the smokeless propellants.

of metal plates but later the new material of Kevlar was the prime choice. It was incredibly tough and could be worked as a woven thread. A number of layers – seventeen was an early number – could be shaped into a sleeveless garment that would resist the penetration of many handgun-calibre bullets. For magnum rounds the number of layers was increased, while for high-powered rifle rounds, ceramic plates were incorporated in the defensive vest. Whenever the armourers made an advance in defence, the weapon makers sought to defeat it and there was a corresponding search for ammunition that was capable of penetrating the new armour.

Greater penetration was achieved by reshaping the bullets, which were mostly round-nosed, and giving them a more pointed profile, as well as increasing the speed of the projectile and using materials that were harder than lead. One type of ammunition, KTW, was specially designed to penetrate body armour. The bullets contain a steel core and are coated with Teflon, or a similar chemical, to help reduce friction and so ensure smooth rapid transit along the barrel. Several brands of such cartridges, such as the French THV (*très haute vitesse*, or 'very high speed') and a Russian round, are now available. These can penetrate over fifty layers of Kevlar but supplies are often restricted to law enforcement agencies. Improvements in the resistance of Kevlar continue to be made and the competition goes on.

Bullets of lead and lead compounds will leave minor deposits on the inside of the barrel. If left uncleaned, these will build up to create serious fouling, which can affect the performance of the ammunition. In order to reduce this effect, bullets are often given a thin coating of copper; such bullets may be described as 'FMJ' (full metal jacketed).

Calibre

The measurement of a bullet is usually given as the internal diameter of the barrel for which it is intended. For handguns, most bullets fall into the range of .22 in. to .455 in. There are other sizes, some smaller and a few larger, but these sizes cover the majority of current handgun ammunition. The size of some bullets is given in millimetres, because they have originated on the Continent, and the commonest of these is 9mm. The size of a bullet is its main identifying feature, but there are other features, such as the shape or construction, which are reflected in the names ('hollow point', and so on). The description of the round may also give the weight of the bullet. It is important to know the weight for this will affect the speed of the bullet or muzzle velocity – as a general guide, the lighter the bullet, the greater the muzzle velocity, and the heavier the bullet, the lower the muzzle velocity. Other factors can influence these figures too.

The most significant change in calibres came with the development of the magnum round in 1935 by Smith & Wesson. Essentially, this was a standard-calibre cartridge case filled with an increased powder charge, giving it more thrust; thus, a .38 cartridge with a longer case became a .357 magnum. The increase in length was a necessary change to prevent the loading of a magnum round into a standard pistol cylinder, which would not be able to withstand the increased pressure. The other most common magnum round is the .44 Magnum, introduced in 1955 and made famous by Clint Eastwood in the *Dirty Harry* films, who called his weapon the 'most powerful handgun in the world'. The claim is no longer valid but it is still a very powerful cartridge and, as with the .357 cartridge, the case is made too big to fit a normal .44 chamber.

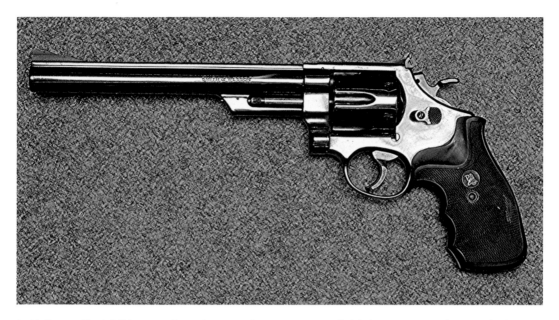

A .44 Magnum Smith & Wesson revolver with contoured composition grips, which help to ensure a good grasp and to lessen the impact of the considerable recoil. The long barrel ensures a high muzzle velocity. The catch unlocks the cylinder assembly so that it can be swung sideways for ejecting the fired cases and reloading.

The choice of calibre is very largely determined by the purpose for which the firearm is to be used. For stopping power a large calibre is probably most suitable, although with the range of bullets now available for different calibres, smaller bullets can be made to achieve the same result. Linked to calibre is muzzle velocity, or the speed at which the bullet leaves the muzzle. The most widely used revolver cartridge is the .38 Special, first produced as long ago as 1902, and, for the self-loader, the 9mm Luger round. In 1985 the US Army abandoned its old favourite, the .45 ACP round, used since 1911, and adopted the 9mm round as its official calibre, together with the Beretta Model 92F self-loading pistol. The main reason appears to have been that the ammunition weighed so much less and the magazine held fifteen rounds, considerably more than the Colt 1911.

In addition to all these examples, there are numerous other cartridges, some designed for specific handguns.

Speed-Loaders

Prior to the introduction of pepperbox pistols, most handguns were single-shot weapons, with a few offering up to four shots. The pepperbox, with its circular barrel, set the pattern of six shots, but there are some pistols that offer up to twenty shots. In action, having six shots without reloading would be more than welcome, but loading was a slow tedious business, with caps to be fitted to nipples, powder to be poured in the chamber and bullets to be rammed home. A few multi-pourer powder flasks were produced for pepperbox revolvers, as all six chambers could be accessed in one operation, but for the percussion firearms there was no easy quick-fit solution.

Even the advent of the metal cartridge case did not solve the problem, as the cylinder had to be rotated by hand until the chamber was clear to take the cartridge. Often there was a loading gate that had to be opened to allow access.

The design of swing-out cylinders and drop-down barrels enabled rapid loading, as it meant that all six chambers were now accessible. The various ejector systems certainly speeded up unloading but the insertion of new rounds was very much a manual operation. The cartridge had to be extracted from a belt loop or pouch and individually placed in the chamber, and it was not long before shooters sought quicker methods and started the development of so-called speed-loaders. These are devices that will, in one action, feed several or all six rounds into the revolver cylinder and one of the most successful was designed by Frenchman William Prideaux, who was granted an English patent for it in 1914. He was a keen patentee and his design of a 'revolver charger' was efficient and soon received official recognition. It was a simple, circular spring-loaded device into which were placed six rounds of revolver ammunition. These were commonly arranged with the same spacing and positions as the chambers on the cylinder of the Webley Army .45 revolver. The rounds were held in place by a series of sprung arms. In order to load the revolver, the cylinder was swung out of the frame and the loader held with the bullets lined up with the chambers. Pressure on a central point opened the restraining arms, allowing the bullets to drop into place. These speed-loaders were available with a leather case to hold one or three. An officer going into action using one of them could maintain a rapid rate of fire.

With the growth of semi-automatic weapons the need for revolver speed-loaders diminished, but it never disappeared completely.

A rare 'harmonica' pistol, so called because the cartridges were loaded into a block of six chambers, which moved sideways as the trigger was pressed and a shot fired. The original design was patented by J. Jarre in 1862 but this is a later version, of 1873. The projection from the top of the butt is a cleaning rod, which screwed into the frame. (Thomas Del Mar Ltd)

Police forces tended to retain the revolver as their side arm and the revolver was favoured in many practical competitions. Variations on the theme of the Prideaux were numerous. In the most basic and simple version, a rubber strip held six rounds in a line. Two rounds at a time were loaded and the strip was pulled away and then the next two were similarly loaded. Some rubber loaders copied the Prideaux by arranging the rounds in a circle and by simply twisting the holder free on all six rounds. Others loaders had a spring catch, which was pressed to release the rounds. Sets of these loaders were fitted to a waist belt, ensuring a conveniently handy supply of cartridges to maintain a steady, fast rate of fire. The loaders were supplied in various sizes to match the calibre of the revolver.

There is less of a problem for semi-automatic pistols that use magazines. These vary in size, from those holding around half a dozen to special ones with a capacity of more than twenty. An empty magazine can be removed by the simple press of a spring catch and a new, full one inserted in a fraction of a second. A number of brands offer larger-capacity magazines, including the Luger with its drum magazine, and the very latest Glock G18, which can be supplied with a double-drum magazine with a thirty-three 9 mm round capacity. The pistol has a selector switch so that it can fire single-shot or fully automatic, and a detachable shoulder stock is also available, making it into a machine pistol. Its devastating rate of fire means that legally it can be owned only by military or law enforcement bodies. In general, fully automatic handguns are ammunition wasters, for it is almost impossible to aim and hold the pistols on target. They have a tendency to rise high and right, making controlled fire difficult.

The usual semi-automatic pistol magazine is of the straight, stick type but large-capacity ones are usually circular and often require a special loading tool to insert the cartridge. There is an exception with the Colt 1911A1 .45 ACP pistol, which was available with a long stick magazine holding twenty-four rounds. It was also supplied in a leather case that held two of the magazines. It is reported that this type of magazine was favoured by fighter pilots in the First World War, before machine guns were fitted to the planes and they still fired handguns at the enemy.

Whether it should be defined as a handgun or not, more and more police forces are using the Taser. It is intended to be non-lethal and on the earlier models a small charge of gunpowder was used, but this has now been replaced by compressed air, to discharge two small barbed projectiles. These darts are connected to the Taser body by two light trailing wires. When the arrows strike the target, a high-voltage electrical shock of several thousand volts is administered, disabling or incapacitating the victim. Although

Modern speed-loader that is basically an updated Prideaux model. The rounds are released by pressing the central button. The strip system was perhaps a little less efficient since the rounds were arranged in a line. They were loaded into the chambers two at a time, and the strip was pulled clear.

the voltage is high, the amperage is very small and, except for very, very rare occasions, will not cause serious or lasting harm to the victim.

The official policy is that the Taser should be used only when the officer is under threat of extreme violence, but there is some

Early Prideaux speed-loader with correct leather carrying pouch. The loader held six .45 rounds and, when located over the cylinder and pressed, released them into the chambers.

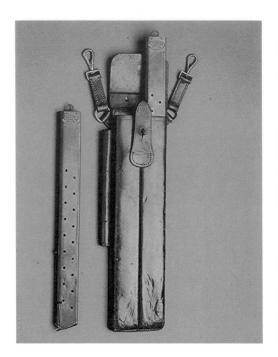

Leather ammunition pouch housing two full-length magazines for the Colt 1911A1, each holding twenty rounds, as well as a cleaning rod. The small straps were used for suspending the pouch from a Sam Browne belt. These pouches are rare and the pistol with such a magazine in place was not easy to handle.

Typical officers belt as carried by many US police forces. The holster has a retaining strap; there are spare round loops, a handcuff case, a leather round holder and pouches for strip loaders. This style has largely been replaced by self-loading pistols and the various ammunition pouches by magazine holders.

The MAC 10. Such weapons have recently figured in some firearm incidents in Britain.

concern that it may be used, indeed is being used, in less hazardous situations. There is also some controversy over whether it should be carried only by specially trained officers or as general issue. At the moment, it is basically a short-range weapon but there is some development work being carried out on a new version, XREP, which will have a range of about sixty feet.

Another firearm that is on the border of the definition of 'handgun' is the MAC 10. It is a small sub-machine gun/pistol with a magazine of about thirty rounds and a rate of fire of 1,000 rounds a minute. It has some similarities with the Liberator, as it is made by the Military Arms Corporation from steel stamp-

ings. It is available in several calibres but was designed for the .45 cartridge. Although it can be used single-handed it is difficult to control and tends to spray the rounds and, surprisingly, or perhaps consequently, has no sights.

CHAPTER 8

Silencers and Holsters

Silencers

Every shot fired from a handgun generates noise and that noise is the result of several effects created by the gas generated by the propellant and the bullet as it leaves the muzzle. At the instant that the bullet leaves the barrel, the report is at its loudest and in the normal course of events the report is accepted as unexceptional. Ear muffs to protect the hearing are now standard wear for all shooters, both indoors and outdoors. (This safety device was ignored by shooters in the past, and there were many cases of deafness.) However, there are circumstances in which it is desirable to reduce the report as much as possible; urban pest control, hunting from a fixed shooting point, indoor shooting and covert action by Special Forces might all benefit from noise reduction. Despite the impression given by many films, it is almost impossible to eliminate the noise of a gunshot completely, and even the most efficient silencer or sound moderator may still leave a popping noise. As well as the report, there is also the sound generated by moving parts such as the breech of the gun.

Commercial silencers made their appearance in the early twentieth century and the first to patent a device was a son of Sir Hiram Maxim, the father of self-loading weapons. The silencer has hardly changed in shape since the first model and most still comprise a cylindrical tube fitted to the muzzle of the handgun. The noise is caused by the expanding gas and it follows that, the more the gas is controlled, the more efficient the silencer. Handguns with a well-enclosed breech area, where the gas is generated, as on a self-loading pistol, can be well silenced. A revolver has a perceptible gap between the end of the chamber and entry to the barrel, through which some of the gas and noise can escape, and consequently it is more difficult to silence. It is a fact apparently unknown or ignored by many film directors, who delight in showing the shooter securing a silencer to the barrel of a revolver. The Russian Nagant revolver is different and can be efficiently silenced, because the mechanism ensures an extremely close fit between chamber and barrel, allowing only a very small amount of gas leakage. The speed of the bullet has some influence on the silencing effect and supersonic bullets will create more noise. Even

Self-loading pistol with attached silencer. The length of the fitting suggests that the sound reduction would be considerable. Revolvers do not lend themselves to efficient silencing.

with semi-automatic pistols, as the breech opens to eject a cartridge, some noise will be generated.

The basic principle of effective silencers is the absorption of the expanding gases before they leave the exit of the silencer. This is done by creating a number of chambers inside the silencer and these are made by a series of baffles, frequently rubber discs. Other methods have been tried, but the baffle seems to be the most practical type.

As a result of their potential use by criminals, silencers are illegal in many countries but sound moderators fitted to rifles and air weapons are usually accepted as legitimate. It is also illegal to manufacture silencers.

During the Second World War there was some research into the use of silenced weapons. The British produced an effective silencer for the Sten sub-machine gun and the USA tried one for the Thompson sub-machine gun. A few pistols, including the Luger, P38 and Beretta, were also fitted with various devices but the only really unusual example was one produced for Allied secret agents of OSS or SOE – the Welrod pistol. This was more a silencer fitted with a firing mechanism than a normal pistol and was very much a short-range weapon. The twelve-inch 'barrel/silencer' was fitted with a magazine grip holding six to eight rounds and the firing mechanism was a hand-operated bolt action. The two sections could easily be disassembled or assembled quickly, so increasing the ease with which the device

could be concealed. It was, perhaps hopefully, fitted with sights but it was essentially a close-combat assassination weapon. The ammunition was either .32 or 9mm Parabellum. According to whispered gossip, it has been retained in service and was used in the Falklands War (1982) as well as in the Iraq campaigns. It was produced in Britain but has no markings to identify its source. It is not known how many were produced, but the number is likely to be quite small. Similar rumour has it that various silenced pistols were used by Special Forces on both sides during the Cold War.

Silencers are most efficient when using low-velocity ammunition and many sub-machine guns, like the Israeli UZI 9mm model, work quite well as silenced weapons.

Holsters

A musket, rifle or shotgun can easily be carried resting on a shoulder, tucked under the arm or suspended from a sling. The pistol may be tucked into a belt or waistband, but this is not necessarily the safest method and some form of container or holster is really necessary. The first step in the development of such a carrier appears to have been the saddle holster. In 1575, Elizabeth I (1558–1603) specifically banned the carrying of personal firearms but made an exception for horsemen. They were allowed to carry pistols on horseback but the weapons had to be clearly visible in holsters that were attached to the saddle. This exemption was, however, not for everybody; it was limited to those people whose character was 'beyond reproach'. This was in effect a licence for the propertied, official and aristocratic class to travel armed. Surviving examples of early Tudor holsters are rare but most probably differed little in shape from later ones. Made of leather, these have a tapered length to hold the barrel, with a wider section at the top to accommodate the mechanism, and the butt stands clear of the open top. Riding holsters were generally made in pairs, with a central joining strap to go across the saddle or the horse's neck.

During the sixteenth and seventeenth centuries, wealthy and honoured owners probably had their holsters covered with rich material such as velvet and embroidery. During the seventeenth century, when the wheel-lock system simplified the weapons and they were more widely manufactured, pistols became general issue for much of the cavalry. Their holsters began to follow a more or less standard pattern and orders for their supply are recorded during the seventeenth-century English Civil Wars. Fashioned from hardened leather, they were fairly basic in construction, with one piece of leather folded and stitched down one side. The holsters were usually plain but were sometimes fitted with a leather cap to cover the top and keep the pistols dry. The design was simple – the top section housing the mechanism was wide enough to hold the weapon no matter which way it was inserted. Most had two or three outside stitched loops through which the straps holding them in the saddle could be passed.

During the seventeenth century there was a marked increase in the manufacture of smaller firearms. Since these weapons were usually carried for self-protection, they were of a size to fit into a pocket in the clothing and

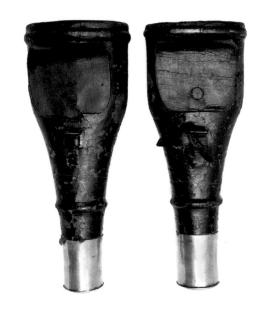

Pair of Russian regulation pistol holsters dating from around 1800. They are wooden framed with a leather covering and a brass cap. (Thomas Del Mar Ltd)

holsters were hardly needed. Interestingly, according to contemporary newspaper reports, it was common practice for mid-nineteenth century Parisian tailors to include a special revolver pocket in men's suits.

The general shape of saddle holsters hardly varied over the centuries, although some were more decorative than others, and some later French patterns had decorative brasswork. In the late seventeenth and early eighteenth centuries, the use of firearms by the cavalry changed and many became dragoons riding to battle but fighting on foot. For these troops a carbine was more common than a pistol and with that change special holsters were developed. In the nineteenth century, many cavalry were equipped with carbines that called for much longer holsters. Following the Great Exhibition of 1851, there was a growing feeling that revolvers were a

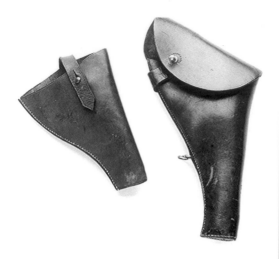

Left: British Army other ranks leather holster for a .38 revolver. Right: Officer's leather holster for a .45 revolver – the small brass 'S'-shaped hook was probably designed to hold a Prideaux speed-loader.

more appropriate cavalry weapon and the Crimean War (1854–1856) provoked still stronger demands.

Although the 'saddle' holster may be traced back to the sixteenth century, the holster specifically designed to be carried about the person seems to be a nineteenth-century innovation. It may well be that its development was stimulated by the introduction of the pepperbox revolver. These firearms, with their often quite substantial multi-barrel blocks, tended to be just a little too large or too heavy to sit comfortably in a pocket. It seems that the introduction of the percussion pepperbox pistol around the 1840s may have been a prime factor in increasing the demand for holsters. Many surviving holsters of the nineteenth century appear to match the period of the pepperbox. However, as early as 1850, Russian cavalry-men were issued with waist-belt holsters and in 1851 the British Government was purchasing holsters for the Colt Navy Percussion revolvers. In 1856, there are references to the Colt revolver being carried in a waist-belt holster by the US Cavalry.

During the eighteenth and nineteenth centuries, an alternative method of carrying pistols became very popular. The belt hook was an angled bar secured on the left side of a pistol about half an inch away from the stock, which was pushed down inside a belt or waist sash. One advantage was that the pistol was reasonably easily available and no holster was necessary, but the hook did not hold the pistol very securely in position. It was commonly used on naval pistols when obviously it was a great advantage to be able to use both hands when manipulating the rigging or managing sails. It is also found on some 'civilian' weapons.

All holsters need to be a little more than just a case to hold the firearm. A good holster must fit the weapon and hold it reasonably securely, but not so tightly as to prevent a quick withdrawal in an emergency. It also needs to be safe and prevent as much as possible any accidental discharge when drawing the weapon. According to illustrations of early holsters, they were usually carried at the waist on some sort of belt. Later in the nineteenth century, with the adoption of the metal-cased cartridge, the waist belt was modified to serve a double purpose by incorporating loops to hold spare rounds and pouches of ammunition. Today, many police have special belts to carry keys, handcuffs, first-aid items and batons. Most holsters, but by no means all, intended for use by the military, have a top, fold-over flap to protect the pistol from wind and weather. There are some contemporary illustrations of the eighteenth century showing the use of a shoulder belt with a number of pistols attached, either with belt hooks or loops on the belt. A further safety precaution found on some pistols and

Colt Navy 1851 percussion revolver made in 1866. The barrel has the New York address but carries British proof marks. The grips are stamped with an official Enfield mark, indicating Government ownership. The holster is typical of the Slim Jim style and is made of pigskin. (Thomas Del Mar Ltd)

revolvers is the lanyard ring fitted at the base of the butt. This was engaged with a spring-operated clip on the end of a lanyard worn around the neck or shoulder. It served the same purpose as a sword knot in preventing accidental loss.

Thanks to TV and films, the Western holster is probably the best-known type, although those seen in contemporary photographs are usually quite plain and far less elaborate than those depicted on the screen. In reality, there were two main styles of holster. The first was the Californian holster, or Slim Jim, so called because it was long and narrow and shaped to hold a long-barrelled revolver such as the Colt Army or Navy Model percussion revolvers. It was made of leather and in contemporary catalogues was offered decorated with incised patterns. The other type was the Mexican loop or Buscadero style, which was fashioned from a single piece of hide. Part was shaped to hold the revolver and this

Top: Belt. buckle, cap pouch and holster for a Colt Navy Percussion revolver, as used by Union forces during the US Civil War 1861–1865. Bottom: Good-quality decorated commercial holster for the Colt Navy revolver and a rather unusual one, probably locally made. If worn on the right side, the belt fitting would cause the butt to protrude forward. If worn on the left it would be more appropriate for a left-handed shooter or a cross-draw style.

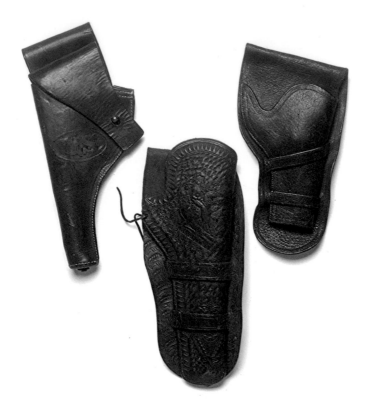

Left: Pattern for the Colt .45 revolver with fold-over restraining flap and embossed 'US'. Centre: Commercially produced Buscadero holster for a long-barrelled percussion revolver, with overall embossed decoration. The short thong could be used to secure the gun in the holster. Right: Simpler version for five and a half inch Colt Single-Action.

section was folded back and passed through a couple of narrow loops to hold it in place and at the same time create a loop through which to pass a belt. On many of the revolver holsters there was often a small leather loop or a slit leather strip fitted by the mouth. This was hooked over the hammer of the revolver to ensure the gun would not fall out of the holster when the owner was mounting or dismounting from a horse.

Another frequent feature of Western films is the twin holster belt. Again, the movie directors were using a bit of artistic licence, as firing two guns simultaneously, one in each hand, with any accuracy calls for skills way beyond the aptitude of any except a gifted few. Proof of their use in reality is hard to find and the vast majority of contemporary photographs show only a single holster. One

iconic photograph of the well-known character, Wild Bill Hickok, does show him carrying two revolvers at his belt, but whether they are in holsters or just tucked into the belt is not clear. In this case, the position of the pistols, with butts projecting forwards, suggests that he might have been using a cross-draw – drawing the pistol on the right with the left hand, and vice versa. Drawing in the normal way would have required a rather awkward twist of the arms. The pistols are thought to be a pair of 1851 Navy Colt percussion revolvers with ivory grips. In any case, those with knowledge of actual combat shooting generally stress that a few careful single shots are worth many quick-fire rounds.

Careful analysis of serious lethal shootings, usually designated fire-fights, indicate that it is exceptional for more than a very few

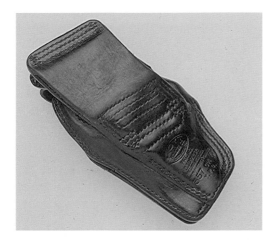

Leather pancake holster designed so that the pistol did not need to be drawn but was simply pushed forward, parting the holster at the front and allegedly speeding the draw.

Two belt holsters for snub-nosed revolvers: one is of plastic and reduced to the bare minimum in the hopes of preventing any snagging as the revolver was drawn.

shots to be fired. This finding is backed up by analysis of recorded fire-fights by American policemen. One common practice for police-trained shooters is the 'double tap', two shots fired one after the other, which increases the chances of a hit and delivers maximum shock to ensure that the target is stopped. It is reckoned that in the well-recorded fire-fights, such as the 1881 shooting at the OK Corral in Tombstone, Arizona, involving Wyatt Earp and several others, probably fewer than twenty shots in all were fired. Contemporary accounts of Western fire-fights paint a very different picture from those portrayed in the films. Shots were fired at almost point-blank range and still missed, guns were dropped, combatants would run for cover and weapons would misfire.

Another feature commonly shown on the screen is a thong or strap fitted at the base of the holster, tied round the thigh to hold the holster firmly in place. However, again it does not seem to figure very often in contemporary photographs. Most of the men seen in the pictures have their holsters quite high at the waist rather than slung low. This tie-down system was used on some cavalry holsters for the nineteenth-century US Army issue .45 revolvers and was, in fact a leather thong. Holsters for the Colt 1911A1 .45 ACP semi-automatic pistols during the Second World War have a hole at the very bottom, which could be used to fit such a thong if necessary. The tie-down thong is also used by some specialist units whose activities tend to be a little more vigorous than most.

Contemporary photographs seem to indicate a very casual attitude towards holsters. They are often seen hanging at an odd angle and certainly lacking any securing thongs – tucking the pistol into the waist belt seems to have been just as popular. As the cult of the quick draw, largely generated by the early films, somewhat imaginative fiction and Wild West shows, gained credence, special holsters were designed and a few experimental skeleton versions were developed. Some modern pistols, such as the Glock semi-automatic pistol, offer a plastic version of this sort of pattern. There was also a fashion for what might be called a 'minimum' holster, on which the item was reduced to the absolute basic, often little more than a strap. Another style that gained a certain acceptance was the 'pancake' or front opening holster. On this model, the outer section was hinged and sprung so that, when closed it looked quite conventional, but instead of lifting the gun out of the holster the shooter simply pushed it forward, causing the holster to spring open.

The myth of the quick draw has largely been perpetuated by the cinema, but it is in fact a rather over-rated action. There are recorded examples of some incredibly fast actions by professionals, such as the FBI agent who in December featured in an article in *Life* magazine. The recorded times for his quick draws were incredible, but he was obviously a 'natural', able to perform amazing trick shooting. His skills were put to good practical use, for he is believed to have been involved in numerous lethal fire-fights during his FBI service. Such incredible skills aside, researchers have in fact shown that the quick draw does not always give the shooter an advantage. The physics of the quick draw have recently attracted some scientific interest and tests have shown that the shooter who waited for his opponent to draw first reacted faster, albeit by just a few milliseconds, and apparently had a slight edge. Another researcher confirmed the result but insisted that, despite a quicker reaction, the second shooter was at a disadvantage and would, all other factors being equal, lose the fight. The general opinion by serious shooters, however, was

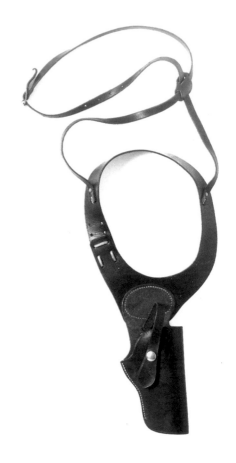

Typical shoulder holster for a revolver, with retaining straps, designed to be worn on the left side for a right-handed draw.

that it was not timing but accuracy that would decide the outcome.

For security and law enforcement officers who need to carry their firearms covertly out of sight, there is a market for holsters hidden about the body. Where concealment is important, the semi-automatic is favoured, since its flat shape is obviously less bulky than that of a revolver, but there are suitable covert holsters for revolvers. The most common type is the shoulder holster, of which there are many styles. They can be made for right- or left-hand use and the pistol can be carried in

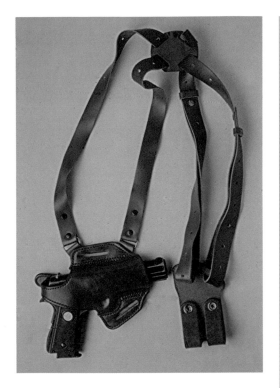

A more elaborate shoulder holster for a self-loader with extra fittings to enable a spare magazine to be carried. The holster is designed so that it can be fitted to a waist belt if desired.

Claimed by the manufacturer to be far superior to leather, Mills webbing equipment was used by many military forces and could be supplied in a number of styles and patterns.

a variety of positions to suit personal taste. Some hold the gun with the butt hanging vertically whilst others hold the pistol horizontally, and many also have a fitting to carry a spare magazine for the semi-automatic pistol or a speed-loader for a revolver. Ankle holsters are favoured for so-called back-up weapons and another type is outwardly a body or money belt but adapted to contain a holster.

Modern shooting catalogues offer a range of holsters that are designed to be as unobtrusive as possible and make use of every curve and recess of the body. The development of the material Velcro has led to the creation of holsters that hold the gun firmly without

straps but can be easily pulled open. There were a few spring-operated devices fitted to the arm that, on operation, deposited a pistol into the open hand. Small holsters to clip to the waist belt of trousers are also favoured by some law enforcement officers. One style dispensed with the holster and used a metal projection fitted to the revolver that engaged with a slotted plate on the belt, but it was not a universal choice. Another rather fanciful idea was a rotating holster from which the gun was not drawn but swivelled, and the trigger pressed, although aimed fire would have been unusual, to say the least.

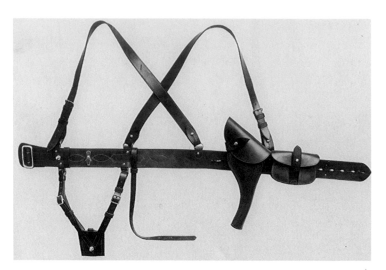

British Army officer's Sam Browne belt for carrying the official .45 revolver, sword and ammunition pouch. It was designed by a Captain Browne, who lost an arm during the Indian Mutiny of 1857 and found it difficult to manage the sword with only one arm. The extra support given by the cross strap improved matters.

Modern technology has been pressed into service to produce holsters designed to be minimal but secure, safe but still allowing a

Illustration from a contemporary magazine showing the Sam Browne belt in use by an officer during the South African War. Note the lanyard attached to the butt to prevent loss of the weapon.

quick draw if required. Most of these use plastic as the basic material but incorporate metal fittings and the Russian Makarov self-loader holster, as used by their Special Forces, is a current example.

The military issue of handguns is now generally limited to officers, cavalry and some specialist units, and most holsters are fitted with a flap to protect the weapon. Many of the early holster flaps were quite decorative, with embroidery and coverings of animal fur. There are a multitude of military patterns and many also have an integral magazine holder. Most carry various markings which can usually identify country of origin. The majority of them are made of leather, but webbing such as Mills Woven Military Equipment, is a cheap but quite durable alternative. Indeed, it has been claimed that it is superior to leather in comfort and durability, especially in hot climates. The USA was the first to use it and Britain followed close behind. Both leather and webbing military holsters were sometimes made with fittings to hold a cleaning rod or a few rounds of ammunition.

Some handguns were supplied with a wooden holster that could be attached to the butt of the pistol, converting it into a carbine for careful aiming. The Mauser 96 is probably the most recognizable, with its distinctive shape, but many others, such as the Browning Hi-Power, Colt .45, Webley, Luger and many other pistols, offered a similar facility, which was a butt-shaped board.

Although not strictly holsters, there are some devices that house a pistol. One of the favourite, fictional secret agent models is the small case or handbag holding a pistol operated by an external trigger. The case is also fitted with an internal laser and the films suggest that it is a simple matter of lining up the laser beam on the target and pressing the trigger to ensure a hit. In fact, it is extremely difficult to hold the case steady in the hand and the laser beam tends to wander, making a sure shot difficult.

Over the years there have been a number of patented holsters and devices for carrying a firearm, some of which bordered on the ridiculous. Although perhaps lacking some of the perceived glamour and romance of the weapons, holsters do offer an interesting collecting and research field. In addition to the standard commercial items made by such firms as Bianchi, there have been a number of 'personal' designs such as the the First World War Captain C.D. Tracey Model, which was specifically intended for quick draw in the circumstances of trench warfare. J. Noel, a renowned pistol shooter of the 1920s, offered two patterns for the Colt 1911 and the variety offered by commercial companies today is amazing.

A wooden holster for an M96 Mauser self-loading pistol. At the tip of the narrow section is the metal catch which allows the holster to be clipped onto the butt of the pistol, so converting it to a carbine. (Thomas Del Mar Ltd)

Leather holster for a 9mm Luger self-loading pistol. It has a magazine pouch at the front and on the inside of the fold-over flap is a small metal tool to assist when loading the magazine. The projecting strap passes, inside the holster, under the trigger guard and if it is pulled it will raise the pistol, making it easier to draw.

CHAPTER 9

Shooting the Handgun for Sport

~ ~

During the Middle Ages, competence in archery was considered essential. Men were expected to practise extensively and part of their training took the form of competitions. When firearms began to replace the bow, it was a natural development for similar competitions to be carried on but using the gun. As the handgun was a late development and difficult to aim, it is likely that the first target shoots were based on using the musket, and inability to aim it must have delayed competition, probably until the fifteenth century. Special areas, 'the butts', had been set aside for archers to practise their skills and the shooters naturally used the same areas.

As the firearm became more sophisticated, the whole system of competitive shooting became more complex. Ranges were lengthened and embellished, special buildings were erected for storage, and regular meetings and celebrations were established. On the Continent there were big changes and some ranges measured over four hundred feet in length. In place of the simple marks used by archers, special targets were introduced; at first, they were no more than painted boards but soon a whole range of scenic, grotesque and comic targets were being manufactured. Some complex examples were fitted with a simple device that fired a shot to indicate when a bull, the centre of the aiming circle, had been hit.

Towns and guilds formed civic shooting clubs, which developed into quite important civic bodies, organizing parades and running well-publicized competitions. In Britain, records seem to suggest that there were apparently fewer such organizations but there was no lack of enthusiasm, coupled with a certain disregard for safety. Both Henry VIII and Elizabeth I found it necessary to issue proclamations reminding the trigger-happy citizens that there were regulations setting out where they were permitted to shoot. In growing recognition of the potential danger presented by firearms, there were proclamations stating that no firearms were to be used anywhere near the Royal Household. Elizabeth issued an edict stating that there was to be no more shooting in churchyards; perhaps the openness of the ground in a graveyard, in contrast to the crowded streets, suggested to enthusiasts that it might be a good place to set up targets.

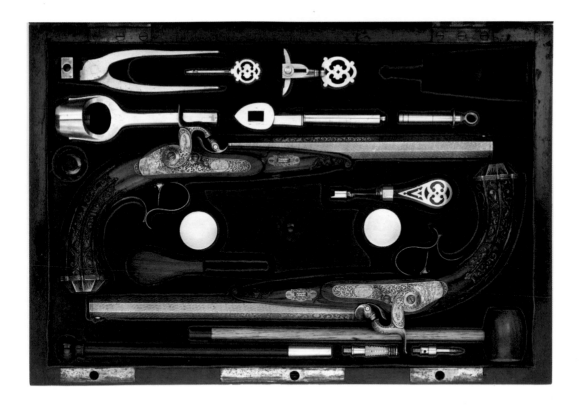

Cased pair of rifled, target percussion pistols in their contoured case with all accessories by a most famous maker, J. Adam Keuchenreuter, who was based at Regensburg. The decorated octagonal barrels are fitted with adjustable sights. The accessories include a wooden hammer, since the rifling made loading the bullet rather difficult. (Thomas Del Mar Ltd)

During the seventeenth and early eighteenth centuries, target shooting was not widespread and hunting was the main shooting exercise, but from the mid-eighteenth century there appears to have been a change, with pistol shooting becoming popular. This change may have been stimulated by the fact that duelling was turning more towards pistols and away from swords. Gunmakers were no doubt swift in pointing out that, in a shooting duel, there was usually only one chance and a miss could be fatal. They began to design pistols to be more accurate and supplied longer barrels, specially shaped butts, set and hair triggers, sighting aids and other devices for the keen shooter. Several gunmakers offered their customer the chance to try out a pistol before making the purchase and some shops accommodated a shooting range.

The advent of the percussion system was keenly adopted on the Continent and elaborate cased pairs of target or duelling pistols were popular and were often fitted with a variety of loading tools. Specialized forms of competition shooting were adopted and one extreme example in the nineteenth century was a practice duel, in which both competitors wore protective clothing and fired at one another using special wax bullets. There was a return to a form of 'duelling' shoots in the 1990s, when turning targets simulated the opponent but did not return fire!

During the nineteenth century there was a tremendous development in target shooting in Britain, with thousands of ranges being established. This was due in part to the growth of the Volunteer Movement, which was at its height around the middle of the century. Since most volunteers were obviously considered to be foot troops, most of the shooting was with rifles and comparatively little pistol shooting was done. Interest

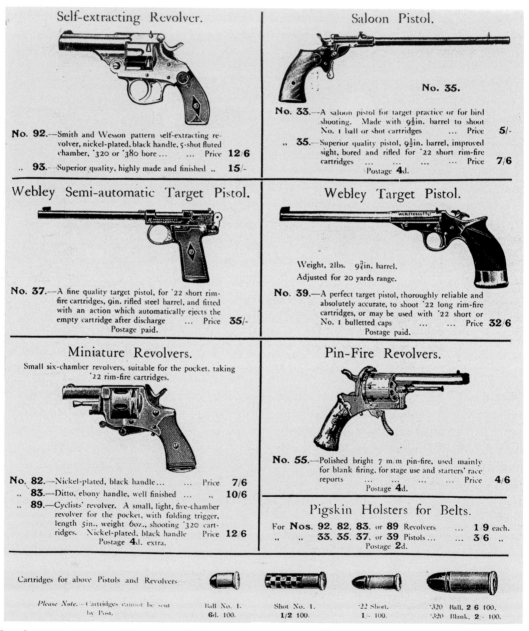

Page from a sales catalogue of the early twentieth century showing a range of firearms on sale. Note the single-shot target pistols with their long barrels, which increase the accuracy and power of the round.

This elegant late nineteenth-century lady in sepia has none of the safety accessories of the modern shooter, such as safety glasses or ear defenders. It is to be hoped that she is merely looking at the pistol rather than firing it, as it is dangerously close to her face.

R. DELL & CO., LTD.
EXPORTERS & IMPORTERS

Telephones: Bishopsgate 4541 & 454

45-51 CHURCH ROW
Bethnal Green Road,
LONDON,

5 MIN. BY No. 8 or 60 BUS FROM LIVERPOOL STREET

Re **Toy Pistols and Revolvers**

Extract from the Speech by Mr. Hacking, the Under Secretary of State, in the House of Commons on November 8th, 1933, in introducing the New Firearms and Imitation Firearms (Criminal Uses) Bill:—

"To deal with the imitation Firearm in the same way as the genuine Firearm is dealt with is not desirable and is in fact not necessary—that is, by way of a firearm certificate or by means of registration as a firearm dealer. To deal with the problem in that way would be exceedingly inconvenient. Imitation firearms have in fact a legitimate and harmless use. There would be, in my submission, an undue interference with industry, at any rate with a certain portion of the toy industry, if dealers and manufacturers had to be registered before they were allowed to sell or to make such articles as, for example, toys capable of firing paper caps, or dummies which might be used for letter weights, or cigarette lighters, or imitation revolvers which are used for theatrical purposes, and many other articles of a harmless nature. If you had to compel the manufacturers of that type of imitation armaments to be registered, I believe you would be interfering with a legitimate and harmless trade. It would in fact be absurd to have to possess a firearms certificate or an imitation firearms certificate before one can carry or use a particular form or a particular shape of cigarette lighter. If one had to insist upon a certificate in cases such as those, obviously the law would be held up to ridicule."

The problem of balancing public safety and private ownership of firearms is long standing and arises regularly as this leaflet clearly shows. The problem is still current today and impinges on apparently innocent items such as toy guns just as it did in 1933.

was growing and in August 1885 a meeting was held in Westminster with the intention of setting up a Metropolitan Revolver Club. It was to be limited to Volunteer and Militia officers and the stimulus for its foundation seems to have been the result of the National Rifle Association holding its first revolver competition that year. According to the report, there were about 1,000 entries and some good scores, but the account deplores the fact that very few taking part knew how to handle a revolver. The number of entries supports the idea that Britain was more gun-conscious than had been previously thought.

As target shooting gained in popularity, many manufacturers such as Colt and Webley turned to producing convertible pistols and revolvers. These were weapons of a normal calibre, such as the Colt 1911A1, which, with the aid of an Ace Conversion kit with alternative barrel, magazine and other parts, could then fire the .22 Long Rifle cartridges for plinking or target shooting. Webley revolvers were also in the same market, with simple fittings such as the Morris tube, which accepted .22 cartridges and was inserted into the normal barrel and with other fittings allowed the revolver to be used for target work. The firm also produced more elaborate conversion kits, which involved changing the cylinder. Webley sold cased sets that included the full-bore revolver and the conversion .22 kit.

Wholesale Price List of
"WALDEN"
Safety Pistols and Revolvers,
Air Guns, Air Pistols, Shot,
— Slugs, Darts, etc. —

No. 5.

DELL & CO.,
45-51, Church Row, Bethnal Green Road, London, E.2.

Telephone: Cables:
BISHOPSGATE 4541.   DELCODELL, LONDON.
        4542.

New Customers supplied with goods
"ON SALE OR RETURN"
for first order only. :: ::

Shooting in its various styles was, at one time, part of the British culture, and most boys were given water pistols, air guns or cap guns. There was a good trade in such items and firms regularly advertised their wares, as shown in the example above dating from the 1930s.

Judging by contemporary photographs, there was a somewhat casual approach to shooting sports during the latter part of the nineteenth century, with few concessions to safety. Ear muffs to protect the ears from sound blast were not commonly worn and neither were safety glasses; both are obligatory in modern ranges. There was apparently a more open-minded attitude and it was not seen as unusual or misguided for children to play with toy guns or even, as evidenced by some material, to enjoy shooting as a game.

Into the twentieth century, too, there seems to have been only limited public opposition to shooting as a sport. Fairgrounds commonly offered visitors the chance to win a prize with a .22 rifle, although tradition had it that the sights of the guns were always slightly 'adjusted' to ensure that the stallholder did not have to give away too much! The fairground firearm was usually a single-shot rifle firing a .22 Short, low-powered cartridge.

Pistol shooting gradually began to appeal to a wider group and its inclusion in the newly regenerated Olympic Games must have had some effect. There was even an acceptance that ladies might well take up the sport. In 1911, world-famous shooter Walter Winans wrote a book called *Shooting for Ladies*, which recommended that a lady would need a light weapon if she was to succeed. He suggested that a .22 would be the ideal round but warned against a self-loader: on no account get an automatic pistol – *the recoil is too great and they are very dangerous for a non-expert to handle*. He also detailed the French system of 'duel' shooting, which utilized a musical metronome for timing. However, the general tone of his book implies that shooting is not yet really an appropriate sport for ladies – one chapter even discusses appropriate ornaments and jewellery to be worn by the shooter. This attitude has long been discarded and competitive pistol shooting is seen as one of a very small number of sports in which men and women compete on equal terms.

Shooting clubs were quite common and sporting shooters tended to use .22 Long Rifle cartridge weapons, which are so much cheaper than full-bore ammunition. Most sporting pistols had long barrels, offering better accuracy, and most were single-shot. The introduction of the self-contained metal-cased cartridge was a further stimulus to competitive shooting, as loading the pistol

Correct Firing Position

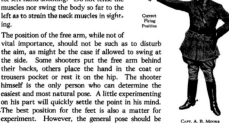

Shooters differ somewhat in their manner of standing, but in many respects there is a similarity in the "stance" of all good shooters. You should stand in a natural easy manner with right foot advanced (for right hand shooting) and your weight evenly distributed. Your body will face slightly to the left of the target, your right arm fully extended in a direct line toward the target. This position is, of course, reversed for left hand shooting. Do not tense the muscles nor swing the body so far to the left as to strain the neck muscles in sighting.

Correct
Firing
Position

The position of the free arm, while not of vital importance, should not be such as to disturb the aim, as might be the case if allowed to swing at the side. Some shooters put the free arm behind their backs, others place the hand in the coat or trousers pocket or rest it on the hip. The shooter himself is the only person who can determine the easiest and most natural pose. A little experimenting on his part will quickly settle the point in his mind. The best position for the feet is also a matter for experiment. However, the general pose should be much the same as that shown in the illustration.

Capt. A. B. Moore
New York State Troopers

Many people think that the expert shot holds his Pistol out with a steady hand, gets it right over the bull's-eye and pulls the trigger. He doesn't. There's no such thing as holding a pistol dead on a bull's-eye and shooting. The Arm is bound to sway to and fro, if ever so slightly. The only way to hit the center of the bull's-eye is to have the hammer fall just when the sight crosses the aiming point. The shooter cocks the hammer with his thumb, extends his arm, raising the Pistol to the line of sight, being sure that the piece is not canted to left or right but held perfectly level: then taking a long breath, takes aim at the lower edge of the bull's-eye, which is known as the "six o'clock hold" and begins gradually to press the trigger. It will be found that the Arm will weave back and forth and around the aiming point. The best shot in the world could not hit a bull's-eye if he had not developed a good "trigger squeeze." Be careful to squeeze the trigger slowly; do not jerk or twist it or you will get a wild shot. If you find that your shots are inclined to go to the left (with a right-handed shooter) or to the right (with a left-handed shooter) increase the thumb pressure on the side of the Revolver.

Page from a Colt publication of the 1930s, detailing the standard firing position of the time. It remained popular until after the Second World War, when the two-handed grip was widely adopted.

Contemporary picture of the famous marksman Walter Winans, author of many books on the art of shooting. He is demonstrating the standard target shooting position in use until the late twentieth century.

was obviously so much simpler. Many target pistols were of the break-barrel type where the barrel was unlocked and dropped down to allow the cartridge to be loaded directly into the breech.

All the main manufacturers produced single-shot target pistols and most went on to make self-loading target pistols. The improvement in design saw higher scores, which in turn led to all manner of refinements to push scores ever higher. Butts were shaped and moulded and could be personally tailored for each shooter. Barrels were fitted with counter-weights, and triggers were electronically controlled. Following these changes, there was a tightening of

competition rules in order to ensure some sort of equality among competitors. Sizes and weight of pistols were defined and special leagues were established. Soon, this style of target shooting escalated and special revolvers and pistols were produced.

Among the new series of competitions were various courses usually known as 'practical', in which the shooter had to follow a set route, dealing with certain set-up situations as they arose. Such shoots were seen by some as unacceptable since the vicarious task was to kill or wound the various figures and it could be argued that they were encouraging violence. Even man-shaped targets were condemned, although these had been in use for many years. Those who took part in the shoots generally failed to discern any problem and saw little difference between practical shooting and fencing, wrestling or boxing.

Beginning in the USA and spreading to Europe, the so-called practical shooting led to special training systems. The beginnings of these were seen during the First World War when shooters of renown such as Captains Tracy and Noel set up Trench Ranges, simulating the Western Front in order to train Army officers. For serious combat training this idea later took the form of rooms with set situations, into which the trainee was thrust with little or no preparation. The whole sequence was videoed so that the action could be analysed at leisure, and technique, reaction and accuracy could be discussed. In another set-up, the shooter walked a course dotted with remotely activated figures that popped up; the skill lay in deciding whether or not to shoot. It was a decision that would be taken in real life in a fraction of a second, with potentially fatal results if it was incorrect.

A third system involved a computerized video projected on a screen and depicted a scenario that called for a 'shoot/no shoot 'decision. When a shot was fired from the electronic pistol, the screen recorded where the shot would have hit. Again it could be stopped and the decision could be discussed for training purposes. There were variations of these and, in some, as the trainee improved, the speed of the video was slightly increased so that the pupil was always shooting against himself.

Today these practices have developed into games in which paintballs take the place of bullets, bursting on impact to mark the protective clothing worn by players. Even more sophisticated are the laser games, with competitors wearing electronically active clothing, pistols projecting lasers, and hits being registered by various means.

At one time there was a fashion for quick-draw competitions, sometimes involving drawing the gun from a holster and firing to burst a balloon. Special holsters, guns and electronic timers were developed and some incredibly fast times were recorded. However, the sequences were so unrealistic as to have no real significance. Fast draws have been featured in so many Western films that they have acquired a largely mythical importance. Some gifted shooters have performed properly controlled and recorded feats that are scarcely believable. *Life* magazine in November 1945 carried an article about an FBI agent named Bryce who could draw and fire his revolver in two-fifths of a second and had been in a number of practical situations in which his skill had been clearly demonstrated. Such skills are beyond the hopes of all but a tiny group.

Sights are obviously of great importance in aimed target shooting and various types have been developed in the hope of improved accuracy, with beads, dots, blades and crosses all having their advocates. The rear sight is usually an aperture, with some favouring a U shape and others a V shape. One newer system incorporates three fluorescent dots, one on either side of the rear aperture sight and the third on the blade of the front sight. In taking aim, the pistol is moved until the front dot sits neatly between the two back-sight dots.

A great breakthrough for improved accuracy was achieved with the discovery of lasers. The ability to generate a bright, narrow, constant-value, thin beam of light was obviously going to be adopted by shooters. Today, a small inexpensive laser can be mounted on the barrel of a firearm and, if correctly adjusted, can achieve near-perfect scores with little or no effort to aim by the shooter. All that is required is to keep the red dot on target – in certain fraught circumstances, a little red dot showing up on the clothing has been known to encourage the target to surrender without the need of further violence!

For those whose life may depend on a rapid, accurate shot, a new style of shooting – sense of direction or instinctive shooting – was evolved in the USA. Until the period following the First World War, the standard recommendation for target shooting was to stand sideways to the target, extend the arm with the pistol and rest the other arm on the waist or put the hand in a pocket, to avoid any unnecessary movement. Take aim, hold breath and squeeze, not pull, the trigger. Most training was done with this stance but a new system, of almost non-

aiming, was evolving. The butt of the pistol is gripped by the strong hand whilst the weak hand supports this grip. Both arms are extended and fairly rigid, although there are two schools of thought on this and the pistol is thrust forward as if it were the forefinger pointing at the target. The trigger finger is extended along the side of the frame but is not touching the trigger; this is a safety measure intended to prevent unintentional shots. Both eyes are open and the pistol is seen relative to the target. If the sight picture is satisfactory, then the finger slips to the trigger and, usually, two consecutive shots are fired. Until there is a strong likelihood of a shot being fired, the pistol is normally carried in a safe position.

As the result of various tragedies, pistol shooting is now virtually banned in Britain,

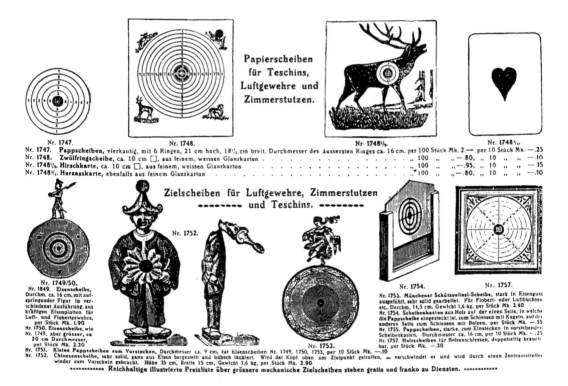

Page from a German trade catalogue of the early twentieth century showing the range of targets of paper, card and cast iron available to indoor shooters. The clown is of cast iron, with a pivoted head that falls back when struck.

with some very minor exceptions – rifle and carbine shoots are permitted. An exception is also made for black-powder shooting, which is still permitted, although under pretty severe restrictions. The 'logic' behind the exception is presumably the belief that no villain would consider carrying out a crime using a nineteenth-century revolver.

In order to meet the demands on the market for those wanting to go back in time and use percussion revolvers, the Italian manufacturers in particular seized the opportunity. Since there is always a risk in shooting an old pistol, collectors are loath to use a genuine Colt, valued at around a thousand pounds; they would much rather purchase a well-made modern replica at a fraction of the cost. Today, with the appropriate authority it is possible to buy replicas of most of the old cap and ball revolvers and pistols, and many of these are Italian-made. These replicas introduce an anomaly in the law: whilst a genuine 1851 Colt Navy Percussion revolver may be owned in the UK without any official permission, a modern-made replica requires a firearm certificate. There are also some restrictions on the possession of percussion caps and black powder. It is only prudent to check the situation with the local police.

Shooting black-powder replica revolvers is undoubtedly satisfying for many enthusiasts but it is a sport that needs to taken very seriously. Powder loads and bullets need to be correctly measured, otherwise accidents are likely. Since the modern powders are not the same as the original gunpowder, it is important to measure them very carefully and the various brand manufacturers usually offer advice and recommendations. It is also a rather dirty sport, since fouling of the pistol is a problem and the revolvers need to be thoroughly cleaned after each use.

There is one other alternative type of competition shooting and that involves using the various air weapons.

Following the First World War, there was a period of relative quiet in the development of handguns but then came a gradual increase in pistol shooting and the number of clubs grew. With this growth came an interest in ballistics, techniques and competition shooting, which probably reached a peak in the 1980s. In Britain, annual shoots at Bisley attracted entrants from all over the country and indeed the world. With this interest there was a surge in experimentation in pistols and ammunition design, with unusual rounds being tested, new-style competitions and an increase in black-powder shooting. In Britain there was a reasonable relationship between shooters and the police, in their capacity as licensing officers, but these relations were much improved when the supervision of private ownership of firearms was made the responsibility of specialist firearms teams. These were manned by officers who had experience of the subject and dealt with all issues relative to certificates, clubs and security.

Unfortunately, a number of tragic events changed the situation dramatically and led to a strong, sometimes ill-informed, anti-shooting movement in Britain. It was supported by a vociferous media, and in the end the Government decided to bow to public demand and take drastic action. The outcome was, in effect, an almost total ban on pistol shooting. Today, the pistol shooter has a limited number of options: non-competitive shooting under severe limitations, black-powder shooting or air weapons. There is now a growing possibility of air weapons being banned or severely restricted, and Scotland is taking a lead in this.

CHAPTER 10

Air Pistols

~ ~

Missiles may be projected manually, by the elasticity of various materials, by chemical reaction or by compressed air. Although some miniature crossbows were made, including some very small models described as 'assassin's weapons', as far as the handgun was concerned there were really only two practical alternatives: gunpowder and compressed air. Elastic and electricity were experimented with but no really practical solutions were achieved. The use of compressed air is an ancient method and many primitive cultures, apparently in no way associated, independently evolved blowpipe weapons. Warriors or hunters perfected a technique of inhaling a good lung-full of air and expelling it in short, sharp puffs, sending darts at a fair speed over a comparatively short distance.

Although firm evidence is lacking, there is some reason to believe that there were shooters experimenting with the idea of air guns and pistols as early as the late fourteenth century. Da Vinci makes passing reference to them in his notes but the majority of these early references seem to apply to long guns or air rifles. In order to function, an air weapon obviously needs a supply of compressed air and this was usually obtained from a strong metal reservoir that was filled by some form of pump. The earliest known surviving air guns date from 1644 and have cylindrical reservoirs that encircle the barrel, whilst the earliest air pistols can be dated a little later, to the 1650s[40].

In shooting an air weapon, pressing the trigger normally operates an air lock, which allows sufficient air for one shot to escape into the barrel and expel the missile. This is an improvement on the very earliest air weapons, which allowed all the air in the reservoir to escape in one burst. Later in the seventeenth century the type of reservoir was changed to a globe and was generally fitted either on top or beneath the barrel, and this style remained in general use. Fitted with an appropriate valve release, several of these reservoirs could be filled and carried as spares. Another early type of air weapon used a butt-mounted bellows system and in the eighteenth century some air weapons had a hollow butt made to serve as the reservoir.

The use of air weapons for target shooting seems to have been an eighteenth-century development but the majority of air weapons of the period were long arms rather than pistols. There was even an attempt to employ an air-powered rifle in the Austrian Army in 1779, using a rifle designed by an Italian,

Page from the catalogue of an early twentieth-century toy shop, showing the variety of projectiles on offer for air weapons. Darts were generally unpopular and tended to be too inaccurate for serious users.

Girandoni. It was a repeating model with a magazine holding twenty rounds and the reservoir was powerful enough to discharge forty shots. It was in service for some years but proved difficult to maintain and demanded prolonged pumping to fill a reservoir.

There is another way, apart from a reservoir, in which bursts of compressed air can be generated, and that involves the use of a spring-operated plunger. This became the most commonly used system on air pistols from the later part of the nineteenth century. The usual method was to compress a strong, spring-operated plunger, which was enclosed inside a cylinder, and then release it so that it slammed forward, compressing the enclosed

air. This could be released in one spurt by means of a one-way valve and diverted into the barrel of the pistol. The compression of the plunger is usually achieved by cocking a lever or, later, on many pistols, by the break-barrel system, whereby the barrel is depressed for loading and in so doing, at the same time, the spring plunger is compressed.

The advent of the plunger system simplified the design of air pistols and their popularity soared. They were now seen as a serious form of a shooting sport. Range was limited but within certain limits they were extremely accurate. Official competitions were established and the number of clubs increased. As interest developed, so did demand for better air pistols and most prime gunmakers soon moved into the field.

One name that was to figure prominently in the development of air pistols and more or less dominate the British market was that of Webley. Already firmly established in the revolver and self-loading pistol-manufacturing industry, the firm took the first steps in 1910. One of its directors, William Whiting, acquired a patent for an air pistol that physically rather resembled the Webley self-loading pistol. Some work was carried out on the design but it was evidently decided that it was not going to be a great success and the project was abandoned.

The Great War then dominated the firearms industry for several years and air pistols were rather neglected. However, in 1917 a Birmingham engineer filed a patent for an air pistol on which the barrel, mounted above the air cylinder body of the pistol, became the cocking lever. This idea was improved by another patent in 1922 and in 1924 a further patent on the system was approved, and the system was to become a feature of Webley air pistols for many years[41].

Webley's Mark I air pistol went into production in 1924 and continued until 1935, with some 50,000 being made. It was not cheap, selling at thirty shillings, but it was immensely popular. An even more expensive, slightly better-quality version, the Mark II Target Model, was introduced in 1915 and ran on until 1930. A smaller, less powerful version intended for the younger shooter was marketed as the Webley Junior, and remained in production from 1929 to 1938, to be followed by a rather superior model the Webley Senior, made from 1930 to 1935.

Different versions of the time-honoured pistol were offered and the final version, the Webley Premier, came on the market in 1964, with production ending in 1975. There were various other models with minor variations and in the 1970s the traditional shape changed. New models such as the Hurricane, the Typhoon and the Tempest were offered, with variously shaped butts but still utilizing the lever-barrel system.

Webley pistols, in fact, the majority of air pistols, were produced in two calibres – .177 and .22 – and shooters were strongly urged to use only Webley lead pellets, which were carefully shaped with a waisted outline. The barrels were rifled and with the correct pellets the pistols were agreeably accurate and began to be used in serious competitions. Darts with flared tails were also used, but these tended to be disapproved of by serious air-pistol shooters. Webley models were sold in cardboard boxes or, more expensively, in small leather cases containing the pistol and other accessories. Muzzle velocities were mostly around 200 to 400 fps.

Although Webley may have dominated the air-pistol market, there were other British makers, including B.S.A. and Accles & Shelvoke. The German maker Haenel produced a well-made series during the 1930s, while makers in countries such as Spain and Japan also entered the field. In the USA, the most prolific supplier of air weapons was Henry Marcus Quackenbush from New York, who first patented a pistol in 1871. He became so successful that he virtually dominated the market and in 1890 spread his influence to Europe, licensing the German Diana Company. Also in USA was the Daisy Manufacturing Company, which in the late nineteenth century flooded the market with cheap air pistols and guns[42] and is still in production.

CO_2 Pistols

As long ago as the late nineteenth century there was some work on using liquefied carbon dioxide gas to power pistols. The work was, in a way, a reversion to the old reservoir air weapons. Small metal cylinders filled with liquid carbon dioxide are usually inserted into a section of the butt, with a trigger operating a mechanism that allows a small amount of the liquid to convert to gas and expel a pellet from the barrel.

Whilst most conventional air pistols are recognizable as such, CO_2 pistols are more 'look-alike' copies of cartridge firearms. Most have a break-open breech action into which fits a circular magazine holding the pellets. There are revolver and semi-automatic look-alikes from Colt, Smith & Wesson and Glock, together with many accessories, such as small pistol-mounted lasers, special targets and holsters.

As with most air weapons, the active range of CO_2 pistols is not very great but at shorter ranges they are quite accurate and do give an impression of what firing a real pistol feels like.

Different Types of Air Weapon

Soft air pistols are mostly single-shot, low-powered pistols activated by some form of spring action. BB pistols are essentially air pistols that fire small BB metal balls.

The self-contained gas cartridge air weapon, which had a comparatively short spell of life, was in effect a 'do-it-yourself' pressured air cylinder system. The case was filled with compressed gas and a bullet was inserted into it. A number of incidents persuaded the authorities that these weapons were too powerful and too easy to convert to more nefarious purposes, and they were banned under Section 39 of the Anti-social Behaviour Act of 2003. Owners were obliged to surrender them or were permitted to keep them only by obtaining a Firearm Certificate with all its incumbent security requirements. Most people felt that the trouble was not worth it and surrendered their guns, while some simply forgot that they had ever had one – in this way, a considerable number of guns and their owners were criminalized.

Air Weapons and the Law

At one time in Britain air weapons were not subject to any control and could be purchased and sold without restriction. The one exception in Britain was based on the power of the air weapon: if the pressure generated exceeded a certain figure – six foot pounds for pistols and twelve foot pounds for others – then a licence was required. In 2006 a new Act made it illegal for a person under the age of eighteen to buy or be sold an air weapon and obliged the dealer to keep details of any transactions. At this time (August 2010) there are plans in hand to modify the law on the possession of air weapons and in Scotland there is talk of banning them completely.

In Britain the law respecting air pistols was made much tighter by the Violent Crime Reduction Act of 2007. It is only possible for people of a certain age to own or use an air pistol and there are tough restrictions on where and how it may be used or carried. It is an offence for someone under the age of fourteen to own an air pistol. An air pistol may be owned between the ages of fourteen and eighteen, but there are restrictions on its use and carrying. Owners of some air weapons such as soft air and CO_2 models could also be subject to legislation dealing with imitation firearms, although this is a slightly grey area. Clearly, it is advisable always to seek the advice of professional bodies or the local police before becoming involved with such items.

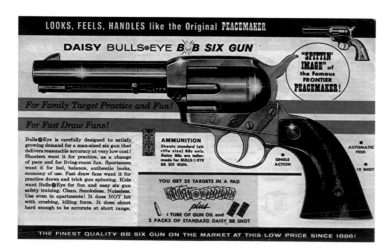

Daisy advert showing a very good replica Colt Single-Action Army revolver. The BB shots were loaded via a modified ejector-rod fitting.

CHAPTER 11

Miniatures and Toys

∾ ∽

The use of miniature versions of weapons for training or simply for children's play can be traced back for centuries. Swords, toy knights and castles from the Middle Ages are familiar in the toy box and with the emergence of firearms it was inevitable that toy or miniature guns would be made. Indeed, they are still made, despite the protests of some. Tiny weapons were made as charms or jewellery and by the sixteenth century many were of top quality. One such wheel-lock piece in London's Victoria and Albert Museum dates to this period and is of enamelled gold and houses three, hinged toilet accessories. During the sixteenth century, fully functioning miniature-style guns were made. A few have survived, mostly of cast bronze and with the barrels and touch holes drilled, indicating that they were indeed intended to be fired. The majority are in the shape of matchlock muskets and were fitted with a small operating lock mechanism, which is now normally missing

In the early seventeenth century, Nuremberg in Germany seems to have become a centre for the production of small wheel-lock pistols, and a number that have survived bear the name or mark of two

brothers, Michel and Conradt Mann. These miniatures were fitted with fully functional wheel-locks and on some of the surviving examples there are clear indications that they were fired. The pistols are of gilt brass and blued steel and well made, although the decoration tends to be less well done.

Miniature flintlock pistols are rare and it may be that, by the seventeenth and eighteenth centuries, pistols were no longer quite so unusual and there was less demand for them as charms or jewellery. The advent of the percussion lock, with its much simpler construction, stimulated the novelty market and examples of percussion and pinfire miniature pistols are not rare. Some were made as cufflinks or watch keys. The French gun trade of the period was noted for the decorative qualities of its work and some top-quality examples incorporated ivory and precious metals. After a while, demand fell away and the supply of miniatures diminished.

During the mid-twentieth century, there was a resurgence in model-making and today some superb miniature firearms are produced by dedicated craftsmen who copy, in exact detail, percussion revolvers, pistols and other weapons to an exceptionally high

Children of all ages and in all ages have played with toy guns and this example dates from either the late sixteenth century or the early seventeenth century. It is four and a half inches long and is a copy of a matchlock. (Thomas Del Mar Ltd)

standard. These are not made as jewellery or toys but simply as superb examples of the modeller's craft. Needless to say, production is very limited and these little treasures command high prices on the rare occasions when they come on to the market. There is a parallel with the superb miniature matchlock guns made by the Japanese, which are perfect in every detail.

During the nineteenth century, the culture of Empire, the West and military glory ensured that large numbers of toy guns and cannons were produced. In the early part of the century, scaled-down examples of sporting guns were often made for the boy of a household, but pistols are far less common. The arrival of the cinema at the end of the century and its cowboy films stimulated a number of toy-makers to enter the market of toy guns, with the Colt Single-Action Army Model taking the lead, and versions using rolls of caps becoming common. Other versions offered plastic cartridge cases, which could be fitted with a cap and loaded into the cylinder. 'Spud guns' were popular and were a cheap substitute air pistol. The barrel terminated in a short cylinder, which was pressed into a potato to acquire a plug, which was then ejected by a simple spring plunger.

Next on the market were replicas that were metal copies of genuine pistols but were totally non-operational. In order to prevent misuse, they were fashioned of a metal that was not strong enough to withstand the shock of a fired cartridge, should one be loaded into a modified item. A replica could often be such a close copy of a genuine weapon that it was impossible to identify it except by picking it up. The next step was to produce some that fired blank cartridges; this may have delighted some re-enactors, but it could, and did, cause alarm to members of the police and the public.

Steps were taken to limit the misuse of replicas and legislation was introduced that was concerned with 'realistic imitation firearms'. As a consequence, examples of handguns pre-dating 1870 are available to anybody over the age of 18, but replicas of a pistol of a post-1870 date are restricted to certain groups and are not generally available[43].

Matters were made even more complex in 1988 when the Home Office allowed firearms to be deactivated and made incapable of firing any shot, which meant that they were no longer firearms as defined in the 1968 Firearms Act: a 'lethal barrelled weapon of any description from which any shot, bullet or other missile can be discharged'. All types of firearms – pistols, self-loaders, revolvers, rifle sub-machine guns, rocket launchers and heavy machine guns – were deactivated. Each was stamped by a special mark and given a deactivation certificate.

A page from a 2008 World Wide Arms catalogue, listing some of the deactivated firearms available on the open market. These included machine guns, assault rifles and self-loaders.

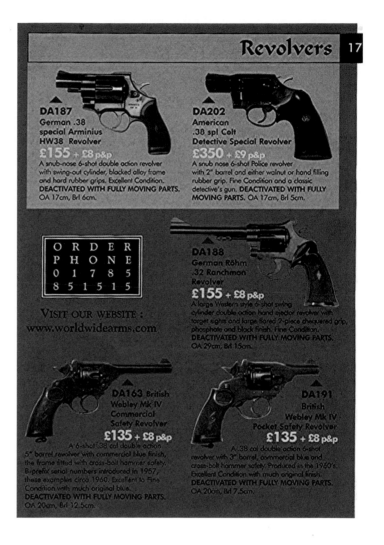

Before long, mechanically competent villains were beginning to devise ways to reactivate these firearms, but the scale was fairly small. In the four years between 2003 and 2007 the Forensic Science Service was asked by the police to examine 246 deactivated or reactivated firearms, and there were only three recorded offences involving reactivated firearms. Deactivation was made more total in 1995 but the regulations were still sometimes circumvented.

At the moment, 'de-acts' are still quite legally on sale but there is a threat that they will be banned and a Home Office Consultation has been launched, seeking opinions. If a ban is introduced it will be a very difficult one to impose, since over many years the number of deactivated firearms sold has been very high. It is not clear how such arms would be dealt with, but one likely consequence would be to criminalize many honest citizens who, either by design or by accident, end up retaining a banned item. Indeed, this is exactly what happened when SAC weapons were banned.

CHAPTER 12

The Handgun and the Law

From the time of its invention the firearm has been subject to some kind of restrictive legislation in most countries and this applies especially to the handgun. The ability to carry a handgun out of sight or disguised in some way has always made it appear more menacing than a rifle or shotgun, although each weapon could achieve the same result.

Until the fourteenth century there were few controls in Britain relating to the possession of weapons. In reality, the ordinary people were expected to arm themselves in defence of the country. By law, the man of a household was supposed to own a longbow and arrows. Knives were a part of everyday costume and the situation during periods such as the Wars of the Roses, when groups of armed men roamed the countryside, must inevitably have ensured that all manner of weapons were freely available. In 1388 an Act of Parliament[44] included a clause that represented a serious attempt to control weapons, but was a class-based restriction:

no servant of husbandry or labourer or servant nor any victualler shall from henceforth bear any buckler [shield], sword nor dagger upon forfeiture of the same but in the time of war for the defence of the realm.

It is difficult to know how effective this ban was. Although such laws were proclaimed publicly in towns and larger villages, it is likely that much of the population would have been ignorant of the ban. It is also interesting to note that the law does not specifically ban possession of the weapon mentioned, only the 'bearing' of it. A further attempt to reduce the number of weapons in circulation was made by Henry VII a century later, in 1487, when he forbade anyone, except 'officers of the law', to carry any weapon in any town or city.

With the sixteenth century came the firearm and it was not well received by Henry VIII (1509–1547), who complained that its use was interfering with the obligatory longbow practice. In 1514/1515 he introduced an Act intended to stop men leaving the longbow and using *crossbowes and handgonnes*[45]. Once again it was a class-based law and only individuals who owned land or had an income of more than 300 marks a year would be permitted to hold either weapon. This was a substantial sum and would have excluded the majority of common folk (although is

Ireland's troubled history led, in 1848, to a law requiring all weapons to be recorded and marked with the county location. This licence allows the owner to have one double-barrelled shotgun, four pistols (possibly two pairs), and a sword.

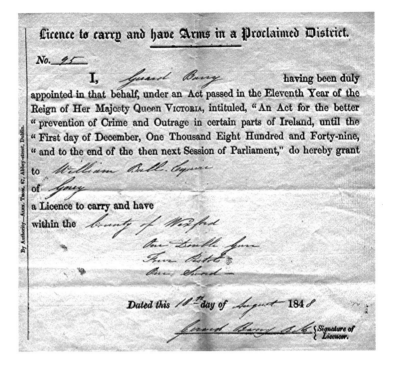

Licence to carry and have Arms in a Proclaimed District.

No. *95*

I, *Gerard Barry* having been duly appointed in that behalf, under an Act passed in the Eleventh Year of the Reign of Her Majesty Queen VICTORIA, intituled, "An Act for the better "prevention of Crime and Outrage in certain parts of Ireland, until the "First day of December, One Thousand Eight Hundred and Forty-nine, "and to the end of the then next Session of Parliament," do hereby grant to *William Bull, Esqre* of *Gorey* a Licence to carry and have within the *county of Wexford*

One Double Gun
Four Pistols
One Sword —

Dated this *10th* day of *August* 184*8*

Gerard Barry {*Signature of Licencer.*}

By Authority—ALEX. THOM, 87, Abbey-street, Dublin.

unlikely that many would have wanted to own a handgun or would have been able to afford one). The income limit was reduced in 1526 to £100 and officials were urged to ensure that the regulation was enforced[46]. Two years later, in 1528, Henry went all the way and banned anybody from having a crossbow or handgun in their house[47]. Law officers were given permission to enter premises and search for any suspected weapon and any gun that was found was to be broken up.

It would seem that eventually Henry realized that he could not halt the incursion of the handgun and in 1533/1534 he cancelled all licences and all relevant Acts were repealed[48]. He tried a new start by bringing back the £100 property clause but at the same time exempted certain people from its restrictions. In 1537 another Act[49] introduced the idea of a *placard*, a document, being issued to all who had permission to hold a handgun or crossbow. In effect, this was the first firearm certificate or licence.

The popularity of the handgun is evident in the next legislation, which complained that people had been shooting off their handguns in inappropriate places and the people were in danger of being hit by their 'pellets'. In future, shooting would be permitted only at properly defined butts. In 1541/1542 a new word appeared in the Act and Clause 2 referred to *little short handguns and little hagbuts*[50]. It is unclear as to what differences, if any, there were between the two weapons, although length seems to be a factor. It deplores the fact that people were going about armed with these weapons, spanned and ready to fire, and it also forbids the ownership of a handgun, *being other than suche as shallbe in the stock and gone of the length of one hole Yarde or any hagbut or demyhawke other than suche as shallbe in the stock and gune of the length of three quarters of one*

GUN LICENCE 10s.   CE 02518

† _Mr V. Y. M. Christian_

of _26 Becking Rd._ in the

Civil Parish or Township of _Putney_ within the

Administrative County* _London_ is hereby authorized to CARRY AND USE A GUN in Great Britain and Northern Ireland from the date hereof until and including the _Thirty-first_ day of _July_ next following; the sum of TEN SHILLINGS having been paid for this Licence.

Granted at _Putney Bo H_ at _4_ hours _40_ minutes _P.m._

o'clock this _9th_ day of _August_ 19 _39_ by _6 Y_

NOTICE.—1. This Licence will not authorize any person to purchase, have in his possession, use, or carry any firearms (as defined in the Firearms Act, 1920) in respect of which it is necessary to hold a firearm Certificate granted under the said Act unless he holds such Certificate.

2. Any permanent change of address should be notified to the County or County Borough Council in whose area this Licence was issued.

† Insert full Christian Name and Surname.
* If the residence is within a County Borough, strike out "Administrative" and insert "Borough" after "County".

This British 1930s gun licence was obtainable at any Post Office, price ten shillings (50p). It made a clear distinction between a gun – generally understood at the time to mean a shotgun – and a firearm, in other words, a pistol or rifle, as defined by the Firearms Act.

Yarde. By definition, a yard was 36 inches or 91.5cm and three-quarters would be 68.6cm, and these measures hardly match the size of the usual wheel-lock pistol. The lengths relate more to short muskets or carbines, or possibly to the petronel, a form of long pistol with a musket-type butt that was held against the chest rather than the shoulder when firing. It was apparently developed in France in the mid-sixteenth century but is thought to have reached England later some time after this Act.

By 1544, Henry apparently gave up his opposition to firearms, and accepted that they were here to stay. In order to ensure that some of his subjects at least were well versed in the use of firearms in the defence of the kingdom, he relaxed the restrictions and allowed anybody over the age of sixteen to shoot a handgun. It was forbidden to shoot at birds or to shoot anywhere near the king's residence, but in fact there seems to have been an outburst of rather thoughtless shooting. In 1548, an Act of Edward VI[51] reiterated the point that the aim of the rules was to get men used to guns so that they were better able to defend the kingdom. Instead, gun owners were blasting away with such abandon that buildings were being damaged and too many birds were being shot. In future, shooting would be allowed only at the butts. It is worth noting that, under Henry's laws, a man was allowed not only to own a handgun or cross-bow, but might also legally use it in defence of the home.

In 1549 there was some national unrest and the king forbade anybody to carry a weapon within the royal courts, or within a three-mile radius of them; the terms 'dag' and 'short handguns' are used in the legislation. With the accession of Mary (1553–1558), the weapons law was much more concerned with swords and daggers, and there were statutory regulations on the length of rapiers. One big change during her reign was the repeal of a very ancient regulation, the Assize of Arms, which defined each man's obligatory possession of weapons for the defence of the realm. It had been in force with various amendments from 1181, but was now replaced. A new Act set out the full details of what armour and weapons each class of gentlemen must possess. Among the items listed are haquebuts and matchlock muskets, but there are no references to handguns. The Act was later repealed in 1562 by Elizabeth I (1558–1603).

In 1559, Queen Elizabeth proclaimed that all regulations introduced by her father concerning the owning and shooting of handguns were still valid and emphasized that, as the number of robberies and murders was increasing, officials were to enforce the restrictions. The situation changed little and only two years later, in 1561, the Queen issued another condemnation of those people who were firing handguns in churchyards.

Despite all these proclamations and prohibitions, it seems that matters did not improve and there was yet another order in 1575, stating that anybody merely holding a handgun was to be taken before a magistrate. Men of quality were still permitted to ride with handguns clearly visible in their holsters, as were their servants, as long as they had a letter of authorization. This edict seems to have been about as ineffective as all the others and in 1579 another ruling was published that was even stricter than previous ones. It once again forbade the shooting of guns anywhere except at authorized butts. In the past, those accused of shooting elsewhere had claimed that they were merely practising for their duty as defenders of the realm, but in future this excuse was not going to be accepted. This particular proclamation went further than previous ones, giving officials the authority to search people's houses when looking for guns, although compensation was promised for any weapon seized. Not only was the carrying of guns prohibited, but also the making, mending and importing of them. It is also worth noting that mention is made in the Act of the ability to carry a dag in a pocket or elsewhere on the body.

The legal situation remained largely unchanged, either because the authorities accepted defeat or the matter was just allowed to drop. In 1594, an order demanded that officials should submit a written report on their efforts to enforce the controls on firearms. In 1600 another proclamation returned to the subject of firearms but this time restrictions were extended to cover 'birding and fowling pieces'. These weapons were included not through a fear of crime or violence, but because the 'common and ordinary people' were shooting too many birds, and that was a privilege reserved for the rich. Some surviving contemporary crime records of the period, such as those for the county of Essex, certainly indicate that, from 1570, poaching with guns did increase.

The death of Elizabeth in 1603 left Britain with a simmering religious problem and a new King, James VI of Scotland and I of England (1603–1625). The situation was further exacerbated by events such as the Gunpowder Plot of 1605. James was perhaps not the best of rulers, but he was a keen hunter and some of his early legislation related to firearms and their use in hunting. His legislation also repealed the various statutes requiring men to maintain stocks of arms and armour as part of their duties. Like his predecessors, James issued a proclamation in 1612/13 forbidding the use of 'dags', and specifying a minimum length of twelve inches (30.5cm). A very similar statement in 1616 mentions a number of weapons – *steelet or pocket dagger, pocket dagge or pistol* – and orders that they be surrendered and destroyed.

In 1625, Charles I (1625–1649) was crowned and began a reign plagued with religious conflict and Civil Wars. The political differences between King and Parliament acquired a religious flavour as the Scots and Irish became involved and old anti-Catholic prejudices or fear came to the fore. In November 1640, the King ordered all Catholics to go home and surrender their weapons, allowing them none the less to keep enough for self-defence. Once war broke out it was a matter of seeking out weapons rather than controlling them.

During the wars the New Model Army that had been created by Parliament became, in effect, a standing (in other words, permanent) army. This was something that the British people had always disliked and feared, so there was much opposition. When the wars ended, in 1649, England became a Republic and the new Commonwealth set up a control system of public order in 1655 known as 'the Major-Generals'. Each of these twelve commanders was responsible for governing a large area of the country and given the authority to raise troops. They collected taxes and were obliged to enforce new laws, including unpopular Puritan regulations such as closing ale houses and curbing popular entertainments. The country was effectively under military law. The much-hated system remained in force for just over a year and was disbanded in 1657.

Parliament recognized that there was a need for a corps of troops that would create a reasonably efficient force in times of war, and turned to the concept of the old locally trained bands, first created in 1573. This corps of troops became known as the Militia, and thus began a system that was to become a familiar part of life, with men being liable, subject to conditions, to serve when ordered to do so. When Parliament sought to create a part-time armed force to call upon when necessary, the regular army opposed it. In 1648, however, the force was officially established by Parliament. In 1650, Parliament stated that for the next year, if required, every citizen of London might be called upon to acquire a horse and arms and had to be ready to serve outside the London area. When the Royalists returned to power in 1660, they supported continuing the Militia and in 1662 it was confirmed as a lawful body. The Militia became something of a political football and, on the rare occasion when it was called to action, its performance was hardly impressive. One effect of setting up the Militia was to ensure that there were now stores of weapons dotted around the country, and some groups expressed fear at the possibility of armed rebellion. Generally, Militia arms were stored in armouries with some sort of supervision.

The next important development in firearms control was the Bill of Rights of 1688, which was the result of the ignominious dethroning of the Catholic King James II. It formally set down the rights of subjects that were to be established under the new King, William III (1689–1702), and opened with a list of the old King's misdemeanours, numbering thirteen in all. One of these was the claim that James had disarmed Protestants whilst Papists, or Catholics, were 'both armed and employed contrary to law'. This claim is a little difficult to square with the serious restrictions placed on the Irish when, in 1673, there was a blanket prohibition on Papists owning virtually any edged weapon or firearm.

The Bill of Rights sought to provide an answer to the charge that James had disarmed Protestants, by allowing that, in future, *the subjects which are Protestants may have arms for their defence suitable to their conditions and as allowed by law.* Clearly, there is still a class distinction, reflected in the phrase 'suitable to their conditions'. However, it did give subjects the clear legal right to arm themselves and is used by many US citizens to support the claim that they are by law allowed to own firearms. The right to own arms was tacitly if not openly recognized in Britain until 1946, when for the first time it was stated in Parliament that the right of citizens to possess arms for self-protection was no longer acceptable in law.

During the late eighteenth and early nineteenth centuries, periods of industrial and social unrest led the Government to become seriously concerned about the possibility of armed rebellion. It was felt that action had to be taken and the next big step was the introduction of the 1820 Seizure of Arms Act. It was accepted in principle that a citizen might legally own arms, but it was felt that in certain circumstances it was permissible to withhold the right, especially in unsettled areas of the country. The Act gave magistrates the power to issue a warrant to search premises for any weapons, including a pistol or gun, which they considered to be 'for any purpose [that was] dangerous to the peace'. The new powers were basically limited to areas in the north of England such as Yorkshire, where industrial unrest was widespread. This Act was the only one whose specific purpose was to control or limit the private ownership of firearms, although the definition 'dangerous

to the peace' was open to all sorts of interpretation. Firearms are mentioned in several other Acts of this period but the legislation primarily dealt with their use in crime rather than with ownership. There were several attempts by individuals to introduce restrictions on the owning and carrying of firearms, but they did not get much beyond their initial publication. Presumably, if the politicians had seen the issue as more important, matters might have been pushed further forward.

Civil unrest in Ireland and general lawlessness resulted in another Act dealing with Irish firearms being introduced in 1843. This required every firearm in Ireland to be registered with the police, and to be stamped with an identifying number and letter, showing where it had been registered. A special licence was then issued to the owner.

England has never been seen as a nation particularly involved in firearms but, around the middle of the nineteenth century, it seems that firearms, especially revolvers, were quite common and regularly carried by many people. Whether the Great Exhibition of 1851, with its numerous and impressive displays of guns, or the publicity evoked by Colt's aggressive marketing had any bearing is unclear.

The newspaper columns of the period carried many paragraphs about the firearms in the Exhibition, as well as letters urging greater use of revolvers by the British Army. Newspapers such as *The Times* carried adverts for all manner of firearms, mixed in with those offering conventional household items, suggesting that firearms were not considered to be in any way special. The letters page in *The Times* confirms this. In August 1865, one irate member of the public, deploring the ineffective Metropolitan Police, wrote that he and his brother slept with loaded revolvers by their beds. The writer

During the various British amnesties, every effort was made to encourage the surrender of illegal or surplus firearms. Sadly, many continued to be held illegally and the fall in gun crime proved to be less significant than had been hoped for.

also vowed that they would no hesitation in shooting dead any intruder found on their premises.

In January 1885, *The Times* published several letters relating to firearms and their control. One writer claimed that the French citizens were far more addicted than the English to habitually carrying a pistol. On 13 January 1885, another writer responded, saying that carrying a revolver in England was more common than was generally thought. He went on to relate how, in a Yorkshire hotel, all eight to ten persons present were able to produce such an item. This provoked another writer to claim that he had for years been pressing for a law to regulate the carrying of revolvers: in his view, 'the possession of a revolver is one thing, carrying it about is another'. Another writer replying pointed out that an Act of 1883 already covered this matter. The legislation to which he referred was the Gun Licence Act of 1870, which, as a means of controlling or restricting ownership, was meaningless. It stated that any person carrying a gun anywhere apart from within a house and its surroundings should have a licence, price ten shillings and obtained from any Post Office.

One interesting diversion generated by this discussion on firearms law was an official enquiry sent to various nations, seeking information on their current firearms laws. It was no surprise to discover that the laws varied greatly in detail, as did efforts to enforce them. During the later part of the century there were several attempts to introduce new laws for Great Britain, but they all failed, through lack of support, to pass through Parliament. It was not until 1903 that new legislation was finally approved, with the Pistol Act, a version of an earlier Act that had been rejected by Parliament.

The Act did introduce restrictions on the acquisition and possession of firearms, but

Following the First World War, men who had served in the Army were allowed, under the Firearms Act, to keep their revolvers as a souvenir. The revolver had to be duly registered with the police and the owner was not allowed to use or carry it and was forbidden to hold any ammunition.

they were fairly minimal. A firearm could be purchased on production of a game licence, which was available over the counter from the Post Office. The stated objective of the legislation was to prevent the sale of firearms to children and drunken persons.

Further developments in legislation were delayed by the First World War and there was no further legal activity until 1920, when a far more comprehensive set of regulations was adopted[52]. It may be that fear of armed revolution in Britain was stirred by events in Russia and this may have played some part in framing the legislation. During its passage through Parliament there were a number of amendments, but the next big step was the setting up of a committee under Sir Archibald Bodkin, to consider the concept and detail of firearms control. As a result of its lengthy deliberations, a Firearms (Amendment) Act was approved in 1936 and the final outcome was the Firearms Act 1937.

The Second World War was responsible for a tremendous increase in the number of legal and illegal firearms in the country. The issue of weapons to the Home Guard and other bodies had often been hurried and rather haphazard, and many had not been surrendered after the war. Returning troops had also brought back trophies and souvenirs, and there was some concern about the number of guns held in households across Britain. In 1946, an amnesty was declared – for a period of six weeks, firearms could be surrendered with the promise that no action would be taken against the donor. A staggering 75,000 firearms of all types, including shotguns, rifles, pistols, machine guns, rocket launchers and air weapons, were handed in. There was further control legislation in 1965 and 1967, but much of it was devoted to shotgun control.

As far as handguns were concerned, the legislation ruled that someone who wanted to acquire and use a pistol needed to have a certificate issued, and these were subject to certain general rules. In order to obtain such a certificate, an application was made to the local police, who carried out enquiries about the applicant and his or her reason for claiming ownership. Enquiries were often cursory, and sometimes officious, but the important point was that the applicant had to be able to justify owning a pistol. Target shooting was generally accepted as a good reason. The certificate imposed certain conditions on the storage and use of the pistol and herein lay one of the problems: the conditions were set by the local police chief and could vary from place to place. One bone of contention was that the local chief police officer imposed the restriction and in the event of a dispute there was no right of appeal except by going to law.

The certificate was normally valid for three years, later extended to five, on payment of a fee. The conditions under which a certificate was issued were strict and it could be revoked by the police at any time if it was felt that the owner was no longer considered safe. Some of the conditions were rather tricky and there were cases in which a certificate holder was prosecuted for breach of security simply because the keys to the firearm locker were left with a person who was perfectly trustworthy, but who was none the less not a certificate holder. In general, the system worked reasonably well, although there were a few problems, sometimes caused by over-officious or firearms-ignorant police and sometimes by over-zealous or prickly shooters.

Various subsequent Firearms Acts were aimed at specific problems, but the broad outline remained in force. A new Act in 1969 was intended to clear up anomalies and clarify definitions, with firearms being split into three classes: Section One included pistols but excluded air weapons unless they were over a certain power. One thorny question was the definition of the term 'antique', since antique firearms kept as a 'curiosity or ornament' were excluded, and this was a phrase that had been used in some of the earliest Acts. The official understanding of what was an antique was vague and there were a number of cases in which police and owner failed to agree on the status of a particular gun. Such cases would be referred to the law, with differing verdicts from different courts. The final position was basically that each case had to be decided individually. The situation is similar today although there are moves to establish a cut-off date at which a firearm officially becomes 'antique'. Section Two of the Act covered shotguns, with slightly less rigorous conditions, while Section Three prohibited certain weapons that could be owned only with special Home Office permission.

Until 1973, matters were reasonably stable but then the Government issued a Green Paper – a document setting out a proposal – which outlined more extreme control of firearms that was, for shooters, very depressing. United and determined opposition led to its demise and the *status quo* was left more or less intact. This state of affairs was shattered in 1987 when a shooter in possession of legally owned firearms went on a killing spree in a small English town. This horrific act confirmed all the worst fears of those who were anti-firearms and led to renewed demands for measures to restrict legal ownership. There were changes in the law but basically pistols were left untouched. This tragedy was followed by another amnesty, which attracted a large number of weapons. These were screened to ensure that items of particular interest were rescued from destruction and handed over to approved museums.

In 1991, the Home Office instituted a study to consider the potential cost of setting up a nationwide Firearms Control Board, as compared with the cost of the current system. The idea had its supporters as well as its opponents, but in the end it sank without trace. The growth of the European Union had led to a desire for a more common approach to firearms control with certain basic conditions. Each country had the right to amend its own rules but only in terms of increased control, with the European rules as the basic standard. Britain officially entered the scheme in 1992. This process is ongoing and in general leads to a much more restrictive control on the private ownership of firearms.

In 1996 there was an almost unimaginable tragedy in Scotland, when a man in legal possession of a number of guns entered a school and shot and killed sixteen children and one of their teachers. In a terrible state of shock, the public called for immediate action. The Government set up an inquiry under the distinguished judge, Lord Cullen, who published his report later in the year. The Government's response was a total ban on the private possession of handguns except .22 pistols, which was later extended to all calibres. Legal owners of pistols were obliged to surrender them; they were paid compensation, but still some unfortunate owners and traders lost large sums of money and stock. Another national amnesty followed, with over 12,000 weapons being surrendered.

The scheme, with its costs for compensation, extra staff, police overtime, storage and other expenses, ran up a bill that is still disputed but almost certainly exceeded £100 million. It also threw up a strange anomaly in that, although the certificate holders had to surrender their pistols, they were permitted to acquire a carbine, which was probably a more powerful firearm.

The Government claimed that its draconian action would take guns off the street and decrease gun crime. Unfortunately, it is certainly questionable whether it has been successful in either respect. In 1997/8, the number of recorded crimes in England and Wales in which a firearm was used was 2,939; by 2007/8, the figure had risen to 4,014. According to most official reports, illegal firearms are becoming easier to acquire.

Today, bans are being seen as an answer to gun crime in the Republic of Ireland and Scotland and many other European countries are also in the process of reforming their controls. Much debate is taking place but the result will almost certainly be that pistol shooting will be even more restricted. One proposal in Finland, previously one of the most liberal-minded countries on the question of private firearm possession, is to ban all self-loaders. However, there is no guarantee that a blanket ban will have the desired effect. For a long time, Britain had some of the most stringent firearms controls anywhere in Europe, but any tightening of the restrictions led to a rise in gun crime rather than the opposite.

The USA is often quoted as a case proving the need for control since annually thousands of citizens suffer injuries and death relating to firearms, but, considering the size of the population and the number of firearms in private ownership, direct comparisons with Europe are misleading. Gun control in America is complex because State laws vary considerably, and Federal and State laws often find themselves almost in opposition. Respected academic Dr John Lott has studied crime and gun-control statistics and his research shows that, if private citizens under the law are allowed to carry concealed firearms, there is a marked decrease in crime in that area. As a result of his work, many states have adopted his system and the results have borne out his claim. Most of the US states now allow licensed citizens to carry a concealed firearm, although there are certain areas, such as bars, where carrying a firearm is still banned. Efforts are being made to remove this restriction too, in states such as Arizona. If the change is approved, a bar owner would have discretion as to whether to allow patrons to carry or not. Recent Federal Court decisions have confused matters even more and their rulings have been contested by several states. The Supreme Court of the USA have recently (2010) voted that the Second Amendment to the US Constitution – the right to bear arms – will now apply nationwide, allowing all citizens to own firearms despite any local prohibition.

At the moment there seems to be no consensus of opinion as to the best way of allowing honest citizens to possess and use handguns, whilst at the same time protecting the community. It is certainly questionable whether blanket bans achieve the desired results; as one American slogan has it, 'If guns are outlawed then only outlaws have guns.'

CHAPTER 13

Collecting Handguns

~ ~

Despite all the changes in the law, the presence of the anti-gun lobby and other factors, handgun collecting is still a fascinating and satisfying hobby. Unfortunately, firearms of any type tend to provoke a hostile reaction in many people; some just cannot believe that an interest in handguns can be anything but unhealthy. This is partly due to a common, but ill-informed misconception that firearms have only one function: to kill or injure. In fact, it is not the object itself that has a purpose, only its user. The vast majority of those with an interest in the pistol see it as a functional piece of design or engineering. Its end purpose may be to discharge a missile but it is the user who determines the target of that missile.

Until the advent of industrial machinery in the mid-nineteenth century almost all handguns were unique because they were hand-made. Consequently, no two items from this period are ever totally and entirely the same. Even on pairs of pistols of the very best quality there will be minor, almost indiscernible, differences of detail. The machine-produced handgun can be of interest in different ways – in its design and in the multitude of ways in which the same problems of design were tackled.

Before extolling the virtues of collecting handguns it is necessary to add a word of warning. Firearms, even antique ones, are potentially dangerous and because of this there are restrictions and prohibitions associated with them. These restrictions become more strict the newer the weapon. Generally speaking, and this is a generalization that requires some qualifying, any pistol made before about 1860 is likely to be, of itself, perfectly legal. Pistols dating from prior to the mid-nineteenth century are officially 'antique', and current UK firearms legislation excludes antiques from any restrictions in ownership or possession. In the words of the main Firearms Act, if the pistol is kept as a curiosity or ornament there is no problem. However, there is no legal definition for the term 'antique', although discussions are under way to arrive at an agreed cut-off date.

No licence or certificate is necessary to own an antique pistol but that exemption is qualified – *using* it in any way may remove the exemption. An owner wanting to shoot an antique would come up against a problem;

A selection of various handguns. From top to bottom: .32 Webley self-loader as issued to many police forces in the early twentieth century; Smith & Wesson .357 revolver; Smith & Wesson .22 target pistol with muzzle brake; Colt Single-Action Army revolver in .357 calibre; Browning 9mm Hi Power pistol.

there are arguments to counter the objection, but it would be a little risky to try.

If a collector has an interest in pistols that were produced after the introduction of metal cartridges in the 1860s, the pitfalls are many but there is one basic guideline: whether ammunition for that particular pistol is readily available. If there is a chance of acquiring rounds of a calibre or design suitable for the pistol, then it immediately makes the pistol subject to restrictions. It is possible to obtain permission to own some handguns that are not officially antique but, as the interpretation of the conditions set down allowing ownership can vary from area to area, it is as well to seek professional guidance.

There is one way in which it is possible to collect non-antique handguns and that is by turning to deactivated pieces. The legal definition of a firearm includes the phrase 'capable of discharging a missile'. If a pistol is altered

so that it cannot do this and it is impossible for it to fire a cartridge, and this conversion is confirmed by a proof house, then by law it is no longer a firearm. If it cannot discharge a missile it is no longer a firearm and may therefore be legally held. This makes it possible for members of re-enactment groups, for example, to use machine guns, rifles, assault rifles or any type of firearm, so long as it is properly deactivated.

The situation of actually shooting antique pistols becomes rather confusing. First the owner will need to seek permission to acquire and store black powder, and caps for percussion weapons, and then the antique will have to be licensed and placed on a firearms certificate for it will no longer be covered by the 'curiosity or ornament' definition. Even more confusing is the fact that, while an individual may own a genuine 1851 Colt percussion revolver without any authority, it is illegal

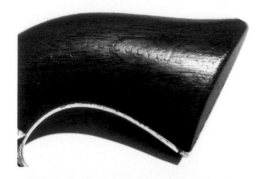

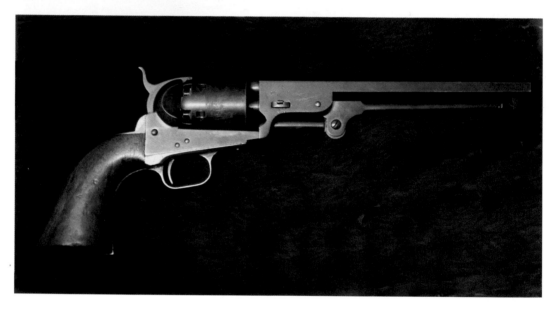

LEFT AND BELOW: Occasionally, an antique pistol can be linked to an owner. The butt of this Colt .36 Navy Percussion revolver has 'H G COLVILL' stamped in the wood, relating it to Captain Hugh George Colvill, who was Governor of Bodmin Prison. On 16 October 1860, Colt revolvers were issued at this prison to special officers for use on special occasions only. (Private collection)

to purchase or own a modern replica, which may be an exact copy but cannot, by any definition, be called an antique.

It is possible to own and shoot, non-competitively, quite modern handguns but special permission and very secure storage are demanded. As police forces vary in their attitudes, permits are not always easy to obtain and expert advice should be sought.

Assuming that an interest in handguns has developed and the idea of owning one or more comes about, what is the first step? Collecting is not a cheap pastime and it is obviously desirable to avoid bad buys. Two

of the best pieces of advice are *caveat emptor*, or 'buyer beware', and 'knowledge is power' – in other words, do as much research as possible before making any purchase.

In the 1950s the number of readable, reliable books on handguns was fairly limited, but today the opposite is true. There are several published magazines that cover collecting and shooting, and it is worth spending some money getting a few copies. Although it is essential, theoretical research is, however, of limited use and whilst it may be possible to identify a particular type of pistol on sight, that is not enough. Familiarity is absolutely vital and there is nothing to equal the experience gained by handling actual specimens; unfortunately, this is not easy to achieve.

Museums are not always keen to allow just anybody to view their exhibits close up, but if such a request is motivated by a genuine interest, many will be ready to help. When asking for such a privilege it is a good idea to prove that interest by referring to some relevant books and, if possible, membership of a recognized society associated with the topic. If there are any such groups in the area, it can help to make contact with them; today's technology makes it fairly easy to locate them online.

Although they are less common than they used to be, there are still many antique fairs and markets dotted about the country, and these offer an opportunity to meet fellow enthusiasts and to handle actual specimens. There is a protocol about handling and it is normal to ask the vendor for permission before picking something up.

Similar opportunities for handling are offered by auction sales when, prior to a sale, the lots are put on view. Again, the internet is invaluable in locating auctions, and there is an added advantage in that they offer some guarantee of authenticity. If after purchase there is some problem with a lot, the auction company will consider whether they have made a mistake and may consequently refund the purchase price. Before any such action they will expect some strong evidence to support the claim. Most sales catalogues are now well presented and, although not cheap, represent an investment for they become a reference source both for the description of the lots and for prices. One other point to remember is that if you have an interest in an item it is possible to contact the salerooms and ask for a condition report and then receive a fairly detailed description as well as answers to any questions.

An auction is a very uncertain event and the prices achieved depend on many factors other than the object itself; similar pieces can sell at very different prices. If two keen bidders go after the same piece, the price may be pushed very high, but if there is only one person in the room who is really interested, that person may get a bargain. Most auction rooms include in their catalogue description an estimate – the price range in which they think there will be bids. For the usual lots that have been seen before, these estimates are a good guide, but for out-of-the-ordinary pieces there has to be an element of guesswork. The cataloguer will have to look through past sales for similar pieces, note the prices, consider the differences in detail, quality or special factors, and then make an educated guess.

One golden rule of bidding at auction is to decide on the absolute top price that you are prepared to pay and stick to it. Being taken over by the idea that 'just one more bid will do it' can be dangerous! Bidding is not a problem – the auctioneer will soon detect a wave of the hand, a nod or other simple signal – but it is not possible to buy something by accident because of a sneeze, despite the stories.

Antique dealers are an obvious source and a trustworthy dealer is very precious and should be cultivated. If they recognize a serious collector they will do their best to help in any way with advice on quality, rarity, condition and market value. They can attend sales on a client's behalf and advise and, if necessary, make bids too. They will charge commission for such a service but it is usually well worth it. It is sound policy when making a purchase to ask for a receipt that clearly identifies the object, so that if a problem arises there is no doubt about the item under discussion.

Having acquired an item for a collection, the first thing to do is to record it. In these days of digital photography it is simple to photograph it from different angles and show specific details. In the unfortunate event of an item being lost or stolen, the insurance company will then have full records. Better than a general overall view, it is worth considering specifically recording minor details, which can make a more positive identification. The computer also makes cataloguing the item simpler and time spent on this task is always worthwhile.

Cleaning and repairing are tricky subjects but one simple practical piece of advice is to do as little as possible. Rust does need to be dealt with – oil and gentle scraping will deal with superficial rusting, but more serious pitting needs more expert attention. Restoration is a ticklish subject and the question of whether broken or damaged parts should be replaced is much debated. It seems to be generally accepted that any restoration should be recorded and in general should be reversible, without damage to the item. There are several books offering advice on restoration procedures and they are essential reading.

Storage is important and simple things such as acid-free paper and similar packing materials are to be recommended. A thin layer of oil such as WD40 is a sound basic process but too much oil leads to grease and sticky dust.

What to collect? The basic answer is, what is affordable to you? It is impossible to lump all types of handgun under various price labels, but it is possible to generalize. Quality costs money and if you are going to follow just one guideline, always buy the very best that you can afford. Condition is all important and next comes provenance as any item with some proven connection with a person, an event or a unit, is always worth more. Pairs are worth more than two singles and rarity is also a very important factor.

It is only the wealthiest collectors who can afford wheel-lock pistols and the earlier a piece the higher the price. Small flintlock pocket pistols are fairly common and can be acquired at a reasonable price; the larger the flintlock, the higher the price is likely to be. The maker's name will also be a factor and well-known London makers will command high prices. Percussion pistols are, piece for piece, likely to be cheaper than an equivalent flint. Single-barrelled pocket percussion pistols are not highly regarded and consequently sell at reasonable prices, but quality percussion duellers and similar pieces are not cheap. Percussion revolvers are popular with collectors and those by well-known makers such as Colt, Adams, Remington and others will be more expensive. Pinfire revolvers tend to be rather plain or even cumbersome and are a cheaper group worth considering.

Bibliography

Adams, R. *Street Survival* Calibre Press, Northbrook 1980

Anon, *The Control of Firearms in Great Britain* London 1973

Applegate, R. *Kill or be Killed* Paladin Press, Boulder 1976

Atkinson, J. *Duelling Pistols* London 1964

Ayoob, M. *Fundamentals of Modern Police Impact Weapons* Springfield 1978

Barwick, H. *A Briefe discourse concerning.. manuall weapons of fire* 1594, reprint E.P. Publishing Wakefield 1973

Blackmore, Howard, L. *A Dictionary of London Gunmakers 1350–1850* Phaidon 1986

Blair, Claude *European and American Arms c. 1100–1850* Batsford Ltd, London 1962

Blair, Claude (ed.) *Pollard's History of Firearms* Country Life Books, Feltham 1983

Brady, Donald *Colt Automatic Pistols* California 1973

Bristow, R. *Modern Police Firearms* Beverly Hills 1964

Bristow, R. *The Search for an Effective Police Hand*gun, 1973, Charles C. Thomas Springfield

Bruce, G. *Webley and Scott Revolvers* Zurich 1988

Bruce, G. *Webley and Scott Automatic Pistols* Zurich 1992

Bruce, G. *Webley and Scott Air Pistols* London 2001

Buchanan, Brenda J. (ed.) *Gunpowder* Bath University Press, Bath 1990

Burgoyne, John *The Queen Anne Pistol 1650–1788* Museum Restoration, Toronto 2002

Chamberlain, W. and Taylerson, A.W. *Adams' Revolvers* Barrie and Jenkins, London 1976

Chase, Kenneth *Firearms: A Global History to 1700* Cambridge University Press, Cambridge 2003

Clede, B. *Police Handgun Manual* Stackpole Books, Harrisburg 1985

Cockle, Maurice *A Bibliography of Military Books up to 1642* London 1972

Collins, S. *The Good Guys Wear Black* Century, London 1998

Collins, S. *The Glory Boys* Century, London 1998

Coombs, Roger *Holsters and Other Gun Leather* Northfield 1983

Corkery, J. *The Theft of Firearms* Home Office, London 1994

Crocker, G. *The Gunpowder Industry* Shire Publications, Princes Risborough 1999

Curtis, Christopher *Système Lefaucheux* California 2002

Dewar, M. *Weapons and Equipment of Counter-Terrorism* Poole 1987

Dunlap, J. *American, British and Continental Pepperbox Revolvers* Pacific Books 1967

Emmison, F. *Elizabethan Life and Disorder* Essex County Council, Chelmsford 1970

George, J.N. *English Pistols and Revolvers* Onslow N.C. 1938

Gould, R.W. and Waldren, M. *London's Armed Police* Arms and Armour Press, London 1986

Greenwood, Colin *Firearms Control* Routledge Kegan Paul, London 1972

Greenwood, Colin *Police Tactics in Armed Operations* Paladin, Boulder 1979

Greenwood, Colin *Police Firearms Training* Harrogate 1966

Hardy, R. *Longbow: A social and military history* Patrick Stephens Ltd, Ambridge 1992

Harman, Greene, et al *The Elizabethan Underworld* London 1930

Hayward, A. *A Complete History of the Highwaymen* London 1926

Hayward, J.F. *The Art of The Gunmaker Vol 1* Barrie & Rockliff, London 1962

Hayward, J.F. *The Art of The Gunmaker Vol 2* Barrie & Rockliff, London 1963

Heard, B. *A Handbook of Firearms and Ballistics* Chichester 1997

Held, Robert *The Age of Firearms* Northfield 1978

Her Majesty's Inspectorate of Constabulary, *Facing Violence* HMSO, London 1995

Hoff, Arne *Dutch Firearms* London 1978

Houze, Herbert G. *Arming the West* Mowbray Publishing, Rhode Island 2008

Ingleton, R. *Arming the British Police* London 1997

Ingleton, R. *Police of the World* Shepperton 1979

Kates, D. *Restricting Handguns* USA 1979

Konig, Klaus and Hugo, Martin *Service Handgun* London 1988

Lavin, James *A History of Spanish Firearms* London 1965

Logan, George *The British Bulldog Revolver* RI 2006

Malcolm, J.R. *To Keep and Bear Arms* Cambridge 1994

Marshall and Sanow, E. *Handgun Stopping Power* 1992

Neal, Keith *Great British Gunmakers 1748–1798* London 1975

Partington, J.R. *A History of Greek Fire and Gunpowder* The Johns Hopkins University Press, Baltimore 1999

Riling, Ray *Guns and Shooting, A Bibliography* New York 1951

Rimer, Graeme *Wheellock Firearms of the Royal Armouries* Royal Armouries 2001

Rosa, J. *The Age of the Gunfighter* London 1993

Schif, Christopher *Remington's First Revolvers* RI 2007

Taylerson, A.W.F. *Adams' Revolvers* London 1978

Taylerson, A.W.F. *The Revolver 1818–1865* London 1968

Taylerson, A.W.F. *The Revolver 1865–1880* London 1970

Taylerson, A.W.F. *The Revolver 1880–1914* London 1970

Taylerson, A.W.F. *Revolving Arms* London 1967

Trench, Charles Chenevix *A History of Marksmanship* London 1972

Waldren, Michael *Armed Police* Sutton, Stroud 2007

Walter, John *The Luger Book* London 1956

Walter, John *The Pistol Book* London 1983

Wilkinson, Frederick *Antique Firearms* Guinness Signatures, London 1969

Wilkinson, Frederick *The World's Great Guns* Leicester 1987

Wilkinson, Frederick *Those Entrusted with Arms* Royal Armouries, Leeds 2002

Winant, L. *Early Percussion Firearms* New York 1959

Winant, L. *Firearms Curiosa* London 1956

Zhuk, A.D. *An Illustrated Encyclopaedia of Handguns* London 1995

Endnotes

1. The shootings at Hungerford and Dunblane were horrific and created demands that there should be tighter firearms controls. The government decided to ban the private ownership of handguns with the result that, with a few minor exceptions, pistol shooting was finished. At the time, 1997, it was claimed that this draconian edict would reduce gun crime despite warnings from well qualified shooters that it would not. Sad to report they were right and British gun crime has steadily increased from that date.
2. Steele, R. *A Bibliography of Royal Proclamations of the Tudor and Stuart Sovereigns 1485–1714* Oxford 1910
3. Ibid.
4. Wilkinson, F. *Those Entrusted with Arms* London 2002
5. Ibid.
6. Library, Christ Church, Oxford
7. Partington, A. *History of Greek Fire and Gunpowder* Cambridge 1960
8. Blair Pollard *History of Firearms* p454
9. *The Art of War and Englands Traynings* by Edw. Davies
10. Needham, J. *Science and Civilisation in China* Vol 7 Cambridge University Press 1980

11. See *Journal of the Arms and Armour Society* Vol 3 A Note on the Early History of the Wheel-lock by Claude Blair
12. For a discussion of this definition see Wilkinson p36
13. *The Manufacture of Gunflints* by Sidney Skertchly 1879
14. See Bibliography
15. *What Wood is That? A Manual of Wood Identification* by Herbert L. Edlin, London 1979
16. See Wilkinson pp72–73
17. *The Code of Honour or Rules for the Government of Principals and Seconds in Duelling* by John Lyde Wilson, Charleston 1858
18. *A Bibliography of Royal Proclamations of the Tudor and Stuart Sovereigns 1485–1713* by Robert Steele, Oxford 1910
19. 1 Geo.st.2c 54
20. See Blackmore pp85–86
21. *The Reverend Alexander John Forsyth* by Maj. Gen Sir Alexander Forsyth Reid, reprint
22. *The Course of Instruction in Laboratory Work and Directions for Making Percussion Caps* Madras 1847
23. *Instructions to Young Sportsmen in all that relates to Guns and Shooting* by Lt

Col. P. Hawker, 6th edition, London 1830

24. *Underhammer Guns* by Herschel C. Logan, Harrisburg 1960

25. For full details of Colt revolvers see *The Book of Colt Firearms* by R. Sutherland and R.L. Wilson, Kansas City, and *Colt Revolvers* by Joseph Rosa London 1988

26. For the full story, see *Colonel Colt, London* by J. Rosa, London 1976

27. See *Arming the West* by Herbert, G., Howe, R.I., 2005

28. See Taylerson *et al. The Revolver 1818–1865* London 1968

29. Hogg *Illustrated Encyclopedia of Firearms* London 1978

30. Comprehensive listing can be found in *Pistols and Revolvers* by Fowler, North & Strong, London 2007

31. For full details, see Wilkinson p169

32. *The Times* 25 January 1885

33. For full details, see Taylerson *The Revolver 1889–1914* pp228–234

34. For details of the various pistols, see *The Book of Colt Firearms*

35. Full list in *Webley & Scott Automatic Pistols* by Gordon Bruce, Zurich 1992

36. For full details of the adoption and use, see Bruce and Wilkinson

37. *Firearms Curiosa* by Lewis Winant, London 1956

38. See *Handgun Stopping Power* by E. Marshall and E. Sanow, Paladin Press 1992

39. See *Exotic Weapons* by Michael Hoy, Mason, Mich

40. Tojhus museum, Copenhagen,

41. For a full and scholarly history, see *Webley Air Pistols* by G. Bruce, London 2001

42. See *Air Pistols* by Dennis Hiller 1982

43. Refer to the Violent Crime Reduction Act of 2006

44. 12 Rich. II

45. 6 Hen.VIII c17

46. 17 Hen. VIII

47. 20 Hen. VIII

48. 25 Hen. VIII c.17

49. 28 Hen. VIII

50. 33 Hen. VIII c.17

51. 3 Edw. VI c.14

52. For full details of the act, see *Firearms Control* by Colin Greenwood, London 1972

Index